"Doing the Music" of Worship

"Doing the Music" of Worship

Regulative Principles Found in the Book of Revelation

THOMAS A. SEEL

Foreword by Robin A. Leaver

WIPF & STOCK · Eugene, Oregon

Wipf and Stock Publishers
199 W 8th Ave, Suite 3
Eugene, OR 97401

"Doing the Music" of Worship
Regulative Principles Found in the Book of Revelation
By Seel, Thomas A.
Copyright © 1995 by Seel, Thomas A. All rights reserved.

Softcover ISBN-13: 979-8-30852-7171-9
Hardcover ISBN-13: 979-8-3852-7172-6
eBook ISBN-13: 979-8-3852-7173-3

Publication date 12/4/2025

Previously published by Scarecrow Press, 1995 as *A Theology of Music for Worship Derived from the Book of Revelation*

This edition is a scanned facsimile of the original edition published in 1995.

Scripture quotations are from the Revised Standard Version of the Bible, Apocrypha, copyright © 1957; The Third and Fourth Books of the Maccabees and Psalm 151, copyright © 1977 National Council of the Churches of Christ in the United States of America. Used by permission. All rights reserved worldwide.

To my wife Diane, whose deep spirituality and unfailing character are an inspiration to me.
And to our sons, Matthew and wife Abby and children Joel and Nora, and Joshua and wife Cheryl and children Logan and Levi.
May your unbridled joy in your dear Lord and Savior Jesus Christ continue to grow throughout your lives.

"For the concert of life no one is given a program"
(OLD DUTCH PROVERB)

And yet, inspired by the Holy Spirit,
Christians were given this view of worship in heaven
that we might seek to replicate it this side of eternity,
albeit imperfectly.

Contents

Foreword by Robin A. Leaver | ix
Preface | xi
Acknowledgments | xvii
Abbreviations | xix

1. Introduction | 1
2. The Origin and Use of Προσκυνέο | 26
3. Music Forms | 41
4. Performing Groups | 61
5. Performance Practice | 81
6. A Theology of Music for Worship | 105
7. Implications for Today's Church Musicians and Worship Leaders | 118
8. Regulative Principles in the Book of Revelation | 131

Appendices | 159

Bibliography | 187

Foreword

IN THE BOOK OF Revelation, there are many passages that imply a liturgical form of worship in which music was a fundamental part. The nature and extent of this liturgical music forms the substance of this study. In the process of evaluating the linguistic and historical background, the author reveals something of the multicultural context in which these musical terms and performance practices developed—an amalgam of Jewish traditions and contemporary practices of the Graeco-Roman world, as modified by the Christological experience and eschatological hope for the early church.

But this book is more than a study of biblical theology set within the historical framework of the first few centuries of the Christian era. In the final chapter Thomas Seel makes the following observation: ". . .contemporary Christianity is historically tied to its past and eschatologically pulled into its future" (see page 130–31). Accordingly, having established the framework of a theology of music in worship from evidence found within the Book of Revelation, the author examines some of the implications of this theology for music in worship of contemporary churches.

The book originated as a DMA-Church Music dissertation at The Southern Baptist Theological Seminary, Louisville, Kentucky, and has been significantly revised for publication. Its respectful biblicism reflects the evangelical perspectives of the author and of the seminary for which the dissertation was written. Nevertheless, the author's findings challenge many of the current presuppositions and practices of evangelical Christianity. There is a widespread short-sighted view that music in worship is simply entertainment or propaganda that is useful for an anthropocentric here-and-now. By contrast, the Book of Revelation presents a more far-sighted view of music in worship in which a theocentric future is anticipated.

Thomas Allen Seel is an experienced church musician. In 1995 he was an assistant vice-president and investment officer of the Presbyterian

Church (U.S.A.) Foundation, and minister of music of Fern Creek United Methodist Church, Louisville, Kentucky.

Robin A. Leaver
Series Editor
Westminster Choir College of Rider University and Drew University

Preface

THE BOOK OF REVELATION is not only a book of doom and gloom for the lost but a book of hope to every generation of Christians. My doctoral dissertation, "Towards a Theology of Music for Worship Derived from the Book of Revelation," was completed in 1990 at the Southern Baptist Theological Seminary. My esteemed dissertation committee was comprised of Drs. Hugh McElrath, Donald Hustad, G. Maurice Hinson, and Ronald Turner and was published by Scarecrow Press, a division of the University Press of America, in 1995 and Dr. Robin Leaver served as my editor. Since then, it has gone out of print.

Since 1990, I have presented my thesis in churches and worship conferences many times and, by so doing, have honed it through additional learning and insight to make it even more practical and relevant for today as a guide for all church musicians and worship leaders of whom the senior pastor is chief. The standards for the use of music in the church have been reasoned out through the centuries based on general theological and musical considerations. This study goes beyond the theological surface of worship itself and delves into the regulative principles about "doing the music" of worship. These regulative principles are historically, biblically, and eschatologically supported and made relevant for the church today. The purpose of this study is to convince you that the New Testament, particularly in the largely ignored book of Revelation, does have practical, "down-to-earth" and specific things to say regarding the use of music for worship in the life of the contemporary church. This study assumes it is no accident that the writer of the Apocalypse chose to portray his eschatological glimpse in terms of the best music traditions that he knew in his past and present time.

This study begins with a discussion of what the only word for worship (Προσκυνέο—*Proskuneo*), found in the book of Revelation, means. Then, the "doing the music" of worship is described and categorized as Revelation and Response. An analysis of the only music forms found in the book and a discussion of the performing groups follows. A study of the Greek verbs that describe "doing the music" of worship informs us as to performance practice that is entirely relevant to today's worship practice. Thus, this presentation illustrates the regulative principles as delineated in the book of Revelation based on my biblical study completed in 1990 that was placed historically from Genesis to the Revelation and was subsequently published.[1]

I have found it remarkable and frankly disappointing that these ten regulative principles for "doing the music" of worship have had little to no attention drawn to them over the years. Whaley reminds us that "worship is not the music, message, or the messenger . . . it is rather our expression of love to the Father, in our Lord and Savior Jesus Christ, by the power of the Holy Spirit."[2] Although this is true, and though many authors concur in their focus on the subject of a broader theology of worship, they have collectively often failed to comprehend that the book of Revelation can in fact inform our "doing the music" of worship.[3] Ron Man asserts that "there

---

1. Seel, *Theology of Music*. References already annotated in this book are not re-annotated here. I repeat my original findings through Chapter 7 and add further illumination I have received since 1990 from having taught the material, including insight from others in Chapter 8.

2. Whaley, *Called to Worship*, 334.

3. Other recent works include the following: Alfonso, *The Billboard Guide* (a detailed critical history of contemporary Christian music from 1950 to today, with interviews from leading artists); Beale, *We Become What We Worship*, 243–44 ("The letters to the seven churches are to all churches and deal with the practice of witnessing for Christ in the midst of a pagan culture. . . and to have ears to hear. . ."); Begbie, *Resounding Truth*, 74 (". . . Perhaps the most important thing to note here is the essentially positive impression of music given in Scripture. . . Overall, we find a warm-hearted acceptance and encouragement of its proper use."); Best, *Music Through the Eyes of Faith*, 204 (He states, "The gospel must be sung, not just preached" and looks at music through the eyes of faith, wherein he addresses the tough questions that come to mind when people of faith reflect on music); Borchert, *Worship in the New Testament* (This study challenges the reader to consider worship as intertwined with one's life as its focus in interpreting the New Testament); Boswell, *Doxology & Theology* (A manual seeking to raise up a new generation of worship leaders who believe that good theology is not just for the trained clergy but for every Christian); Brooks, *Worship Quest* (It serves as a guide to understanding foundational questions about worship and leading in Christian worship); Hill, *Enter His Courts with Praise!*, 82 (Hill sets forth a biblical theology of time as it is understood in the Old and New Testaments); Kauflin, *True Worshipers* (Discusses the importance of biblical truth in worship songs); Bob Kauflin, *Worship Matters* (An important text in the season of worship-style wars and points us to the point of it all—pointing to the Savior of the gospel); Old, *Themes and Variations* (Through the history of Christian worship, Olds weaves a biblical doxology as found in a variety of church traditions); Risbridger, *The Message of Worship*, 9, 87 (As neither a professional theologian nor a seasoned musician, the author is intent on seeking to acknowledge the "power of music. . .to address biblical truth to the human heart and to carry the response to that truth that the Holy Spirit brings forth." I agree with Risbridger

is no one 'right' way to do worship."[4] Peterson concurs and says that ". . . primitive worship was intended to be parallel to the worship of heaven." He goes on to say that

> the doxologies, acclamations and hymns of praise in John's Apocalypse have found their way into many Christian songs and liturgies throughout the centuries. This has happened because of the form as well as the content of these segments . . . Observing this, some scholars have proposed that John must have employed sentences and phrases taken from pre-existing liturgical sources in the first century . . . including contemporary Jewish practices in the synagogue and temple and syncretized with Hellenistic ruler cults . . .[5]

Man then goes on to list twelve biblical principles of worship for which we need to aspire, yet he cites these principles generally at the broader level of corporate worship and not at the actual "doing the music" of worship, as espoused in the book of Revelation.[6]

Peterson says the elements of heavenly worship have their own special function in the structure of this book.

> They interpret the apocalyptic events, the peculiar meaning of which would not be completely clear without such interpretation . . . John has made eschatological drama unfold from a heavenly, cultic setting . . . The gathering of the church is meant to be an anticipation of the heavenly or eschatological assembly of God's people.[7]

If our primitive "doing the music" of worship this side of eternity is indeed to parallel that in heaven one day, then this study of what we learn of heavenly worship in the book of Revelation is relevant for fashioning the music in our worship today.

---

that throughout Scripture, worship is "clearly much broader than singing God's praise"; rather, it is about living whole-heartedly our movement to lyrical theology evidenced in the eighteenth century whole lifelong for the glory of God); Wainwright and Tucker, *The Oxford History of Christian Worship* (A compendium covering the traditions of the Christian faith and their respective worship practices); White, *Documents of Christian Worship* (A compendium illustrating the organization of teaching liturgical pedagogy); and Young, *Music of the Heart* (This is a companion to St. Augustine's treatise, *On Music*, wherein Young has shown the importance of the unique contributions of John and Charles Wesley and the Methodist movement).

4. Man, *Let Us Draw Near*, 414–15.
5. Peterson, *Engaging with God*, 275–76.
6. Man, *Let Us Draw Near*, 439–96.
7. Peterson, *Engaging with God*, 276.

This study does not analyze the contextual contents of the texts of the ᾠδή (*oda*) in the book of Revelation. Rather, this study goes down a level into "doing the music" of worship in the Apocalypse.

Ross quotes my old mentor, Donald Hustad, by saying,

> Music. . . is to be biblically accurate, spiritually uplifting, honoring to God, and edifying for the congregation. The music is supposed to lift the worshippers out of their experience, focus their attention on Christ, and transport their spirits to realms of glory. But if the music draws attention to the musicians rather than the Lord, centers on human experience instead of divine acts, mimics the style of entertainment that the world offers, or becomes routine and predictable so that the mind and soul are not engaged, then it fails to be an effective means of praising God.[8]

Ross then goes on to say what my other mentor, Hugh McElrath, who with Eskew, said in consonance with Hustad.[9] Ross provides basic principles for more glorious worship. Many of them, especially principle seven, speak to the singing, chanting, playing of musical instruments, and dancing done to the glory of God as part of the praise from the people of God.[10] But Ross says little about how to do same. Williamson adds to this practice and states that "the choir is potentially the most powerful worship leader in almost any congregation." While the choir can lead the congregation, "the primary role as a choir is not to impress people. It is rather to inspire their hearers to worship the Living God."[11]

My published work in 1995 delineated ten principles for the "doing the music" of worship that are derived from the book of Revelation. They may be considered to be regulative principles, as commonly attributed to Calvin, and cover the gamut of the attitude and general practice of how Christians should worship corporately by the "doing the music" of worship. While other authors have broadly provided parameters around a theology of worship in heaven, this study seeks to go down a level to uncover and to identify regulative principles that describe the "doing of music" of that worship, which can then provide guidance to our doing worship on this side of eternity. Whaley asserts that the book of Revelation is "God's worship

---

8. Ross, *Recalling the Hope of Glory*, 441–42.
9. McElrath and Eskew, *Sing With Understanding*.
10. Ross, *Recalling the Hope of Glory*, 501–12.
11. Williamson, *God's Singers*, 23, 58.

manual that delineates perfect worship as offered in heaven."[12] So why do we not aspire to it, albeit in our imperfect way?

Owing to the fact that the Apostle John's authorship was inspired by the visions he received while imprisoned on Patmos, can it not be assumed that the writer recorded the visions he received as the Holy Spirit prompted him? These visions went well beyond the Apostle John's education and experience, and thus, well beyond the comprehension of the average person during his and even our time. The writer of the Apocalypse drew on his early Jewish upbringing in the synagogue, and, after Jesus's work on the cross and resurrection, migrated to Ephesus. Ephesus likely provided him the most diverse, multi-cultured church in the world of its time and introduced worship ideas that were influenced by both pagan and Hellenistic rites. Thus, John transcribed these visions using his own background in combination with the vast and various backgrounds of Ephesus in order to fully capture what he beheld. In other words, "doing the music" of worship presented in the book of Revelation is syncretistic, drawing from all of the Apostle John's life experiences. Therefore, assuming the writing was inspired by the Holy Spirit with the specific choice of words used to transcribe his vision, I humbly submit these regulative principles of music for worship again and challenge other church music scholars to a dialogue as may warrant discussion.

A perusal of the related literature concerning music in worship in the book of Revelation has found that no one has gone into the topic at this level of developing regulative principles for the "doing the music" of worship. No recent scholarship has thoroughly reviewed nor spoken of the music forms presented, the performing groups, nor the implications of the Greek words used to identify vocabulary surrounding the doing and performing of the music used in worship in the book of Revelation.

Christian worship practices over the centuries have been formulated by regulative principles and normative principles. Webber reminds us that: "according to Calvin, only that which is explicitly taught in the New Testament was permissible in worship; whereas Luther believed that whatever was not explicitly rejected by Scripture was permissible for worship."[13] The former practices used in worship are specifically directed in Scripture, while the latter practices used in worship are those that are not strictly forbidden in Scripture, as long as they are consonant to maintaining peace and unity within the church. If so, then why is that that which is recorded in the book of Revelation not part of our New Testament legacy for "doing the music" of worship? Why do we ignore it?

---

12. Williamson, *God's Singers*, 23, 58.
13. Webber, *Worship is a Verb*, 177.

This attempt to create a set of principles in "doing the music" of worship in order to help church professionals increase their understanding of music is based on the large amount of musical material in the book of Revelation. So many before have considered this glimpse of the future as unattainable today and have dismissed it as enviable and unattainable. While I agree that perfection this side of eternity is impossible, how dare we not try.

Balancing life has to be a growing experience where the only constant is God. My inspiration comes from seeking to please my Lord and Master Jesus Christ, doing it ". . .heartily, as serving the Lord and not man." (Col 3:23). One must be consumed with his/her knowing God and willfully fashioning his/her lifestyle after Christ's excellent example on a moment-by-moment basis daily; poring over scripture and the Christian traditions and applying insights thereby gained into daily living is my willful aim as I seek to fulfill the Great Commission in my life.

Acknowledgments

APPRECIATION IS EXTENDED TO Mark Hamilton and his staff at Liberty University Library for moving this transcript from its 1995 pdf version to an editable version. Special appreciation is extended to the talented Gracie Owens whose copy editing skills were patiently applied to update and add additional material to this extended version. And, grateful appreciation is given to Jason Robeck at my publisher and to my son, the Rev. Dr. Matthew Seel, who provided additional edits and suggestions.

Abbreviations

ASJ	Henry Barclay Swete. *The Apocalypse of St. John*. London: Macmillan, 1909.
ATM	Alfred Pike. *A Theology of Music*. Toledo, OH: The Gregorian Institute of America, 1953.
BI	Anthony Baines. *Brass Instruments: Their History and Development*. London: Faber and Faber, 1976.
DD	Robin A. Leaver and James H. Litton, eds. *Duty and Delight: Routley Remembered*. Carol Stream, IL: Hope, 1985.
DH	John Julian, et al. *A Dictionary of Hymnology*. Revised, London: Murray, 1908.
DOX	Geoffrey Wainwright. *Doxology: The Praise of God in Worship, Doctrine and Life*. New York: Oxford University Press, 1980.
ECB	James Strong. *The Exhaustive Concordance of the Bible*. New York: Abingdon, 1890.
EIHM	Johann Ernst Altenburg. *Essay on an Introduction to the Heroic and Musical Trumpeters' and Kettledrummers' Art*. Translated by Edward H. Tarr. Nashville: The Brass, 1974.
GEL	Henry George Liddell and Robert Scott. *A Greek-English Lexicon*. Edited by Sir Henry Stuart Jones. Oxford: Clarendon, 1948.
GELNT	William F. Arndt and F. Wilbur Gingrich. *A Greek-English Lexicon of the New Testament and Other Early Christian Literature*. Edited by Walter Bauer. Chicago: University of Chicago Press, 1958.
GGNT	A. T. Robertson. *A Grammar of the Greek New Testament in the Light of Historical Research*. New York: Hodder and Stoughton, 1914.
HMI	Curt Sachs. *A History of Musical Instruments*. New York: W. W. Norton, 1940.
IB	George A. Buttrick. *The Interpreter's Dictionary of the Bible*. Nashville: Abingdon, 1962.
JLD	A. Z. Idelsohn. *Jewish Liturgy and Its Development*. New York: Holt, Rinehart, and Winston, 1967.

MAI	Alfred Sendrey. *Music in Ancient Israel*. New York: Philosophical Library, 1969.
MHBT	Don L. Smithers. *The Music and History of the Baroque Trumpet*. Carbondale, IL: Southern Illinois University Press, 1988.
MSR	Alfred Sendrey. *Music in the Social and Religious Life of Antiquity*. Cranbury, NJ: Associated University Presses, 1974.
NED	Merrill Unger and W. White, Jr., eds. *Nelson's Expository Dictionary of the Old Testament*. Nashville: Thomas Nelson, 1984.
NGD	Stanley Sadie, ed. *The New Grove Dictionary of Music and Musicians*. London: Macmillan, 1980.
NGDMI	Curt Sachs, ed. *The New Grove Dictionary of Musical Instruments*. London: Macmillan, 1984.
OTP	James Hamilton Charlesworth, ed. *The Old Testament Pseudepigrapha and the New Testament*. Garden City, NY: Doubleday, 1983.
PIW	Sigmund Mowinckel. *The Psalms in Israel's Worship*. Translated by D. R. Ap-Thomas. Nashville: Abingdon, 1979.
RD	James L. Blevins. *Revelation as Drama*. Nashville: Broadman, 1984.
SIA	R. H. Charles. *Studies in the Apocalypse*. Edinburgh: T. & T. Clark, 1915.
TDNT	Gerhard Friedrich, ed. *Theological Dictionary of the New Testament*. Grand Rapids: William B. Eerdmans, 1971.
THM	J. Murray Barbour. *Trumpets, Horns and Music*. East Lansing, MI: Michigan State University Press, 1964.
TSB	Eric Werner. *The Sacred Bridge: The Interdependence of Liturgy and Music in Synagogue and Church During the First Millennium*. London: Dennis Dobson, 1959.
VED	W. F. Vines. *Vine's Expository Dictionary of Old and New Testament Words*. Edited by F. F. Bruce. Old Tappan, NJ: Fleming H. Revell, 1981.
VGNT	James Hope Moulton and George Milligan. *The Vocabulary of the Greek New Testament*. Grand Rapids: William B. Eerdmans, 1982.
WSE	John E. Burkhart. *Worship: A Searching Examination of the Liturgical Experience*. Philadelphia: Westminster, 1982.

1

Introduction

Music abounds in the Revelation. When the writer of the Apocalypse chose the nomenclature that could best describe the visions he received, he chose to portray a certain type of music in worship. It can be no accident that he chose to couch the music of his visions in traditional Jewish, Greek, Roman and early Church, as well as pagan terms. This study will seek to develop a theology of music in worship as discerned in the book of Revelation.

Key terms that will be used in this study are defined in the following manner.

MUSIC

A common definition of music is "the science or art of incorporating pleasing, expressive, or intelligible combinations of vocal or instrumental tones into a composition having a definite structure of continuity."[1] Dr. Hilda Schuster, an expert on the views of Emile Jacques-Dalcroze, defines music as an activity that consists of three primary elements: time, space, and energy.[2] Epperson equates the term "music" with "musical symbol." He claims that a definition for a musical symbol less general than "an intelligible structure of sound, apprehended through actual hearing in its own modality of virtual time and motion" would entail "qualifications appropriate only to specific

---

1. Gove, "Music," 1490.

2. This writer studied for a summer at the Dalcroze School of Music, New York City, in 1973. Dr. Hilda Schuster, president, used this definition repeatedly.

examples."[3] In summary, music can be defined as an "aural art" that gains meaning through acculturation.

THEOLOGY

Revelation, as a source of theology, is "God's act of disclosing himself by his 'Word' and actions through time."[4] Faith is the human acceptance of this revelation.[5] Scripture is the written record of God's revelation of himself, and the Articles of Faith that Christians espouse are creedal declarations that preserve our witness of and to God.[6] Then, theology springs as an "overspill of divine faith into all levels of human reasonableness... and search[es] for reasons why, whence, how, and what it is all about." Theology embodies all that makes the theologian someone other than God, the angels, and the beasts.[7] Although the term "theology" appears nowhere in Scripture, it has been said that it is the church thinking "aloud."[8] The purpose of theology is to study the tenets of one's belief by means of "reason enlightened by faith" in order to promote a deeper understanding of it.[9] The broad categories of theology consists of (1) biblical theology, which uses the Bible as its only source, and (2) systematic theology. While it uses the Bible as its primary source, systematic theology can use other sources as well.[10]

Systematic theology attempts

> methodically and in the light of faith... to organize all divinely revealed truths and their explanations according to some form of regular, intrinsic, and rational plan, connection, and/or interdependence. It is based on the comprehensive exhibition essential principles, or dogmatic, historico-salvation, moral, and/or existential facts and attempts to form one organized and intelligible whole.[11]

Systematic theology leads to a synthesis. In synthesizing, systematic theology's task is to locate the "nexus" between the mysteries of faith and

---

3. Epperson, *The Musical Symbol*, 292.
4. Meagher, "Revelation," 3:3498.
5. Meagher, "Revelation," 3:3498.
6. Meagher, "Revelation," 3:3498.
7. Meagher, "Revelation," 3:3498.
8. Cross, "Theology," 1363.
9. Cross, "Theology," 1363.
10. Karleen, *Handbook to Bible Study*, 363.
11. Meagher, "Revelation," 3:3498.

to establish harmony between faith and reason by "illuminating the unity among the ontological, logical, and semantic orders."[12] Theology is that "ultimate speech about the nature and the works of God which is mankind's response, however halting, to God's revelation."[13]

THEOLOGY OF MUSIC

A philosophy of music within the context of the book of Revelation becomes by its nature a theological endeavor. The church musician needs to have a value system that is based upon Christian theology.[14] Yet, nowhere within Scripture is a specific theology of music to be located. Still, "music is the accompanying counterpoint to the divine message and in the mighty acts of God music is never very far away."[15] Music is evident from Genesis to the Revelation, from creation to the Song of Moses, to the angel's proclamation of the Messiah's birth, to the end of time. Music is therefore "bound up with theology and theology with music."[16] A reciprocal relationship exists between theology and music. When the two become separated, music in worship becomes (1) entertainment, (2) music to set the mood, or (3) an "aural lubricant" that serves as a transition between other parts of the service. Without music, theology likewise suffers. It can become "dry, soulless, and brittle."[17] A theology of music begins with the notion that worship is an attitude of the inner self. Everything else, including music, is an outward display of this inner self. Thus, music provides worship with both expression and experience.[18]

WORSHIP: ΠΡΟΣΚΥΝΕΟ (*PROSKUNEO*)

Eight Greek words for worship occur in the New Testament. The exclusive Greek word for worship, which the writer of the Apocalypse employs in his visions, is προσκυνέο (*proskuneo*—see Revelation 4:10). In patriarchal times, this term implied the literal prostration of oneself before a person of dignity, a person of royalty, a god, or Yahweh. By the time of Christ, however, it will

---

12. Meagher, "Systematic Theology," 3:3442–43.
13. Routley, *Church Music and Theology*, 13.
14. Johansson, "Some Theological Considerations," 34.
15. Leaver, "Theological Character," 48.
16. Leaver, "Theological Character," 48–51.
17. Leaver, "Theological Character," 48–51.
18. Wright, "The Place of Music in Worship," 329.

be shown that this word for worship implied only a mental or spiritual prostration to a god or God.[19] The early church of the first century did not view the work of worship, liturgy ("the work of the people"), as a secular cultic practice. The early Christian community viewed liturgical worship as the realization and participation in the "kingdom of God," which was at hand.[20]

While this study is limited to the development of a theology of music in worship in the book of Revelation, the rest of the Bible and other sources are incorporated. In order to do this, it seeks to discover the origins of the music that the writer of the Apocalypse employed. The study seeks to categorize the various types of music found in the book of Revelation, but it is not an in-depth study of them. The study analyzes various song traditions, including the ode, hymn, and psalm, which were used in early worship. This study is not a full exegesis of the Revelation. Not all levels of musical structure are analyzed except only those contributing to an overall theology of music. In order to arrive at a theology of music, a brief overview of the concept of worship in the book of Revelation is discussed. The study centers on the biblical writer's reason for using the music he employed. This study entails a consideration of the origins of the music and the performance practices that he implied, based on his music sources.

Although John Wick Bowman supposes that the book of Revelation utilizes the combined formal structure of letter and drama, this study assumes the dramatic approach to the interpretation of the book as set forth most recently by James Blevins in *Revelation as Drama*.[21] It is Blevins's contention that the writer of the Apocalypse could not express the visions that he received from the Holy Spirit in prose. Rather, he chose a medium that requires the utilization of all the senses, i.e., Greek tragic drama. Blevins, Bowman, Fiorenza, and others divide the Apocalypse into a multi-act drama.[22]

Some biblical scholars dispute the Apocalypse's authorship. Culpepper holds the position that the book of Revelation is the result of a collection of assorted writings assembled by a "Johannine School," an informal group who followed the writings of the Apostle John.[23] Others believe that authorship is uncertain and cannot be pinpointed precisely. Ford conjectures that the writer could be John the Baptist or John the Apostle.[24] But, regardless

---

19. *WSE* 104.
20. Leaver, "Theological Character," 39.
21. Bowman, *First Christian Drama*, 11; *RD* 26.
22. Fiorenza, *Invitation to the Book of Revelation*.
23. Culpepper, *The Johannine School*.
24. Ford, *The Anchor Bible*.

of any particular author, the writer would have to exhibit the following characteristics: (1) one who understood the prophetic tradition of Israel, (2) one who believed in the "imminence of the kingdom," and (3) one who was able to speak the language of the prophets.

Kümmel shows that Dionysius of Alexandria (bishop ca. 247–265 CE) believed that the Apostle John could not have written the book of Revelation and the other books (the gospel and the epistles) based on the linguistic and stylistic differences between them.[25] By holding this position, Dionysius hoped ultimately to have the book of Revelation excluded from the canon.

However, both Buttrick and Guthrie support the view that the Apostle John was the author of the Apocalypse.[26] Guthrie shows that the following writers from the second and third centuries CE assumed that the Apostle John was the author of the book of Revelation: Justin, Irenaeus, Clement, Origen, Tertullian, and Hippolytus.[27]

This study assumes that the Apostle John, inspired by the Holy Spirit, received the vision of the Revelation while a prisoner on the Island of Patmos in CE 95. The Apostle John was born and reared a Jew but became "Christianized" by his close association with Jesus Christ. Following Pentecost, John traveled extensively throughout the world of his day and ultimately settled down in and around the area of Asia Minor known as Ephesus. As a result of his multicultural background, incorporating primarily Jewish, Christian, and Greek lifestyles, it is not unlikely that these elements heavily influenced his writing of the book of Revelation.

By studying the origins of the music of the Revelation, it is posited that the writer of the Apocalypse combined some original first-century "Christian" elements within a greater context of borrowings from other cultures of his time. These other cultures are primarily Jewish and Greek. Music in the book of Revelation is the result of this blending of cultures, which resulted in the creation of a "new" theology of music. This theology of music also includes elements of the seer's eschatological vision.

The purpose of this study is to develop a theology of music in worship in the book of Revelation so that the contemporary church professional can glean greater spiritual understanding and appreciation of music in worship in the first century. Many church professionals today look back as far as the early church for instruction in the practice of music in worship. Few consciously consider that Jewish music traditions, principally derived from patriarchal, tabernacle, temple, and synagogue times, carry any musical

---

25. Kümmel, *The New Testament*, 15.
26. *IB*.
27. Guthrie, *New Testament Introduction*.

weight. Nor do many contemporary church professionals consider that music from other cultures, whether Roman, Greek, or other pagan, could influence the music that is performed on a week-to-week basis in this century. But if the writer of the Apocalypse chose to couch his visions in Jewish and other traditional music of his time, then why should today's church professional continue to ignore them? The development of a theology of music in worship through the book of Revelation will provide a tool that can be used as a possible aid in grasping a hitherto mysterious and hard-to-interpret mass of apocalyptic material.

An attitude of complacency from the leaders in the churches exists today regarding well-balanced worship and music in worship. Many Christian circles have reduced the act of worship to a matter of academic, mentally disciplined rhetoric, and the laity have become passive. Music serves largely to pacify and break the tedium of an otherwise too-routine monologue. It becomes the worship leader's role to entertain the laity in an easily understood, largely non-liturgic and non-threatening manner.

Often, today's congregation is a generation of "takers." Sitting on the sidelines, contemporary Christian consumers want easy answers. They want to feel good and to "have it their way." They represent "easy consumerism" to eliminate boredom. In his day, Kierkegaard experienced much the same problem.[28] He criticized his church by observing that its ministers and musicians were the actors, the congregation was the audience, and God was the absentee playwright. But corporate worship is more than a period of entertainment with a reasoned, comprehensible lecture at the close. Kierkegaard spoke of worship as drama.[29] He described a model worship service consisting of the congregation as actors, the ministers and choir as leaders, and God as the audience. Not often enough in contemporary American Christian corporate worship does the congregation depart the worship service drained of all its corporate and individual energy because it "gave" so much in the service. Perhaps every congregation should desire actively to "give and take" in this manner during every act of corporate worship.

Worship is a two-fold process. It is both "theocentric" and "anthropological"; it is God-centered but God-centered from mankind's point of view.[30] This process should ". . . awaken the [whole] person to the capacity of God."[31] Raymond Bailey calls on the Christian community of the twentieth century to allow worship to touch our whole being—our "head, hand, heart,

---

28. Kierkegaard, *Purity of Heart*, 164.
29. Kierkegaard, *Purity of Heart*, 164.
30. Leaver, "Theological Character," 40.
31. Leaver, "Theological Character," 40.

and imagination."[32] Perhaps this can best be realized through the holistic process called drama.

The Scriptures have much more to teach us concerning the act of worship than we have been willing to accept in the past. Although effective worship can and does occur in both "low" and "high" liturgical traditions in different locations every week, perhaps what Scripture still has to teach us could somehow connect the diverse traditions together by appealing to the whole person and the whole community of believers. Perhaps if we perceived well-balanced worship as drama, we would be better able to experience the Spirit's fullness within the community of the church at large and within God's temple—the whole person.

As important as music is to any worship service, and as important as it is that the church professional be skilled in the practical skills of his or her endeavor so that he or she can produce the aesthetic and pragmatic objectives that the local church and his or her conscience demands, it is critical that he or she and the congregation understand that music is a means to a greater spiritual end. To that end, this church professional is obligated to continue his quest by searching the Scriptures for greater insights.

Every church professional should develop a philosophy or theology of music and worship. This provides him or her a value system with definable boundaries.[33] Many wish to espouse "this or that" philosophy or theology; some even claim to be guided by none. But just as a "nonconformist has to conform to his or her nonconformity," the church professional who chooses to adopt no theology has indeed made his or her choice.

The historical background of this study is rooted in the field of comparative liturgies, which is two to three centuries old. Werner's study is the first comprehensive volume on the topic.[34]

A brief survey of the general use of music in early pagan, Jewish, Greek, Roman, and the early church follows (see Appendix A for a timetable of these cultures).

EARLY PAGAN

Sumerian and Assyrian hymns and secular songs contain similar first lines of many poems and songs of various types. These various types of poems and songs consist of royal psalms, festival songs and lamentations, poems of

---

32. Bailey, "From Theory to Practice," 33.
33. Johansson, *Music and Ministry*, 3–7.
34. *TSB* 577.

"victory and heroic acts," and also love songs.[35] A wide variety of liturgical music exists because of the major role that cultic and religious ceremonies played in the lives of the Sumerian people. The largest temples had schools of music associated with them. The liturgists (*kalu*) and psalmists (*naru*) led the temple services by administering the daily sacred ceremonies to which they also provided vocal background. These sacred singers were members of their own guild and consisted of male and female singers. They were led in performance by a "special officer," while another leader was responsible for rehearsing them.[36]

Sumerian temples employed all types of instruments, although the psalmists used principally stringed instrumental accompaniment only. The harp (*al* or *zag-sal*) and the seven-stringed lyre (*shebitu*) were favored. In sacred music, the Sumerians preferred the *balaggu*, the flute and the drum. The most often cited wind instruments were the

> "covered" pipe (*kanzabu*), the single-pipe, an oboe-type (*mali-lu*), [and] the double-pipe (*shem*)... sometimes combined with the timbrel (*me-ze*).[37]

Among instruments extant from this period are harps, lutes, and double oboes. Written records do not exist, but other evidence indicates that these same instruments were used widely in Babylonia as well.[38]

According to Galpin, lyrics in Sumerian song "were put to music in a free recitative style."[39] Word accent determined the rhythm of the melodic line. These accents were given instrumental emphasis by accompanying harps and drumbeats. However, Sachs rejects Galpin's theory as "untenable." Sachs indicates that

> there are no signs for single notes. They indicate intervals, ascending or descending.... The vocal notations used in connection with religious texts indicate stereotyped groups of notes. They provide evidence of that particular ornamental style that we roughly call "Oriental."[40]

Sumerian music is believed to have provided much of the impetus to the development of early Jewish music even though the Sumerian empire predated the Jewish culture in time. The Sumerian culture is dated from the

---

35. *MAI* 35–36.
36. *MAI* 37.
37. *MAI* 37.
38. Ulrich and Pisk, *History of Music*, 10.
39. Galpin, *Music of the Sumerians*, 62.
40. Sachs, "The Mystery," 1:68.

third millennium BCE (ca. 3000–2300 BCE) when "organized temple music with singers and players existed."[41] Ulrich and Pisk attribute the great number of similarities between the two cultures' music to a common musical ethos that they shared. Each contained similar uses of emotion even though time separated them so widely. The Sumerian music of the third millennium BCE is often religious in character. It also possessed a "vigorous" folk tradition.[42] The music that survives from the Egyptian era is very scant.

Little more than pictorial representation survives. Interestingly, most of what is known of Egyptian music comes from foreign sources. While Babylonian and Assyrian monuments reveal instruments from all nations, the types of Egyptian instruments were more diverse and richer sounding than those of other cultures during their time. The harp (*ben* or *bin*) was the most prominent instrument used, followed by the lyre.[43]

Sacred Egyptian music was dominated by the soft and mellow timbre produced by stringed instruments. Sendrey conjectures that this was the character of the music in order to match the "*claire-obscure*" of the temple halls.[44] This type of music could provide the type of tonal background necessary for their mystic ceremonies.[45]

Music of the Babylonian cult was performed by the priest (*kalu*), the singer (*zammaru*) and for lamentations, the singer of wailing (*lallaru*). The most important Babylonian and Assyrian evidence that survives today portrays the victorious return of their conquering kings after battle. Musicians and singers are praising the king while the king reviews his prisoners. Other bas-reliefs show palm trees being felled in a war-torn city while the musicians are performing their ritual dances. They accompany themselves on drums and cymbals. Also pictured are women clapping their hands as they sing and dance.[46]

Babylonian music is not very different from that of the Egyptians. The principal instruments from the two cultures are the horizontal and vertical angular harps, different types of lyres, the double-oboe, drums, cymbals, and other percussion instruments. The ten-stringed instruments and flutes were commonly reserved for love songs. Similar to the music tradition of

---

41. Ulrich and Pisk, *History of Music*, 10.
42. *MAI* 35.
43. *MAI* 39.
44. *MAI* 40.
45. *MAI* 40.
46. *MAI* 44.

Sumeria, the Babylonians trained their young priests in special schools that were attached to the largest temples.[47]

The Phoenician religion was based on the cult of Ishtar. It praised the cruel service of Moloch who demanded appeasement via human sacrifice.[48] Plutarch recorded that these sacrifices were accompanied by flutes and drums "so that the cries of the wailing should not reach the ears of the people."[49] The "dedicated ones" (*kedeshot*) were responsible for the music and singing in the morning and evening sacrificial rites. They also raised money practicing religious prostitution that they presented to their goddess as offerings.[50]

Aristides Quintilianus (ca. 1-2 century BCE?) wrote of Phoenician music in *De Musica* that

> in the realm of (musical) education there are two degenerate trends: one is the entire lack [of] (*amousia*) and the other the wrong practice of art (*kakomousia*).[51]

This view of Phoenician music is perhaps too narrow. Aristides is perhaps speaking of only one special aspect of the music. Unfortunately, he does not address the other musical practices of the Phoenicians.

Early Phoenician music possibly was descended from the classical Egyptian tradition, which was "solemn, sedate" and full of dignity.[52] Likewise, the Assyrians and Lydians had music of nobler character, apart from the music of their respective orgiastic rites.[53] The basic trend in Assyrian music was toward "refinement" during the period of the great kings, just as it was in the "golden" age of the Egyptians.[54]

JEWISH

Generally speaking, Jewish music is a utilitarian art form. From its beginnings, the Jewish culture demanded that its music exhibit a "heteronomous

---

47. *MAI* 45–46.
48. *MAI* 54.
49. *MAI* 54.
50. *MAI* 54.
51. *MAI* 54.
52. *MAI* 54.
53. *MAI* 54.
54. *MAI* 45.

artistic phenomenon," which subsequently developed into a music with a "strong spiritual and ethical significance."⁵⁵

More so than in other languages, the Hebrew language is designed to express the human vocal sound in a roughly physical manner. But the Jewish tradition borrowed heavily from the Greek in order to express instrumental musical terms. This can be shown by comparing Greek and Hebrew transliterated terminology for similar instruments:

English	Greek	Hebrew
Lyre	*kithara*	*gathros*
Strings	*nema*	*Ninim*
stringed instrument	*psalterim*	*psanterin*
consonance, ensemble	*symphonia*	*sumponia*⁵⁶

The first attempt to catalog Jewish song was begun by Idelsohn in the first part of the twentieth century. In the liturgies of both the Babylonian and Yemenite Hebrews, he found song tune patterns very close to the chants used by the Catholic Church many centuries later. Because the Babylonian and Yemenite Hebrews were separated physically from their Palestinian counterparts and separated from the Catholic tradition in time, Werner contends that the existence of these tunes in later Catholic traditions must be attributed to the passing of the tunes by the Jewish-Christians communities of the first century. One "can rely on the analyses and the resulting conclusions" derived when "at least one of the Jewish or Christian sources is based... upon a well-authenticated [oral] tradition."⁵⁷ This oral tradition was fostered and nurtured in the early church by Jewish cantors who migrated to the church.⁵⁸ Many of Werner's specific conclusions are now called into question, though there is clearly a general affinity between the liturgical music of Judaism and early Christianity.⁵⁹

The pervasive use of Greek music in the Jewish culture caused many Jewish leaders to consider it detrimental to Israel's faith. In fact, after the destruction of the temple in the sixth-century BCE, instrumental music was forbidden in Jewish practice, except for restricted use as expressions of mourning for the destruction of the temple. It was shunned by the Jewish

55. *MAI* 32.
56. *TSB* 334.
57. *TSB* xviii.
58. *TSB* xiii.
59. See McKinnon, *Music in Early Christian Literature*, 335 and Smith, "The Ancient Synagogue," 1–16.

leaders because of the syncretistic manner in which it had been used. Vocal music was exempt from this exclusion as long as it maintained a purely spiritual function.[60]

Early Judaism (from the third-century BCE to the end of AD second-century) believed in a cosmic theology. Above the earth were the heavens. The heavens were not silent but always full of activity. Pseudepigraphal literature of the day (see the *Ascension of Isaiah* and the *Testament of Adam*) portrayed the heavens as full of singing angels. The harmony of the heavens was occasionally interrupted while sinners were being punished.[61]

GREEK

The surviving corpus of Greek melody consists of fewer than six hundred measures. The main features of the monophonic music are described in the writings of Aristoxenus (fourth-century BCE),[62] and in the *Harmonics* of Claudius Ptolemy (from the second-century BCE). The primary type of music in Greek life was choral music. It was used in the cult worship of the gods, at marriages, at funerals, and to celebrate famous men or athletes. The choirs consisted of unskilled musicians who had received rudimentary music instruction as part of their general education.[63]

Pythagoras viewed music as "a microcosm" of sound and rhythm within the greater mathematical laws that affected the whole of creation. These different sounds developed into modes with their own unique character (ethos).[64] The two primary divisions of the doctrine of ethos consist of music that could either create calmness and be uplifting or create excitement and be enthusiastic. The former became characteristic of those who worshiped Apollo and is spoken of in connection with classical style. The Apollonian school strove for clarity and moderation in their music. The latter became characteristic of those who worshiped and followed Dionysus. This is often referred to as romantic style. Characteristic of the Dionysian school was the perpetual drive towards the fantastic and orgiastic.[65]

---

60. McKinnon, *Music in Early Christian Literature*, 335.

61. Charlesworth, *Old Testament Pseudepigrapha*, 59–65.

62. See Appendix B for a summary of the dates of the Greek philosophers and others mentioned in this study.

63. Winnington-Ingram, "Greece, Ancient," 7:659–60.

64. Anderson, *Ethos and Education*, 52–53.

65. Grout and Palisca, *A History of Western Music*, 7–10. This citation is not in later editions.

Plato wrote in his *Republic* that "music can affect not only the emotions temporarily but also can permanently affect one's character."[66] In his *Laws*, he rejects music styles that are "plaintive" (as portrayed in the Mixolydian and Syntonalydian modes) and "effeminate" (as portrayed in the Ionian and Lydian modes) in favor of the Dorian and Phrygian modes, which he believed portrayed "courage" and "sobriety," respectively.[67]

On the contrary, Aristotle wrote in his *Politics* that "carefully selected music" can help one attain "virtue." Aristotle tended to be less "puritanical" than Plato because he allowed for music of relaxation and he claimed that rhythms and melodies "represent[ed] moral qualities" that could directly influence and "affect" the soul.[68] Both Aristotle and Plato's highest ideal was to preserve the "purity" of their music.[69] Music, for the Greek mind, was aesthetically representative of the qualities of "beautiful" and "good." Καλόκαγαθια (*Kalokagathia*)— καλός (*kalos*) meaning "beautiful" and αγαθος (*agathos*) meaning "good"—was the union of beauty and virtue.[70] Plato wrote that music leads the arts in importance. In *Timaeus*, Plato said,

> The philosopher sees an analogy between the movements of the soul and the musical progressions; therefore, the aim of music cannot be mere amusement but a harmonic education and perfection of the soul and the quieting of passions. The primary role of music was a pedagogical one, which implied the strengthening up of one's morals and character.[71]

Music was also used:[72]

1. as accompaniment to sacrificial worship;
2. to provide ἀποτροπαικ (*apotropaic*) protection from evil gods;[73]
3. as an ἐπικλεσε (*epiclese*);[74]

---

66. Arnold, *Companion*, 67. See also Henderson, "Ancient Greek Music," I:336–39.
67. Arnold, *Companion*, 67.
68. Arnold, *Companion*, 67.
69. Hall, *Therapeutic Value of Music*, 33.
70. Lang, *Music in Western Civilization*, 1.
71. Lang, *Music in Western Civilization*, 13.
72. *TSB* 322.

73. The ἀποτροπαικ (*apotropaic*) function of music can be illustrated by: (1) the *sistra* of the Egyptians that were used to drive away the evil Typhon; (2) the bells of the Phrygians that were used to chase away evil shadows and dreams; and (3) *Paamonium* on the dress of the Jewish high priest that were worn when he entered the holy of holies (see *HMI*).

74. A person in a posture of prayer commonly used music to invoke the gods

4. as a καθαρσις (*katharsis*) before and initiation into the mysteries;[75]
5. at funerals;[76]
6. during the performance of magic; and
7. as an accompaniment to sorcery.

ROMAN

Roman music was influenced early by the Etruscans. Later, as the Roman Empire grew, it was influenced by the Greeks and "assimilated, modified, and extended the music of the nations they conquered," including the Orient.[77] After the second century BCE, they overtook the Macedonians, Syrians, and the Egyptians.[78] However, the Roman culture never achieved as high a cultural independence in its music as did the Greeks. This is due largely to the fact that the doctrine of ethos never appeared in Roman music.[79] The high point for Greco-Roman music existed during the reigns of Augustus (27 BCE–CE 14) and under the subsequent dynasties of Julius and Claudius (CE 14–68), the Flavians (CE 69–96) and the Antonines (CE 96–192). During this period,

> professional virtuosi, mainly of Greek origin, sang and played instruments; outstanding Egyptian and Syrian *pantomimi* performed in public; Greek and Roman musicians and actors were active in organized bodies at Rome and elsewhere; dancers and musicians were imported as slaves from all parts of the empire; musical instruments and musical scholarship were developed; and the participation of music lovers in public events increased.

to lend aid and assistance (ἐπικλεσις—*epiclesis*). In the Rhea Kybele cult (a popular religion in Asia Minor), cymbals and bells were used. It has been speculated by H. Gressman in *Musik und Musikinstrumente im Alten Testament* (Gieszen: J. Ricker'sche Verlagsbuchhandlung, 1903) that the *shofar* and trumpet served the same function in the Old Testament period. .

75. The utilization of music for a cathartic purpose is a primary characteristic of Pythagoreanism. Catharsis is the "purification or purgation of the emotions primarily through the arts that brings about spiritual renewal or a release from tension." Woolf, "Catharsis," 345.

76. Flutes and cymbals were used at funerals in all the religious cults of Asia Minor and Palestine.

77. Fleischhauer, "Rome," 16:146.

78. Fleischhauer, "Rome," 16:146.

79. Ulrich, *A History of Music*, 10.

At the same time philosophers and historians, including Seneca, Quintilian, Plutarch, Juvenal and Tacitus, attacked the demoralizing and effeminate effects of theatrical music, and the 'decline' of music in the service of luxury, on national, social, musical and moral grounds. Many actors, dancers, and musicians continued, nevertheless, to enjoy public favour, despite their low legal and social position.[80]

The ritual music of the Romans was influenced by the mystery religions of Cybele (the *magna mater* in Phrygia), Dionysus (Bacchus in Greece) and Isis (in Egypt). The cult of Cybele, introduced in Rome in 204 BCE, held a several-days-long festival with scenic games (*ludi Megalenses*). This festival was held annually

> to commemorate the dedication of her temple on the Aventine. Priests carried the cult-idol of the goddess in triumphal procession to the music of the bronze *cymbala*, frame drums or *tambours* (tympana), *cornua* (horns) and 'Phrygian auloi' or 'Berecyntian *tibiae*' whose deeper-sounding left pipe had an upturned horn-shaped bell.[81]

These same instruments were used at the orgiastic dances of the priests in the temples. The purpose of this music was partly practical. The loud beating of the drums and cymbals muffled the cries of those being violated![82]

When Rome conquered Egypt in 30 BCE, the cult of Isis spread through the empire. The traditional and characteristic instrument of the Isis cult was the *sistrum*—a bright-sounding metal rattle, used to dispel the influence of evil spirits. Other instruments used by the cult were Egyptian vertical long flutes and angle harps. As in the Cybelian and Dionysian cults, instrumentalists and hymn singers were employed by the temple priests.[83]

EARLY CHURCH

"Early church" refers to the Christian Church of the first century up through the writing of the Apocalypse. The early church did not have to travel outside of Palestine in order to be significantly influenced by Greek, Roman, and other pagan ideas. The terminologies of the mystery religions were well-known, although the influence of these mystery religions should not be

80. Fleischhauer, "Rome," 16:146.
81. Fleischhauer, "Rome," 16:148.
82. Fleischhauer, "Rome," 16:148.
83. Fleischhauer, "Rome," 16:148.

overestimated. For the most part, the mystery religions did not succeed in Palestine because of their "offensive idolatrous base." Hengel theorizes that the mystery religions were thwarted from too much influence over the early church because "the solution of humanity's predicaments and the explanation of human existence" had already been "attractively elaborated" via the crucifixion and resurrection of Christ.[84]

The principal references to music in the New Testament are found in Colossians 3:16, Ephesians 5:19, and "certain heraldic references in the singing of the heavenly hosts in the book of Revelation."[85] Vocal forms are referred to and consist of:

1. psalms—"scriptural praises set to music";
2. hymns—"non-scriptural spontaneous songs of praise" to God; and
3. spiritual songs—"ecstatic utterances of joy."[86]

The Pharisees' views on music during the time of the Apostle Paul's writings were the strictest in relation to both synagogue and temple worship. The Pharisees' "antimusical" views consisted of:

1. an opposition to the more liberal attitudes of the Sadducees;
2. an opposition to the use of instruments, because of the "clarinet [sic], cymbals, gong and drum's association with the mystery cults of Asia Minor"; and
3. the general overall historic association of instruments with pagan cults.[87]

Perhaps the Apostle Paul portrayed a new appreciation for the use of music in the early church since he was found to be singing in the Philippian jail with Silas. He also encouraged the Corinthians "to sing with understanding," and he exhorted the Colossians to "sing with grace."[88]

The early church adopted attitudes towards Hellenistic music similar to their contemporary Jewish counterparts. While both utilized instrumental music, both were reluctant to use instrumental accompaniment in their respective religious services. The early church fathers from the second

---

84. Hengel, *Judaism and Hellenism*, 1:202; OTP 81–82.
85. Routley, *Church Music and Theology*, 23.
86. Appleby, *History of Church Music*, 20.
87. Appleby, *History of Church Music*, 19–20.
88. Appleby, *History of Church Music*, 19–20.

century CE considered vocal music more pleasing to God than instrumental music.[89]

Because the early church's vernacular contained Greek and Latin phrases, the infiltration of these pagan fragments into their liturgy was more likely. Consequently, the early church fathers sought to limit the texts of their songs to biblical passages, primarily from the psalter.[90] Eventually, the early church gave up on their exclusion of "pagan influences" as exemplified in their acceptance of the Κύριε Ελεισον (*Kyrie Eleison*—"Lord have mercy"). The origins of this first song of the Ordinary of the Mass stem from an *Helios-Mithra* hymn.[91]

Music was used not only in the various religious cults of the time, but also in the symposia, the theater, in concerts, in recitals and in the secular processions and parades. Between all of these religious and pagan practices of music, the early church existed. It is interesting to note that while the early church basically forsook instrumental music in favor of pure vocal music, the book of Revelation portrays the elders, prostrate before the lamb, playing a new song on their harps.[92] Present-century concepts of the aesthetic and the moral are not at all comparable to Jewish and early church ideas. While "beauty" may not be mentioned in the 1 Kings 5–8 description of the Temple, it is heavily implied-accurate stonework, carved cedar wood, the overlaying of gold, the depiction of lilies, pomegranates, etc. But in Old Testament literature, for example, the idea that music was beautiful was unknown. While music had a decided place in the temple ritual and served as a spontaneous expression of a person or a group, it was nowhere aesthetically intended to be beautiful as a lower human virtue. Rather, music served in the role of a higher virtue under the locus of worship.[93]

IN THE BOOK OF REVELATION

Characteristic of the music and worship of Revelation is that it is lacking entirely of any introspection on the part of the participants, and it focuses exclusively on the characteristics and acts of God.[94]

In his first-century study of hymns, Michael Harris indicates that contemporary authors are reluctant to show a direct relationship between

89. *TSB* 335–36.
90. *TSB* 336.
91. *TSB* 336.
92. *TSB* 344.
93. McKinnon, *Music in Early Christian Literature*, 5.
94. Guthrie, *The Relevance of John's Apocalypse*, 85–89.

hymns and liturgic practice of the first century.[95] David Carnegie argues that the hymns of Revelation are specifically original creations of the writer of the Apocalypse, not borrowed or assimilated from the surrounding cultures.[96]

However, the fact remains that the author of the book of Revelation did use specific types of music and implied specific modes of musical performance, which this author will show contain multicultural roots. According to Werner,

> All Christian liturgies of the Churches which originated during the first millennium have evolved around the same nuclei. Yet the differing languages, regional customs, and specific folklores have wrought vast cleavages between them, both in form and content.[97]

According to Werner, the starting place of early Christian liturgy was neither the Scriptures nor the Jewish temple but rather the synagogue.[98] The early Christian community borrowed its substance and other musical practice from the synagogue and borrowed various musical forms, such as the canticle, response, and refrain from the Jewish temple.

More recent scholarship demonstrates there was no musical borrowing of synagogal tradition in the early church before the destruction of the temple in CE 70, or, at best, several synagogal traditions coexisted. Mowinckel states that "services in the synagogue in ancient times had no singing."[99] Musical texts were recited, not sung. McKinnon further states that temple psalmody was not used in the synagogue tradition: "recitation of Scripture in the ancient synagogue was not a dry reading in the modern sense but rather some sort of elemental declamation or cantillation."[100]

The singing of psalms occurred domestically and in the temple. Two types of singing occurred in two Jewish sects, the Essenes and the Therapeutae. The first consisted of the president's solo singing before a meal accompanied by choral responses. The second occurred as all those present formed an antiphonal "single choir" during the vigil. Smith conjectures that the early church may have borrowed singing and fellowship at meals from

---

95. Harris, "The Literary Function of Hymns," 3.
96. Carnegie, "Worthy is the Lamb," 246–47.
97. *TSB* xvi.
98. *TSB* 19.
99. *PIW* I:4.
100. McKinnon, "The Exclusion of Musical Instruments," 85. See also McKinnon, "On the Question of Psalmody," 159–91.

private Jewish religious gatherings.[101] Two examples are the Last Supper, which ended with a hymn (Matt 26:30; Mark 14:26), and the account of Pentecost, as concluded in Acts 4:25 with the singing of psalms and hymns.

Smith claims that "no relevant notational remains or technical descriptions of Christian song sufficient to provide specific information about the style of the singing during the first or even second century" exists. Smith further argues that songs in the book of Revelation, as well as in "other hymnic passages in the New Testament, are unreliable as evidence about the nature of early Christian singing and therefore also about whether early Christians sang Jewish material."[102] Regardless, this study will clearly show that the writer of the Apocalypse used the breadth of his multicultural life experiences to portray the fullness of the vision he received from the Godhead.

The early Christian community absorbed and modified many regional and pre-Christian traditions they primitively sought to develop an organized liturgy. Cullinan suggests that the entire book of Revelation is couched in and full of allusions to the liturgical usages common to the early worshiping community of the first century. The seer (Rev 1:1) sees his visions on the Lord's Day. This is the time when the Christian community traditionally gathered.[103] The seer sees the entire drama of the last days in "the context of the early Christian service of worship."[104] The use of the church's oldest songs, coupled with Pliny's mention of antiphonal singing by the early church, suggests that "liturgically ordered singing" was already prevalent and practiced by the church as early as the late first century.[105]

In spite of the fact that the writer of the Apocalypse wrote what he saw, "this fact does not preclude the possibility of his visions incorporating established patterns of worship in the church," just as freely as he had incorporated many passages from the Old Testament.[106]

Little work, beyond some text-related hymnological studies (see Bibliography), has been done primarily dealing with the music of the Revelation. Klaus-Peter Joerns has identified thirty hymns within the text of Revelation, but he focuses the bulk of his attention on the hymn texts of chapters 4 and 5.[107] Other authors have identified a different number of hymn texts in the

101. Smith, "The Ancient Synagogue," 6, 11, 16.
102. Smith, "First-Century Christian Singing," 2, 13.
103. Cullman, *Early Christian Worship*, 7.
104. Cullman, *Early Christian Worship*, 7.
105. Cullman, *Early Christian Worship*, 7.
106. Coleman, *Songs of Heaven*, 17–18.
107. Joerns, *Das Hymnische Evangelium*. For a summary listing of hymn texts by

book. Cullman has identified six hymns (5:9, 12, 13; 12:10–12; 19:1–2, 6), while Harris has most recently enumerated seven (4:8–11; 5:9; 7:10; 11:17–18; 12:10–11; 15:3, 4b).[108] Harris's study of the hymns is typical of that of the other authors. He approaches the hymns from a purely literary viewpoint. His study primarily uses narrative criticism to argue for the hymnic unit divisions within the text.[109] Church and Mulry identify eleven hymns in the Revelation (Rev 1:5–8; 4:11; 5:9–11, 12–13; 11:17–18; 12:10–12; 15:3–4; 18:22–23; 19:1–9; 22:16–17, 20).[110] While hymnological studies in the book of Revelation are valid, they only peripherally touch on the topic at hand. They address neither the nature of the music itself nor its performance practice.

During the first century, both hymnody and psalmody were widely practiced within the Greek world. According to Didymus (ca. second half of the first century BCE), it was common for "the man of practical life [to] prefer psalmody; [and for] the man of theoretical life [to] prefer hymns."[111] That is, psalms should be sung by the common man every day, whereas hymns held a place of higher esteem. They were used by others in a more discriminating manner.[112] Where and when did musical concepts, forms, and aesthetic values emerge and develop to produce a synthesis between the temple and other Jewish practice and early church traditions of music? The same question could be asked regarding the relationship between the music of the early church, the Greeks, and the other cultures of the first century. If it were possible to conclusively answer this type of question, we could gain a much deeper insight into the history of religious music.

Since 1936, there has been an increased desire to educate ministers and the laity concerning the act that Christians call worship. Segler defines worship as "man's loving response in personal faith to God's revelation of himself in Jesus Christ."[113] A trinitarian formula for worship might augment the preceding definition with ". . . through the Holy Spirit." While this definition might satisfy the reasoned, rational mind of a technological, scientific-age person, perhaps contemporary Christianity has failed to comprehend the full spectrum of what the act of worship, using music, embraces.

---

various authors see Appendix C.

108. Cullman, *Early Christian Worship*, 8; Harris, "Hymns of the Apocalypse," 305.

109. Harris, "Hymns of the Apocalypse," 3–7.

110. Church and Mulry, *Earliest Christian Hymns*, x.

111. *TSB* 319.

112. *TSB* 319.

113. Segler, *Christian Worship*, 12.

The thesis of this study is that there is a discernable theology of music that the writer of the Revelation assumed. The book of Revelation does not consist of a collection of unrelated visions and music. Rather, the music provides the basis of a well-conceived theology of music in worship. The thesis of this study breaks new ground and has not been addressed directly in any other study to date.

A theology of music in worship in the book of Revelation has not been dealt with as a topic, except for peripheral glances in a few articles, such as R. Bauckham's "The Worship of Jesus in Apocalyptic Christianity."[114] By dividing the book of Revelation into seven acts and suggesting that the book be acted out as a performable drama, James Blevins has shown that the music serves both pragmatic and aesthetic roles.[115] Classical musical works, such as *Messiah* by Handel, draw heavily on the hymn texts of the book of Revelation. All of these works pertain directly or indirectly to music, yet none hypothesize a theology of music related to the book of Revelation.

While Benson discusses the New Testament backgrounds of music in a general overview, he fails to mention any of the music of the Revelation.[116] Neither do other authors. Perhaps most authorities think of the music in Revelation as future oriented and not suitable for contemporary practice.

Several authors have written histories of worship, philosophies of music or worship, or theologies of music or worship in the twentieth century. Representative histories of early Christian worship include Martin's *Worship in the Early Church* and Webber's *Worship: Old and New*.[117] Martin brings to light New Testament teachings concerning early Christian principles of worship and discusses at length the practice of corporate worship, but he makes no attempt to apply the principles to the worship of today. While Webber discusses Jewish and early Christian worship practices, he ignores Greek and pagan worship practices altogether.

In *Jubilate II! Church Music in Worship and Renewal*, Hustad seeks to develop a practical working philosophy for twentieth-century American church musicians from the perspectives of ethnomusicology.[118] He judges music in worship by whether or not it fulfills its best function as a means to a greater spiritual end. Franklin Segler indicates that "all churches are mutually indebted to many historic treasures to which no one denomination

---

114. Bauckham, "The Worship of Jesus," 322–41.
115. *RD* 3–24.
116. Benson, *Hymnody*, 25–53, 233–36.
117. Martin, *Worship in the Early Church*; Webber, *Worship: Old and New*.
118. Hustad, *Jubilate II!*.

or tradition can lay exclusive claim."[119] Segler concerns himself with the meaning of worship, the means of expressing worship, and the planning and conducting of worship in today's church.

Perhaps the bedrock of theological writing on worship and music in worship in the twentieth century has been accomplished by Underhill. Her aim was "to explore those primary realities of man's relation to God which our devotional action is intended to express."[120] She dealt with worship at its very core, as response to the Godhead. She does not specifically bring up the shortcomings of all the different worship traditions within Christianity. Rather, she believes that although the various traditions contain negative traits worthy of ridicule, all pale in comparison to what she calls "the positive element" of each: "man's upward and outward movement of adoration, self-oblation and dependence. . ."[121]

Several theological works on music and worship have appeared within the last fifteen years. Burkhart seeks to sketch a theology of worship by incorporating evidence from the anthropological, biblical, historical, and theological disciplines as well as from a compendium of liturgical experiences.[122] Martin, following up on the basis that he laid in *Worship in the Early Church*, constructs a model or philosophy of Christian worship that is both theologically and pastorally helpful.[123] He touches on the components of both the traditional and contemporary worship service.

Johansson provides one of the freshest and most insightful theologies of music to date.[124] He considers that "no single doctrine or theological topic is intended to stand alone." He juxtaposes opposite ends of the music-practice spectrum in a counterpoint that results in a well-balanced look at the development of a theology of music.

Paul Hoon states that "a viable liturgical theology" must be tested against "the empirical life of the Church" where the central issues are the "gathered congregation" and the need for "a pastoral liturgy."[125] In his Christologically-conceived theology of worship, Hoon analyzes many aspects of the Church's life in worship.

---

119. Segler, *Christian Worship*, 12.
120. Underhill, *Worship*, vii.
121. Underhill, *Worship*, viii.
122. WSE 104.
123. Martin, *Worship of God*; Martin, *Worship in the Early Church*.
124. Johansson, *Music and Ministry*, 3–7.
125. Hoon, *The Integrity of Worship*.

The pinnacle of contemporary writing in the area of worship has been compiled in Wainwright's systematic theology of worship.[126] It is written from a liturgical perspective and proceeds to show "a liturgical way of doing theology." He claims that

> a historical community, in this case the Christian Church, can transmit a vision of reality which helps decisively in the interpretation of life and the world.[127]

Donald Pass uses several key Scripture passages, most notably Genesis 1:3, Acts 2:46–47, Colossians 3:16 and Ephesians 5:18–20, to formulate a "theological theory of church music." Pass shows that music has played a vital role in each of the historical "orders" of God's dealings with humankind: creation, preservation, and redemption. His intention is to show how the whole of Scripture can speak directly to the contemporary church musician.[128]

Idelsohn has been able to illustrate the similarities between isolated Jewish groups with various Gregorian chants. Following on Idelsohn's idea, Douglas shows that the relationship between these two traditions' musical types are:

1. chanting;
2. the use of inflected monotone in Scripture readings;
3. congregational refrains in the singing of the psalms;
4. "festal jubilations" of the alleluia type;
5. the use of prose rhythm;
6. some "practically identical" melodies; and
7. a general similarity of style, which has noble dignity. This characteristic is quite unlike the secular music of its day.[129]

While Idelsohn is able to relate the similarities between the Jewish tradition and Christianity from the patristic Age, no one has attempted to do the same with the music of the first century.[130] Appleby contends that the types of music in worship were not seriously debated before the fourth century CE. Consequently, endless speculation has occurred in the centu-

---

126. DOX.
127. DOX 1–2.
128. Pass, *Music and the Church*, 7–8, 23, 36–38, 88–91.
129. Douglas, *Church Music in History*, 18–19.
130. JLD.

ries that followed concerning music of the church in the pre-fourth century CE period. Although the New Testament has little to say concerning particular stylistic characteristics of music, Appleby cites several examples that indicate that Jesus "had little quarrel" with the forms and types of music and worship that he observed in the temple.[131] His objection arose with the attitude that produced it.

.These works represent the literature related to the topic at hand. They provide the guidelines from which this writer will attempt to develop a theology of music in worship in the book of Revelation. This study analyzes the book of Revelation and identifies all musical references to worship. Once identified, this study then categorizes each musical reference according to its specific or blended origins. By studying the music and practice of the various origins, this writer will show that these various elements meld into a unified whole that subsequently is summarized in a theology of music within the context of the book of Revelation. By studying the role that the writer of the Revelation ascribes to music in worship, it is shown that the music and performance practice implied in the Apocalypse have origins both from other times and cultures as well as from within the early church.

The primary methodological tool implemented in this study is philosophical and theological research. This procedure consists of three steps:

1. identify musical occurrences in worship within the Apocalypse;

2. analyze them in an attempt to codify not only their nature or type but also to show their origins; and

3. interpret them in order to formulate a theology of music that can assist the church musician in the present century.[132]

In pursuing this methodology, a historical study through the earlier and contemporary cultures endeavors to find borrowings from them.

The Revised Standard Version of the Bible is used to study the text of the Revelation.[133] In order to discover the philosophical tenets of Jewish, Greek, and other pagan music, this writer utilizes both primary and secondary sources. The primary Greek sources consist of selected writings. The primary Jewish music sources consist of selected sections of the Old Testament, the Torah, Old Testament Pseudepigrapha, including Apocalyptic writings and the Apocrypha, as well as various authors of the first century, such as Josephus.

---

131. Appleby, *History of Church Music*, 18.
132. Phelps, *Research in Music Education*, 103.
133. May and Metzger, *New Oxford Annotated Bible*.

Sources for the study of first-century Christian music have included the New Testament and writings of patristic authors, as well as secondary authors. After this introductory chapter, chapter 2 focuses on the exclusive Greek word used for worship in the book of Revelation. Προσκυνέω (*Proskuneo*) has Jewish patriarchal and other-culture origins that differ greatly from its usage in the first century after Christ's birth. An understanding of worship in the Revelation has influenced both the type of music as well as the performance practice that is implied in the text.

Chapter 3 focuses on the music inherent in the text. The types of music found in the book of Revelation are discussed. Examples of these include accompanied and unaccompanied odes and songs. The background of the types of music found in the text are analyzed according to their respective early pagan, Jewish, Greek, Roman, and early church origins. Chapter 4 seeks to discover the various musical ensembles that are evident in the text. Chapter 5 studies the types of sounds that were made in producing the music for worship based on a study of Greek verbs found in the text. It also discloses the manner in which those sounds were made.

Chapter 6 summarizes and lists the characteristics of the various elements of music for worship found in the book of Revelation. This summary and subsequent dialogue comprises a theology of music for worship derived from the book of Revelation. Chapter 7 then shows how this theology of music might be woven into the fabric of contemporary Christian music and worship practice. The musical references in the book of Revelation have been dealt with in a topical manner. The culminating theology of music consists of a list of the key characteristics of the music of the Revelation. This list constitutes a synthesis of the music and music practices in the book of Revelation. From it, the contemporary church professional may be able to understand better the methodology of music and worship practice in the Apocalypse and thereby find a way in which he or she can incorporate it into his or her present-day worship services.

2

The Origin and Use of Προσκυνέο

Eight Greek words occur in the New Testament that imply the process of worship. Of these, the most common forms are σέβομαι (*sebomai*—"to revere"), λειτουργία (*leitourgia*—"liturgy"), and λατρεία (*latreia*—"worship").[1] All eight words speak of a human response to the Lord and Maker of all creation. Inclusive in this list is προσκυνέο (*proskuneo*—verb: "worshiping"). It is the only word for worship used in the book of Revelation.[2]

DEFINITIONS

The Greek word προσκυνέο (*proskuneo*) appears fifty-eight times in the New Testament, with twenty-three of those occurrences in the book of Revelation. Προσκυνέο (*Proskuneo*) is a compound of two roots: προς (*pros*) meaning "towards" and κυνέο (*kuneo*) meaning "to kiss."

Κυνέο (*Kuneo*) is analogous to the Latin *os*, as in "osculate," or *ora*, as in "oral," "orate," and "adoration."[3] In combination, προς (*pros*) and κυνέο (*kuneo*) mean "to do obeisance to" and "to worship."[4] A note to Matthew 2:2 in the Revised Standard Version of the *Passages, IV*, says that the word denotes an "act of reverence, whether paid to man [sic] (Matt 18:26) or to God (Matthew 4:10)."

---

1. Martin, *Worship of God*, 11.
2. Strong, "Worship," 1190.
3. *WSE* 103.
4. Moulton and Milligan, "προσκυνέο," 549.

STYLE OF WRITING AND SYNTAX IN REVELATION

Professor Moulton says of the Hebraic style of Revelation,

> That even the Greek of the Apocalypse itself does not seem to owe any of its blunders to Hebraism. The author's uncertain use of cases is obvious to the most casual reader. . . We find him perpetually indifferent to concord. But the less educated papyri give us plentiful parallels from a field whose Semitism cannot be suspected. Apart from places where he may be definitely translating a Semitic document, there is no reason to believe that his grammar would have been materially different had he been a native of Oxyrhynchus, assuming the extent of Greek education the same. . .[5]

Charles agrees and further states that he believes that the language of Revelation differs from that of the Septuagint and other versions of the Old Testament—from the Greek of the Apocrypha and the Pseudepigrapha to that of the papyri. Although the language of the Revelation is basically consistent with the standard Greek of its day, it nevertheless possesses a unique character. The most notable difference is the high number of solecisms that occur in the Revelation text.[6] Charles supposes the reasons for this could be that the writer purposefully "set at defiance" the grammarian and the ordinary rules of syntax. Because the writer was successful in this, Charles does not believe that the writer did it intentionally. Or, the writer of the Revelation wrote in Greek, but likely thought in Hebrew. Charles contends that the writer probably never mastered the Greek language idiomatically. Still, despite the numerous solecistic irregularities of its form and syntax, in the process of translation, these difficulties disappear, leaving "its essential greatness alike in thought and expression."[7]

The writer uses προσκονενε (*proskonene3*—present infinitive: "to worship") with the dative case and implies only the worship of God. When the accusative form is used in the text, it is rendered "homage" or a lesser form of worship is implied. Such a usage is consistent with Septuagint language, although Abbott showed that the Synoptics reserve the accusative case for the worship "due to God or God's Son."[8] In the Samaritan Dialogue and in the Temptation Narratives, the Synoptics employ "a deliberate differentiation of

---

5. *SIA* 79–80.
6. An inconsistency in grammatical usage.
7. *SIA* 81.
8. Charles, *Critical and Exegetical Commentary*, cxli.

the two Greek constructions" (προσκυνενε [*proskunene*] is translated as the "worship of" in the accusative case and "prostration to" in the dative case). The synoptic writers "appear to use προσκυνέο (*proskuneo*) with the accusative [case] as meaning that such worship should be paid to God alone."[9] In Ptolemaic inscriptions it is used with the accusative case only and means "to do obeisance to" a god.[10]

Robertson indicates that προσκυνέο (*proskuneo*) can be used freely in both the accusative and the dative cases. He proposes no excuses for the syncretism of the cases as do Charles and Moulton. Robertson points out that προσκυνέο (*proskuneo*) occurs approximately sixty times in the New Testament with thirty instances in the dative case and fourteen in the accusative case.[11]

In summary, the five positions mentioned of the use of προσκυνέο (*proskuneo*) in the book of Revelation are: (1) Septuagint usage of προσκυνέο (*proskuneo*) in the dative case was reserved for the worship only of God or gods, while the verb in the accusative case was used "to pay homage" to a person; (2) Charles excuses the writer for his inconsistencies of syntax due to his supposed Hebraic background; (3) Moulton believes that the casual use of προσκυνέο (*proskuneo*) is either the prostrating of oneself before kings or queens, other superiors, or the gods and images of the people. Its use in either the dative or accusative cases was typical of the cross-cultural syntax of the first century Greek and Jewish worlds; (4) Abbott contends that the Synoptics reversed the Septuagint's usage; and (5) Robertson argues that προσκυνέο (*proskuneo*) was used indiscriminately in either case to render obeisance to a god or a person. It will be shown that Septuagint usage was normative for the writer of the Apocalypse.

ORIGINS OF ITS USAGE

Origins of προσκυνέο (*proskuneo*) follow.

Early Pagan

The earliest use of the root προς (*pros*) comes from the oriental fashion of the physical κυνέο (*kuneo*) act of either throwing a kiss to the recipient or kissing his or her feet, his or her garment, or kissing the ground. The

---

9. Charles, *Critical and Exegetical Commentary*, cxli.
10. Moulton and Milligan, "προσκυνέο," 549.
11. GGNT 476.

Persians performed this act to honor their deified kings or queens, and the Greeks performed this act before a god or deified image only.[12] The gesture of throwing a kiss is represented in Sumerian and Babylonian monuments which have been uncovered from ancient times. Later, προσκυνέο (proskuneo) would come to signify merely a greeting of welcome and respect to a person, as well as an act of adoration and obeisance to a god.

Jewish

In the Septuagint, προσκυνέο (*proskuneo*) is the only translation of the Hebrew word *shetachavah* and the Aramaic words *sagad* and *segid*. All translate "to bow." Other Jewish uses imply a translation of "to the earth" or "to do obeisance." Most often the verb is used in respect to the worship of Yahweh or other gods, with the remaining percentage of the time owing to other people whom the chosen people honored or who appeared as the elect of Yahweh. By way of explanation, Greeven points out that what is appropriate for Yahweh is also appropriate for his chosen people. Even the most casual Hebraic use of προσκινεσις (*proskynesis*) to a person recognized "that the one thus honored is God's instrument."[13] Illustrative of this are the following examples: Moses before Jethro (Exod 18:7); David three times before Jonathan (1 Sam 20:41); David before Solomon's ministers (1 Kgs 1:47); and Solomon before Bathsheba (I Kgs 2:19). Other examples of προσκινεσις (*proskynesis*) before superiors follow: Jacob before Esau (Gen 33:3–7); Jacob's sons before Joseph (Gen 37:9; 42:6; 43:26, 28); the Egyptians falling down at Moses's feet to petition pardon (Exod 11:8); David before Saul (1 Sam 24:9); Bathsheba and Nathan before David (1 Kgs 1:16, 23, 31); and Ruth before Boaz (Ruth 2:10).[14]

Gestures of deference were common in the ancient world. "Bowing, kneeling, throwing a kiss, kissing someone's feet or the hem of someone's garment, biting the dust, or prostration" represented the recognition of the power of someone or something over another. The act of bowing or prostration expressed not merely a physical attitude but also a mental attitude of submission.[15]

The Hebraic *shetachavah* ("bowing down") and the Greek προσκυνέο (proskuneo) are linguistic equivalents. According to George E. Mendenhall,

---

12. Arndt and Gingrich, "Πρός," 716.
13. Greeven, "Προσκυνέο (*Proskuneo*)," 6:761.
14. Greeven, "Προσκυνέο (*Proskuneo*)," 6:760–61.
15. *WSE* 102.

The symbolic action denoted by the Old Testament Hebrew term *shetachavah* (Greek equivalent—προσκυνέο [*proskuneo*]) consists of kneeling before the god or person having power, and then leaning forward until the face rests on the ground, or sometimes becoming completely prostrate. Sometimes the act is completed and acknowledged by the god's or king's placing his foot on the head or neck of the worshiper"[16]

It is interesting to note that the Islamic term *mosque* is derived from the Arabic *masjid*, which means the "place of prostration."[17]

Wainwright appears to have a broader view of *shahah* (the root of *shetachavah*). He believes it covers both the oriental idea of homage to one's superiors and the attitude of reverence towards a deity, in this case, Yahweh. He points out that in New Testament times Jesus embodied both points of view within his resurrected body.[18]

Rabbinic Judaism utilized προσκινεσις (*proskynesis*) as an attitude of prayer. Though the standard of prayer in public is upright, when one prays in private it becomes one of physical prostration. Rabbinic Jews expand on this idea to include prostration before a rabbi, with the thought that those who study the teaching of the Torah have a particularly privileged relationship with Yahweh.[19]

Josephus generally followed the Septuagint in connoting προσκυνέο (*proskuneo*) to mean the worship of persons, gods or God. However, to differentiate between Jewish and non-Jewish worship, Josephus preferred to ascribe προσκυνέο (*proskuneo*) to the non-Jewish practice and to implement *serene*, *threskefene*, and *timan* for Jewish worship. Also, while Josephus readily ascribed προσκυνέο (*proskuneo*) to Jewish kings and prophets, he restricted the honor he paid to other people of his day to one of mental acknowledgment only, without the physical gesture of prostrating himself before them.[20]

Philo disdained the worship of wealth and material power in the work of his day. He had no misgivings in ascribing obeisance to men or women, as the ten brothers to Joseph, but he preferred to use προσκυνέο (*proskuneo*) only when relating to the veneration of holy things like the temple, the Day of Atonement, and Holy Scripture. But in worshiping these material images,

---

16. Mendenhall, "Biblical Faith," 240.
17. *WSE* 103.
18. *DOX* 47.
19. Greeven, "Προσκυνέο (*Proskuneo*)," 6:763.
20. Greeven, "Προσκυνέο (*Proskuneo*)," 6:762.

Philo recognized the potential idolatry in these, and he "censures men [sic] who have idolatrously yielded to the pomp and arrogance of city life."[21]

By the first century, Jewish thought, as per Josephus and Philo, ascribed προσκυνέο (*proskuneo*) only to a god or deified image alone. Προσκυνέο (*Proskuneo*) to persons was no longer practiced. This, προσκυνέο (*proskuneo*) had been transformed to a higher, more specifically spiritual dimension.

Greek

Originally, the word meant "nothing more than the Greek term for a phenomenon of Oriental life." Προσκυνέο (*Proskuneo*) was an act of "casting oneself to the ground." General consensus indicates that it originated in the tragedians, with Persian origins presupposed. But those against this position argue that the Greeks would not have employed a term from another culture to express as high and noble a thought of their own worship, because the Greeks "rejected and regarded" this form of worship as "undignified." Secondly, there is no conclusive evidence to satisfy the debate of whether the "blown kiss to one of higher rank" is an original part of the gesture of προσκυνέο (*proskuneo*).[22]

The "adoration of chthonic deities"[23] provides an early source of the derivation of προσκυνέο (*proskuneo*): "the man [sic] who wants to honour an earth deity by kissing must stoop to do" it.[24] An example of the origins of προσκυνέο (*proskuneo*) can be found in Greek drama: Odysseus and Agamemnon prostrated themselves and kissed the earth after successful seaship landings.[25]

During the Tragedian period, the early usage of the physical act of prostration and kissing the earth was transformed directly to a mental or spiritually inward attitude. This is supported with documentation that shows that προσκυνέο (*proskuneo*) was used to express respect for the bow (archery) of Heracles (Hercules). Further evidence comes from the following examples: (1) an Aesulapius aretalogy of the second century begins with an exact description of the process of healing; (2) a female slave from the

---

21. Greeven, "Προσκυνέο (*Proskuneo*)," 6:763.
22. Greeven, "Προσκυνέο (*Proskuneo*)," 6:759.
23. The Greek gods that predate the Olympians.
24. This pagan practice was probably the origin of the liturgical practice in Christianity of the "altar kiss," according to Dölger, "Zu den Zeremonien," 217–21.
25. Greeven, "Προσκυνέο (*Proskuneo*)," 6:759.

second century in a letter to her master who became ill on a journey; and (3) from a son asking his father to correspond with him.[26]

Early Church

In the New Testament, προσκυνέο (*proskuneo*) occurs fifty-eight times, with twenty-three occurrences in Revelation. The general tendency in New Testament thought is to deify the object of προσκυνέο (*proskuneo*). To utilize the verb with action towards something or someone not divine would be "to devalue the meaning. The word is found often in the Gospels, Acts, and Revelation but generally is absent from the Epistles with the exception of Old Testament references in Hebrews 1:6 and 11:16 and 1 Corinthians 14:25. The Corinthian passage is the only instance illustrating προσκινεσις (proskynesis) in the primitive Christian community. But Greeven argues that Paul's usage here is for the "unconditional subjection which the ἀπιστοσε [apistose—"unbeliever"] confesses."[27] By doing this, the Apostle Paul borrows the Old Testament usage of προσκυνέο (*proskuneo*).

While other New Testament passages, which refer to "kneeling for prayer (Acts 9:40; 20:36) and "raising the hands in prayer". (1 Tim 2:8), might appear by their physical action to imply προσκυνέο (*proskuneo*), it is interesting to note that the Greek word προσκυνέο (*proskuneo*) is not used. Its omission is consistent with New Testament usage. In the Gospels, Acts, and especially Revelation, προσκυνέο (*proskuneo*) is used only in the presence of the exalted Jesus.[28] New Testament authors are consistently careful to distinguish between the ministry of the man Jesus on the one hand and the resurrected Lord on the other. With the resurrected Christ, his lordship is recognizably manifested by the use of προσκυνέο (*proskuneo*) when he is addressed.[29]

A listing of the New Testament passages that incorporate προσκυνέο (*proskuneo*) supports the claim that the object, whether in the accusative of the dative cases, is generally always a divinity or a deified image:

1. God the Almighty

    Matthew 4:10

    Luke 4:7; 24:52

---

26. The worship or praise of the gods of Aesulapius. Greeven, "Προσκυνέο (*Proskuneo*)," 6:759–60.

27. Greeven, "Προσκυνέο (*Proskuneo*)," 6:763–65.

28. Greeven, "Προσκυνέο (*Proskuneo*)," 6:765.

29. *DOX* 47.

John 4:20 (twice), 21, 22, 23, 24

Acts 8:27; 24:11

1 Corinthians 14:25

Hebrews 11:21

Revelation 4:10; 5:14; 7:11; 11:1, 16; 14:7; 15:4; 19:4, 10; 22:8, 9

2. Jesus Christ

    Matthew 2:2, 8, 11; 8:2; 9:18; 14:33; 15:25; 20:20; 28:9, 17

    Mark 5:6; 15:19

    John 9:38

    Hebrews 1:6

3. A man (person)

    Matthew 18:26

    Acts 10:25

4. The dragon

    Revelation 13:4

5. The beast

    Revelation 13:4, 8, 12; 14:9, 11; 19:20; 20:4

6. The image of the beast

    Revelation 13:15; 14:11; 16:2

7. Demons

    Revelation 9:20

8. Idols

    John 12:20

    Acts 7:43

9. Satan

    Matthew 4:9

    Luke 4:8

Other instances of προσκυνέο (*proskuneo*) appearing in the Greek world of the first century find the object to be in the idol-worshiping of polytheism and, particularly common, in the worship of angels.[30]

As the angel rebukes the writer of the Revelation in chapters 19 and 22, so Peter turns away the προσκινεσις (*proskynesis*) which Cornelius attempts to give him when he says in Acts 10:25, "I am too a man." When Jesus is met by the Samaritan woman in John 4:20–24, προσκυνέο (*proskuneo*) seems to take on a new meaning. It is implied in a wholly figurative sense because Jesus speaks of the act "in spirit and in truth." The previously restricted προσκυνέο (*proskuneo*), which is physically bound in place and gesture, is lifted to a new dimension-the realm of "spirit and truth." Jesus is perhaps ushering in the concept that there is no longer to be an exclusive place of worship, though prayer, an element of worship, can still occur at prescribed places and with "specific gestures."[31]

Reicke observes that "nowhere in the New Testament does προσκυνέο (*proskuneo*) mean technical worship performed by Christians on this earth." Reicke argues that because προσκυνέο (*proskuneo*) involves physical directionality, those who had prostrated themselves to Jesus during his lifetime suddenly had no place toward which to turn after his final ascent to heaven.[32]

In the New Testament, there appeared to be a move from the idea of God as a "conquering hero" (as he was perceived in the Old Testament) to that of a "generous host" (through Jesus's atoning work). In the ancient world, human worth was dependent upon the number of slaves or subjects one had; thus, more slaves implied greater worth. By the first century, the image of God appeared to have shifted, and the model was no longer "master/slave," but rather "host/guest." The good host was now measured in terms of his love for his guests. When Christians gathered in the New Testament period, their characteristic gesture towards Christ was not προσκινεσις (*proskynesis*). Burkhart argues that προσκινεσις (*proskynesis*) is abandoned by God because God no longer seeks the abasement which προσκινεσις (*proskynesis*) implied. It is Burkhart's contention that the "salute" for New Testament Christians was the greeting shared among the community of believers. The act of προσκινεσις (*proskynesis*) was transformed from one of vertical obeisance to a horizontal "holy kiss."[33] Προσκινεσις (*Proskynesis*) was transformed into ψιλέμα (*philema*), that is, abasement was replaced by

---

30. Arndt and Gingrich. "Πρός," 716.
31. Greeven, "Προσκυνέο (*Proskuneo*)," 6:764.
32. *WSE* 104.
33. *WSE* 104.

companionship. In his treatise on prayer, Tertullian spoke of the "holy kiss." This "kiss of peace" (*osculum pacis*) was, according to Tertullian, the "sealing of prayer" (*signaculum orationis*) for "what prayer is complete without the bond of a holy kiss?"[34]

Supported by Jewish thought of the first century, New Testament usage of προσκυνέο (*proskuneo*) witnessed two transformations: (1) the object of προσκυνέο (*proskuneo*) was delimited to include only gods or deified images, and (2) the physical act, which earlier only "casually" implied spiritual assent, predominantly assumed an internally spiritual context. The act of physical prostration became obsolete for the writers of the Gospels and Acts.

In the Book of Revelation

All Apocalyptic literature contains a considerable amount of contemporary liturgical fragments, but none nearly so much as the Revelation. Underhill observes that in Revelation there is an example of the worship services of the Christian churches of Asia Minor in the late first century.[35] There existed a developed form of worship performed by the "whole company of the faithful" (generally congregational), and it was centered around and upon the altar of the Lamb. All of the participants were doing something. The "sensible accompaniments of an ordered cultus" (song, music, incense, ritual movements and prostration) were evident and "taken for granted." Thus, liturgical worship was a true part of primitive Christianity, at least ideally, "though we may suppose that the circumstances of the early church seldom allowed that ideal to find adequate expression."[36] Where else could the writer of the Apocalypse have obtained the liturgy that he used? And what would have appealed to his readers more than being told that the elements of their own familiar worship were used in heaven?[37]

Greeven's observation that the object of προσκυνέο (*proskuneo*) in Revelation is generally a deity, whether good or evil, can be witnessed in the following categorization:

---

34. By the Seventh Ecumenical Council at Nicaea (787 CE) a differentiation between τιμετικε προσινεσις (*timelike proskenesis*—physical prostration) and αλετινε λατρεία (*aletine latreia*—true "spiritual" obeisance) will be made. The former may be offered to icons and only the latter can be paid to the θεια ψυσις (*theia fusis*—natural deity, "God"). See Greeven, "Προσκυνέο (*Proskuneo*)," 6:765.

35. Underhill, *Worship*, 231.

36. Underhill, *Worship*, 55–91.

37. *IB* 12:410.

Addressed to:	Text:
God Almighty	4:10
The Lamb	5:14
God Almighty	7:11
Temple of God	11:1
God Almighty	11:16
God the Creator	14:7
Lord God	15:4
God Almighty	19:4
Angel	19:10
Angel	22:8
God	22:9
Demons	9:20
Image of the Beast	14:9
Image of the Beast	14:11
Image of the Beast	16:2
Image of the Beast	19:20
Image of the Beast	20:4

Revelation 4:10. Before John's eyes the worship of heaven consisted of "constantly repeated" προσκυνέο (*proskuneo*—see also Revelation 5:14; 7:11; 11:16; 19:4).[38] Beasley-Murray contends, however, that it is more consistent with the idiomatic language to interpret "whenever" as a simple "when." This implies not an unbroken process of προσκυνέο (*proskuneo*) but rather notable occasions when God "'comes' and manifests his sovereignty in judgement and redemption."[39]

Until this point in the book of Revelation the elders have been silent observers. But now they "fall upon their knees and prostrate themselves on the floor of heaven" in "readiness" (preparation) to offer praises and their crowns of victory at the foot of the throne. Swete implies that this act of offering crowns is done either to pay homage to an overlord or to seek mercy from a conqueror. In Jabbuk 1:55, the pharaoh and Kings of the Feast took off their crowns in the presence of Moses and Aaron. This was consistent with Old Testament usage. The crowns of the elders in Revelation are not σιασεματα (*siasemata*) but στεψανόι (*stefanoi*—"wreaths, crowns, rewards"),

---

38. Greeven, "Προσκυνέο (*Proskuneo*)," 6:764.
39. Beasley-Murray, "Book of Revelation," 118–19.

and thereby are symbols of victory and eternal life.[40] This supports the argument that Burkhart advances. Προσκυνέο (*Proskuneo*) is no longer concerned with the physical act of adoration or submission. For the writers of the New Testament, particularly the Apostle of the Apocalypse, προσκυνέο (*proskuneo*) had become imbued with a higher spiritual notion which theses crowns of "victory" and "eternal life" connote. Προσκυνέο (*Proskuneo*) is the exclusive word used for "worship" in the Revelation. Other words which imply προσκυνέο (*proskuneo*) are "to bow down" and "to fall down." The former does not occur in Revelation, but the latter occurs once. In this verse, the "four elders 'fall down' before him who is seated on the throne and worship him who lives for ever and ever. . ." Because προσκυνέο (*proskuneo*) has been divorced from the physical act of "falling down," the writer specifically couples this action with the spiritualized προσκυνέο (*proskuneo*). The writer is fusing the spiritual act with the physical one.

Revelation 9:20. In both the Old and New Testaments, heathen worship is regarded as paid to demons. New Testament thought rigorously maintained this old Hebrew protest against idol worship. And though Paul proclaimed that "an idol is nothing in the world" (1 Cor 8:4 RSV) and has no spiritual meaning, it was, however, a visible symbol of men and women's revolt against God. The writer of the Apocalypse used Old Testament terminology here to exhibit his scorn for this demonic worship.[41]

Revelation 11:16. The angels, as they did in Revelation 11:1, and the elders, as creatures, share common προσκινεσις (*proskynesis*) before the throne.[42]

Revelation 14:7. God is established as the ultimate Creator, and as a result, all peoples of the earth are called to bow down and worship him.[43]

Revelation 14:9. Worship of the beast is always idolatry (see also Revelation 14:11; 19:20; 20:4), whereas worship of God is always selfless. The beast continually encourages self-indulgence, not so much for the reason that one should prostrate him or herself before Satan, but rather, to reject God. To worship Satan, self, or any other object or person is to reject God.

Both those who fear God and those who worship the dragon and the beast are called προσκυνουντες (*proskunountes*—participle, third declension). At the end of the existence on this earth, however, "not only will [all] nations come and worship before God (Rev 15:4), but those who serve

40. *ASJ* 74.
41. *ASJ* 125.
42. *ASJ* 142.
43. Blevins, *Revelation*, 68.

Satan... will also come and worship before the angel of that [God's] church" (Rev 3:9).[44]

Revelation 15:4. This passage looks forward to the time in which all nations will willingly προσκυνέο (*proskuneo*) in submission to God in the kingdom of Christ.[45]

Revelation 16:2. Those who choose to worship Caesar will bring upon themselves the ulcerous sores of their punishment.[46]

Revelation 19:4. All the peoples literally "...fell down on their faces."[47]

Revelation 19:10. The practice of προσκινεσις (proskynesis) can be seen from the "repeated rejection of this gesture by the interpreting angel" (see also Revelation 22:8). Why did John prostrate himself before the angel? Was John overcome with the majesty of the angel or did John misinterpret the angel's form as being the resurrected Christ? Swete says that John "can [could] scarcely mistake an angel for Christ or for God." In either case, John's error was soon corrected. Because angel-worship lingered long in Asia Minor, John's inclusion of this "reprimand" could say much to his audience. The obvious conclusion from the passage is that it is wrong to offer religious homage to an angel.[48]

Revelation 22:8. So "astounded by his [the] whole vision," the writer "not improbably entertained some suspicion that it was the Redeemer himself who had manifested himself to him."[49] Primasius agrees and maintains that the writer believed himself to be worshiping Christ even though the angel speaks in the "person of Christ."[50]

The angel rejects John's προσκινεσις (proskynesis) again. Swete says "still less can it be maintained that it is Christ who refuses the worship." Swete concludes again, as he did in the previous passage, that the writer is discouraging angel-worship by the example of his own lapse.[51] It is implied that the writer should προσκυνέο (*proskuneo*) only to the ultimate deity, the Godhead. This remains consistent with the views previously concluded in the discussion of προσκυνέο (*proskuneo*) in the New Testament.

---

44. Greeven, "Προσκυνέο (*Proskuneo*)," 6:764–65.
45. Beasley-Murray, "Book of Revelation," 236.
46. Blevins, *Revelation*, 76.
47. Conybeare, *Armenian Version*, 49.
48. *ASJ* 248.
49. *ASJ* 458.
50. *ASJ* 304.
51. *ASJ* 304.

Summary

The form of worship which προσκυνέο (*proskuneo*) implies has been traced from its earliest beginnings up through its usage in the early Christian church. Προσκυνέο (*Proskuneo*) is a compound of the two roots: προς (*pros*) meaning "towards," and κυνέο (*kuneo*) meaning "to kiss." When united, the roots imply the honor, respect, and obeisance which an inferior demonstrates to a superior. The inconsistent use of syntax which προσκυνέο (*proskuneo*) experiences in the Apocalypse does not present a problem of consequence to Robertson, although Charles disagrees.

Early use of the word in the Semitic and non-Semitic world required a physical prostration before the one to whom προσκυνέο (*proskuneo*) was addressed. The object could be equally a god, king, or another person. But by the first century CE, a transformation of the word seemed to occur. Prominent Jewish evidence, primarily from Josephus and Philo, tells of an initial discrimination in the use of προσκυνέο (*proskuneo*). Both scholars demonstrate a narrower application of the word which allows it to be enacted in front of either a deity, deified image, or kingly personage. No longer is προσκινεσις (*proskynesis*) implemented as "casually" as it had been before. It can no longer be directed to a "mere" person. New Testament thought acquiesces. Thus, the object of προσκυνέο (*proskuneo*) becomes a more specific personage. Both Apostles Peter and John illustrate this new use of προσκυνέο (*proskuneo*). For them this form of worship is worthy of only the ultimate and highest deity, the Godhead.

Another metamorphosis transpired in New Testament times: the purely physical προσκινεσις (*proskynesis*), which included prostration, acquired a thoroughly more prominent spiritual dimension.

Jesus's ministry and resurrection together provide the transition from the physical (Jesus the Incarnate) προσκυνέο (*proskuneo*) to the spiritual (the resurrected Lord) use of the word. The Gospel writers and Paul illustrate this well, as Burkhart points out. But Burkhart fails to recognize that the writer of the Apocalypse fuses the physical and spiritual continuum of προσκυνέο (*proskuneo*) together in his vision. For the writer of the Apocalypse, the highest form of spiritual worship includes physical activity.

CONCLUSIONS

Although the writer of Revelation arguably may not have been a keen student of Greek syntax, he did, however, specifically employ προσκυνέο (*proskuneo*) to display the type or worship activity which he witnessed in his vision. Was the writer aware that the idiomatic usage of προσκυνέο (*proskuneo*) in the New Testament at times excluded the physical act of prostration in favor of the spiritual, mentalized act of adoration and obeisance? It seems so, or why would the writer have included "falling down" with προσκυνέο (*proskuneo*) in Revelation 4:10?

What form of worship will be practiced in heaven through all eternity? Does John provide a hint as to what it will consist of? Some contend that John's visions are limited to what he had actually witnessed in the churches of his day; when he wrote his vision down, he was idealizing contemporary worship practice of the first century. Perhaps the writer was attempting to revitalize the spiritual lives of the Christians in the churches of Asia Minor. However, one could contend that what John described was not limited to a summary of the best of worship practice of his day. Possibly what he transcribed was his "glimpse" into eternal heaven via the Holy Spirit. If so, then maybe his "glimpse" was merely coincidentally similar to the idealized practice of his day. In either case, it is clear that the writer's visions do require a balance between the physical and spiritual acts of worship. Inclusive in these finite and infinite realms are embodied the emotional, mental, and social worshiper of God. To forego one for another is not complete worship.

The type of worship activity expressed in Revelation calls for a balance between physical, mental, social, emotional, and spiritual worship. We are exhorted to examine our intellectual spiritualism and discern whether there is room for other expressions of worship activity. The appeal of worship to our whole being seems to be desired by the writer of the Apocalypse. There needs to be more balance in the use of our minds, hearts, hands, and imaginations.

Music falls within the context of worship in the book of Revelation. But this music no longer fills a functional void as it did in the early pagan, Jewish, Greek, and Roman cultures preceding the early church. Functionalism gives way to music for worship which possesses a largely doxological character. Music and worship possess an "intrinsic spiritual quality."[52] While music can be regarded as a practical art, worship is an end in itself. But both seek a common end. They both seek "the experience of worship itself."[53] It is only in this environment that every worshiper truly will be able to focus solely on the Godhead.

---

52. Wright, "The Place of Music," 329–43.
53. Wright, "The Place of Music," 342–43.

3

Music Forms

Within the book of Revelation exist both direct and indirect references to music. In most cases these references are obvious, but in some instances they are not. This study seeks to determine differentiations of both music forms, performing groups (chapter 4) and musical practice (chapters 5) within the text of the Revelation. A sequential listing of all music and musical practices found in the book of Revelation can be found in the Appendix. In the book of Revelation two forms of music occur—the ode and the trumpet call.

Ὠδή (*Oda*—"Ode")

The exclusive Greek word used to imply "song" in the book of Revelation is ᾠδή (*oda*—"ode"). Throughout ancient times, it was generally defined as "a fresh song of praise." Odes were newly composed songs to commemorate special occasions.[1] Generally synonymous with the terms ᾠδή (*oda*) and song in the time preceding the early church are hymns and psalms. A song is "a piece of music for voice or voices, whether accompanied or unaccompanied, or the act of singing."[2]

---

1. *ASJ* 80.
2. Chew, "Song," 17:510.

EARLY PAGAN

In early pagan times, an ode was a poem which was sung, usually to honor a special event or as part of a play. It was the generic term for song and could be performed either solo or chorally.[3]

Both solo singers and choral groups, accompanied by a variety of instruments, performed in the "private settings of the homes of nobility" as well as in sacred and secular courts. Extant evidence, however, cannot show whether vocal music predominated as a main cultural force in early pagan times, as it did in later Jewish times.[4]

JEWISH

Jewish religious song consists primarily of psalms from the temple tradition and hymns from domestic worship. Early instances of singing occurred around the golden calf (see Exodus 32:18–19). Later, instances of singing took place at secular occasions. When King Saul returned victorious following a battle with the Philistines, he found the Israelites singing and dancing (see 1 Samuel 18:6–7). By the time of King David, the music that was used in religious temple observances had become codified.[5]

Jewish songs consist of religious songs of praise (doxological) or repentance, psalms, hymns, elegies, educational songs, plus all types of secular songs including cradle songs and children's songs. All of the foregoing types of songs are mentioned in the Old Testament.[6]

Traditional Jewish song can best be represented by the book of Psalms. This collection of psalms implied various styles of performance based on their respective textual structures. These appear in later Christian practice (beginning from the second century AD) via the church's use of direct, responsorial, and antiphonal psalmody and litanies with refrains.[7] But they also appear in the book of Revelation.

The psalms can be classified into two categories:

1. "I" and "we" royal psalms that contain a corporate personality; and

---

3. Tilmouth, et al., "Ode," 13:497.
4. *MAI* 40.
5. *MAI* 167.
6. *MAI* 169.
7. Chew, "Song," 17:512.

2. hymns of Praise. At the heart of the hymns of praise is the idea that the congregation, while singing them, is in the presence of the Almighty. Characteristics of hymns of praise are as follows:

a. the exhortation to sing praise to God;

b. the exhorters are mentioned;

c. the laudatory attributes of God are mentioned; and

d. reference is made to Yahweh's special deeds in history.[8]

Traditional Jewish and Christian interpretation held that the psalms had "a more private, individual origin" and, consequently, had no place in public worship. Mowinckel says that scholars, such as Wette, Wellhausen, and Briggs, believe that the psalms originated from individual life experiences. However, Smend found a "poetical personification" of the corporate Jewish body in the "I" psalms.[9] He called his theory the "collective I" psalm. Through the "form historical" (*formgeschichtliche*) and "type-critical" (*gattungsgeschichtliche*) methods, Hermann Gunkel was able to prove that much of the psalm poetry of the Jewish tradition could be found in the public religious rites of the people, not in their individual experiences. Various types of psalms were composed that recalled the acts of Yahweh as He dealt with the Jewish body as a whole.[10]

Psalm singing provided the bridge to higher aesthetic artforms for the Israelites. According to Riehm,

> Psalm-singing was the starting point for the higher development of Jewish music. Like poetry, tonal art, too, was governed by the supreme influence of religion; therefore, singing and playing have had primarily a serene, solemn, but by no means dull or gloomy character.[11]

The primitive psalter became the "liturgical hymnal of Israel." In early temple practice, psalms were performed by the Levitical singers as soloists and grouped-in choirs. As time transpired, Sendrey speculates silent worshipers desired to participate more actively in order to satisfy a longing. Initially, the participation by the laity consisted of single word acclamations. In time, the acclamations became refrains. This process could illustrate the

---

8. *DH* 7.

9. Smend, *Vorträge*.

10. *PIW* 12–13. See also Brueggermann, *Message*; Brueggermann, *Astonishment*; Miller, *Interpreting the Psalms*; McCann, *Theological Introduction*; Westermann, *Living Psalms*; Westermann, *Psalms*.

11. Reihm, *Handwoerterbuch*, 1029.

beginning of active lay participation in liturgical singing. From this practice developed the antiphonal and responsorial styles. This is speculative as there are signs that psalmody was congregational from its origins in both tabernacle and temple worship.

The psalter contains the following hymns: Psalms 8, 19, 29, 33, 46, 47, 48, 76, 104, 135, 136, and 145–150. Other hymns in the Old Testament are found in Amos 4:22, 13; 5:8; and 9:5. Two main types of hymns exist in Jewish tradition:

1. a general type of hymn that singles out Yahweh's lasting qualities and glorious deeds (see Psalm 136); and

2. a specific type of hymn which directs its attention to a particular feature of Yahweh or one of his acts (see Psalms 46, 48, 76, and 114).[12]

Occasionally, hymns end with a short wish or prayer for the "future prosperity of the congregation" (see Psalms 29:11; 104:3; and 135:19). This prayer or wish was usually general in nature. Hymns were recited and accompanied by stringed instruments, cymbals, and the flute (see Psalm 150). Hymns were also accompanied by cultic dance.[13]

The hymns of Israel "clearly show its [their] place of origin to the holy place." The hymn belonged in the cultic festival where the people congregated and witnessed Yahweh's presence and repeated his mighty acts. Hymns were later used in the daily rites of the "great temples" (see Psalm 89:17; 1 Chronicles 9:33; and Sirach 47:8). They also played a major role in the daily morning sacrifices, in temple processions and around the altar (Pss 24; 118). Within Jewish corporate religious practice, the hymn always had a "prominent place." The book of Psalms is often referred to as "hymns of praise."[14]

A constantly recurring theme in the "hymns of praise" is creation, where Yahweh demonstrated his "omnipotence, wisdom, and loving kindness." Yahweh is revealed in nature throughout the psalms. He is shown in storms, thunder and lightning, fire, and earthquakes. Yahweh is represented in nature to show his "awful majesty, his merciful care and his flaming wrath when he comes to judge his enemies." Yahweh's mighty voice continues to be able to "ring out... thunder."[15]

---

12. *PIW* 81–85.
13. *PIW* 89.
14. *PIW* 89–90.
15. *PIW* 101.

Sacred singing poured over into more private settings. It became common to sing at the Passover celebration in the home. The use of the *Hallel* (Pss 113–118) in this setting is an example of the domestic use of psalms.[16]

The Song of Moses (see Revelation 15:3–4) was regularly sung at each Sabbath evening's worship in the synagogue as a remembrance of the time when Yahweh had delivered his people from the land of Egypt (see Exodus 15:2–18).[17] This social event caused the people to burst into antiphonal and responsorial song, and it also resulted in Miriam's leading the women in dancing.[18] Because this particular song originated uniquely in the Jewish faith, it had no connections whatsoever with pagan ritual, other than the fact that both sacred and secular incidents of a significant nature in the life of any corporate body of people were often commemorated or memorialized in song.

The "talent for improvisation of [or by a] Jewish singer" was continually mentioned or alluded to in the Old Testament. Specific reference to "the prophesying of the prophets with a psaltery and a harp" (1 Sam 10:5; 19:20; 2 Kgs 3:15) were probably instances of improvised music. However, the practice of free improvisation in the doxological sense in subsequent Christian liturgy has no support. This is due to the fact that the music of the temple came about on a "rigorously traditional basis." No portion of the sacred ceremonies was left to chance. They were programmed meticulously in every detail. The freedom to improvise simply did not exist in the temple tradition.[19]

The psalms and hymns of the Jewish traditions in the period 100 BCE to CE 200 which directly influenced the early church are the *Psalms of Solomon*, *Qumran Hodayoth*, the *Hellenistic Synagogal Prayers*, and the *Odes of Solomon*. Although the canonical Old Testament in Hebrew (the Masoretic Bible) is composed of 150 psalms, modern scholarship has uncovered five more psalms of David and a part of a sixth (Ps 151B). Four of them (Pss 151A; 15lB; 154; and 155) are present in the Qumran Scrolls and date from the first half of the first century CE. Because five more psalms of David are contained within the Qumran psalter, it is conjectured that the entire psalter was basically set by the second century BCE.[20]

---

16. *MAI* 172–74.

17. Coleman, *Songs of Heaven*, 176.

18. *MAI* 72, 167.

19. *MAI* 150–51.

20. *OTP* 2:607–9. Old Testament pseudepigraphal passages are taken from this two-volume compilation.

The *Psalms of Solomon* number eighteen and are the response of the Jewish people to the capture of Jerusalem in the first century BCE by the Romans. Modern scholarship asserts that the odes of Solomon represent very early Christian hymns. Although the character and tone of them appear Jewish, it is evident that their content is inherently Christian. They exhibit the Christian characteristics of a "joyous tone of thanksgiving for the advent of the Messiah who had been promised" (see 7:1–6 and 41:3–7) and "for the present experience of eternal life and love from and for the beloved" Savior (see 3:1–9; 11:1–24; 23:1–3; 26:1–7; and 40:1–6). The *Odes of Solomon* date from the late first to the early second century CE.[21]

Pseudo-Philo 32:1 demonstrates a Jewish faith familiar with hymnody: "Then Deborah and Barak the son of Abino and all the people together sang a hymn to the Lord on that day, saying. . ." (RSV). In *Testament of Job* 14:1–5, hymns are accompanied by a lyre (see a parallel reference in Job 21:12).

> And I used to have six psalms and a ten-stringed lyre. I would rouse myself daily after the feeding of the widows, take the lyre, and play for them. And they would chant hymns. And with the psaltery I would remind them of God so that they might glorify the Lord. If my maidservants ever began murmuring, I would take up the psaltery and strum as payment in return. And thus I would make them stop murmuring in contempt. (RSV)

Other examples of hymns in Old Testament pseudepigrapha are found in *Joseph and Aseneth* 14:8; 16:20–22; 18:9; and 21:10–21.

GREEK

In Greek aesthetic philosophy, music occurred at "the height of the intensity of feeling and excitement" when the spoken word could proceed no further. Music alone was able "to express the emotions when the deeply stirred soul of man [sic] can [could] utter only inarticulate cries."[22]

Although Greek sources lean more heavily toward instrumental music than vocal, it cannot be assumed that instrumental music stood apart from vocal music. In fact, while vocal music was the constant or the given in Greek society, instrumental music provided the variable element. While chanted or sung words provided the liturgy, instrumental accompaniment provided the ταλεα (*talea*—"color").[23]

---

21. *OTP* 2:639, 725.
22. Lang, *Music*, 12.
23. *TSB* 331.

Basically, all of the extant ancient songs are of Greek origin and come from the Hellenistic period. Although the quantity is small, "certain limited conclusions" can be drawn from the literary and art sources from the period. From these sources it is possible to ascertain the types of songs which were performed and to speculate about the method of accompaniment. The chief type of song employed in Greece before 700 BCE was the oral bardic tradition of epic song. Other simpler functional songs were used which were "presumably unrehearsed and often sung by a leader with choral refrains." These types of songs can be found in Greek, Roman, and Old Testament Jewish literature. These songs were basically secular in character and consisted of work songs, lullabies, victory songs, songs for weddings and funerals, and songs of a mocking or satirical nature. These kinds of songs were later absorbed into the art and music of Greece.[24]

Beginning in the seventh century BCE, accompanied song was lyric, either for solo or choral groups, and accompanied by either the lyre or the aulos. Solo lyric song or monody could relate to the modern strophic song which represents the "personal feelings of the composer in a series of shortish stanzas identical in meter [sic]."[25]

Choral lyric song was characteristically religious in nature and included dancing. It expressed the feelings of a community or citystate. It consisted of elaborate patterns (*systemata*) "of strophe, antistrophe and epode, and the component parts were much longer than the stanzas of choral [sic] lyric [song]"[26] Both solo lyric song and choral lyric song were the main original elements in Greek drama from the fifth century BCE.

The Greek ode is a generic term for song. Choral odes became very important in early Greek drama. Odes were classified by the Greeks according to their respective function rather than their structure: Paean; Epinikian; Threnody; Dithyramb; Hyporchema; Encomuim; and Parthenian. Paean and Hyporcheman odes were used at festivals to honor the Greek god Apollo or a city. Encomuim odes were sung to honor a guest at a banquet. Parthenian odes served as processional hymns, and Epinikian odes were performed to celebrate either war or Olympian victories.[27]

By the late fifth century BCE, a "new music" tolerated "unprecedented modal and rhythmic variety." It also allowed for instrumental interludes and melismatically set texts (pathogenic). Prior to this time the music always

---

24. Chew, "Song," 17:511.
25. Chew, "Song," 17:511.
26. Chew, "Song," 17:511.
27. Tilmouth, et al., "Ode," 13:497.

served the text (logogenic). Evidence indicates that this "new music," however, was not "universally adopted."[28]

The song up to the fifth century BCE exerted the most influence on music of subsequent centuries. The music of the Hellenistic period was considered too decadent. From the Hellenistic period the song of the Greek theater spread to Rome and elsewhere, and song composition reached a high point in the cantica of the comedies of Plautus.[29]

ROMAN

The Roman religion believed that music had magical qualities. Companies (*sodalitates*) of priests known as the *salii* flourished in the Era of the Kings (ca. 750–510 BCE). By Imperial times (the Early Republic 509–265 BCE), this group consisted of twelve members of nobility. A lead singer (*vates*) and a lead dancer (*praesul*) performed archaic militaristic dances and responsorial songs (*carmina*) in honor of the Roman gods Mars and Quirinus. Numerous folksongs and work songs were used in common everyday situations. They included table songs, songs of mourning, lullabies, nursery rhymes, soldier's victory songs, birthday and wedding songs, songs of love and joy, and songs of satire. From the middle of the third century BCE, Roman theatrical music was influenced heavily and increasingly by the Greek theater.[30]

EARLY CHURCH

An important event in the gathering together of the early church was corporate singing. Pliny was asked by Emperor Trajan in the early second century if he knew of "any possible crimes" which the Christians might be guilty of. Pliny wrote,

> The sum total of their guilt or error amounted to no more than this, they had met regularly before dawn on a fixed day to chant verses alternately among themselves in honor of Christ as if to a god and also to bind themselves by oath, not for any criminal purpose, but to abstain from theft, robbery and adultery, to commit no breach of trust and not to deny a deposit when called upon to restore it. After this ceremony it had been their custom

---

28. Chew, "Song," 17:511–12.
29. Chew, "Song," 17:511–12.
30. Fleischhauer, "Rome," 16:147.

to disperse and reassemble later to take food of an ordinary harmless kind.[31]

Ephesians 5:19 provides evidence that perhaps the early church differentiated between various types of song: psalms, hymns, and spiritual songs. The early church borrowed the psalms from the Jewish tradition. They used hymns of the Jewish and Greek cultures. And perhaps the spiritual songs were original musical compositions composed within the early church. They were the "new songs" which spoke of the "new" work which Christ bad accomplished at the cross and resurrection. But Martin says of both the Ephesians 4:19–20 and Colossians 3:16 passages that it is

> hard to draw any hard-and-fast distinction between these terms; and modern scholars are agreed that the various terms are used loosely to cover the various forms of musical composition. "Psalm" may refer to Christian odes patterned in the Old Testament psalter. "Hymns" would be longer compositions and there is evidence that some actual specimens of these hymns may be found in the New Testament itself. "Spiritual songs" refer to snatches of spontaneous praise which the inspiring Spirit placed on the lips of the enraptured worshipper, as 1 Corinthians 14:15 implies. These "inspired odes" would no doubt be of little value, and their contents would be quickly forgotten.[32]

The "psalms, hymns, and spiritual songs" mentioned in Ephesians 5:19 and Colossians 3:16 "were probably unaccompanied," for

> the poor and frequently clandestine Christian assemblies can hardly have boasted instruments. If stringed music (*phallein*) is referred to, it is "in the heart only."[33]

As a Greek word, "hymn" needed neither to be religious nor sung by a corporate body. It was nothing more than a

> song of a serious kind making use of poetry and music in a way which tends to exalt the mind of the singer and listener towards lofty subjects-whatever subject may be recognized by that particular community as lofty.[34]

In the early church the hymn was not always a congregational song.[35]

31. Church and Mulry, *Earliest Christian Hymns*, ix.
32. Martin, *Worship in the Early Church*, 47.
33. Moule, *Worship*, 65.
34. Routley, *Christian Hymns Observed*, 5.
35. Routley, *Christian Hymns Observed*, 5.

Hymns are "a kind of song; but they differ from a professional song, or an art-song, in being songs for unmusical people to sing together."[36] Routley defines hymn tunes for the early church as "the folk songs of the Christian faith."[37] Because hymns are "communal" songs, they are much like folk songs. People care little who composed folk songs; consequently, people have little critical concern about them. As a result, people have little appreciation for folk songs in comparison to the appreciation which a professional musician would exhibit toward them.[38]

Early church hymns "appear to have been sung from a very early date" in the first century.[39] Textual evidence points directly to Jesus's singing of a hymn at the supper in the upper room (see Matthew 26:30). Jesus's utilization of a hymn (probably the Jewish *Hallel*) in this setting leads one to believe that this was not a new practice for Jesus and the disciples.

Within a generation after Pentecost, Christians were singing hymns regularly. Before this time, they had primarily sung psalms. When the writer wrote the Apocalypse, he chose to "punctuate the narrative with snatches of ceremonious poetry" (see Revelation 5:13).[40] Routley contends that the writer "may" have quoted what was familiar to his audience (the Christians in Asia Minor), but even if he did not, the writer was quoting what he knew they would perceive as being a familiar style.[41] The most hymnic sections in the New Testament are Ephesians 4:14; 1 Timothy 3:16; Philippians 2:6–11; Colossians 1:15–20; Hebrews 1:3;[42] and Ephesians 5:14 (an ancient baptismal hymn).[43]

According to St. Augustine,

> Hymns are praises to God with song. Hymns are songs containing praises to God. If it is praise, and not to God, it is not a hymn; if it is praise, and to God, but it is not sung, it is not a hymn. It is essential therefore that, if it is a hymn, it have these three qualities: praise, and to God, and song.[44]

---

36. Routley, *Christian Hymns Observed*, 1.

37. Routley, *Christian Hymns Observed*, 4. See also Adey, *Hymns*; Adey, *Class*; Church and Mulry, *Earliest Christian Hymns*.

38. Routley, *Christian Hymns Observed*, 1.

39. Chew, "Song," 17:512.

40. Routley, *Christian Hymns Observed*, 5–7.

41. Routley, *Christian Hymns Observed*, 7.

42. Martin, *Worship in the Early Church*, 47.

43. Moule, *Worship*, 58.

44. Augustine, *Enarrationes*, quoted in Trench, *Synonyms*, 298.

According to McKinnon, however, Augustine refers to "a category of psalm not a non-biblical hymn" with the above definition.[45] Similarly, Augustine further states,

> Would you know what a hymn is? It is song with praise to God. If you praise God, and do not sing, you speak no hymn; if you sing, but you do not praise God, you speak no hymn; if you praise something which does not pertain to the praise of God, even if you are singing praises, you speak no hymn. A hymn therefore has those three qualities: song, and praise, and to God.[46]

Historically, however, these definitions come too late. Originally, in early pagan and Jewish times, a hymn was simply a song of praise. The Hebrew pattern of hymnody consisted of (1) the thesis which recognized the Creator God; (2) the antithesis which focused on mankind's dilemma; and (3) the synthesis which spoke of man's righted relationship with Yahweh. This pattern was used early in the psalms and was consequently employed in the early church where it incorporated the crucifixion and resurrection of Christ.[47] Werner states that

> the few hymnic passages of the New Testament were considered canticles in the early church. . .[and] are generally recognized to be, in spirit as well as in form, a direct continuation of Old Testament poetry or apocryphal verses, such as Ecclesiasticus 51. At which point then, is it proper to speak of hymnody? Later fragments, such as the communion hymn of the *Didache* or the poetic part of the *Epistle to Diogentus*, can here be mentioned only in passing, since they were, in all probability, not rendered musically.[48]

The Apostle Paul distinguished between canonical poems and free hymns (see the Prayer of Jesus in the apocryphal Acts of John).[49] Several authors, such as Joerns and Harris, have indicated that as many as thirty hymns occur within the confines of the Revelation.[50] Apparently, these authors have assumed a very liberal definition of the term hymn, perhaps as ". . . original, spontaneous outbursts of religious emotion."[51]

45. McKinnon, *Music*, 158.
46. Trench, *Synonyms*, 298.
47. Price, "Hymn Patterns," 436–37.
48. *TSB* 207.
49. *TSB* 208.
50. Joerns, *Hymnische Evangelium*; Harris, "Literary Function."
51. Harris, "Literary Function," 250.

We may assume that the early church sang songs at their services. Some were newly improvised solos (see 1 Corinthians 14:26), while others had refrains on which others could join in singing. Consequently, the early church reflected the *Imago Dei* ideal by composing songs for use in worship. Berkouwer describes the narrow *Imago Dei* as "the image of God in man as it is restored in Christ."[52] Routley theorizes that extended congregational works did not exist in the early church because they would not have easily been memorized. They would have had to have been written down, and no extant manuscripts have been unearthed.[53] But this begs the question that in non-literate societies, the capacity to memorize extended accounts was prodigious.

IN THE BOOK OF REVELATION

The exclusive word used specifically in the original Greek text of the Revelation is ᾠδή (*oda*). This study has already related the manner in which the ᾠδή (*oda*) has come down through the divergent music cultures studied, that is, the psalms of the early Babylonians could have been passed along to the Jewish faithful. From there they were passed into the early church. The songs of early tradition became odes in the Greek culture. The odes of Revelation have been interpreted in modern times as hymns. Because the writer of the Apocalypse does not distinguish between ode, song, hymn, and psalm as music forms in the text, it could be assumed that differentiation was unnecessary. For the writer of the Apocalypse, perhaps the terms ode, song, hymn, and psalm were synonymous. Smith agrees.[54] In order to differentiate the possible vagaries of distinction, an in-depth textual study would need to be done, as Harris, Carnegie, and others have attempted.[55] Such a study is outside the scope of the present research.

Mowry focuses on the "four utterances of hymnic character" in Revelation 4 and 5. Mowry contends that three of these four passages rely on Old Testament texts and are consequently "linked" with Jewish worship services of the first century CE. They are as follows:

1. Revelation 4:8 is sung by the four beasts. The Old Testament parallel is Isaiah 6:3.

---

52. Berkouwer, *Man*, 99.
53. Routley, *Christian Hymns Observed*, 7.
54. Smith, "First-Century," 9–10.
55. Carnegie, "Worthy is the Lamb."

2. Revelation 4:11 is sung by the twenty-four elders. Its Old Testament reference is found in Psalm 19:1.

3. Revelation 5:9–10 and 12 is performed antiphonally between the four creatures and the twenty-four elders. Because it is a "new" song, no earlier Scripture passage is alluded to.

4. Revelation 5:13b is intoned by all creatures in heaven and on earth. The biblical reference is Psalm 41:13.[56]

Hymn and psalm texts from the temple and synagogue traditions used in Revelation (see 4:8, 11; 11:17, 18; 14:7; 15:3–4) were "borrowed directly from the synagogue (*sic*, Jewish tradition) of the Greek-speaking Jewish world" and adapted to the early church. The focus of these songs was to

> the holy and righteous God of Judaism which is extolled. . . in the synagogue liturgy as Creator and Sustainer of the world, and Judge of all.[57]

In Revelation 14:3 the "new song" is sung by the ζοα (*zoa*—"the creatures") and the elders. They represent creation and the church. This song is actually sung before them and, consequently, not by them. It is sung by the angels. Although the angels do not benefit from the redemptive work of Christ, they appear to be seriously concerned for the salvation of humanity (see Ephesians 3:10 and 1 Peter 1:12). The angels lead the "new song" which "the redeemed themselves have yet but imperfectly learnt."[58] It is not easily sung by the 144,000 either. The "music of the heart" (see Ephesians 5:19 and Colossians 3:16) cannot "be acquired without a receptivity which is a Divine gift."[59]

The "new song" symbolized Christ's completed work. This song attests to the fact that through his work he has purchased all people of all race, "new works of grace call forth new songs of praise."[60] The "newness" of this song is akin to "a qualitative sense of something previously unknown, unprecedented, [and] marvelous."[61]

The new song is characterized by "stainless souls" who produce "stainless beauty."[62] New songs are also mentioned in Psalms 33:3; 40:3; 96:1;

---

56. Mowry, "Revelation," 77.
57. Martin, *Worship in the Early Church*, 45–46.
58. *ASJ* 178.
59. *ASJ* 178.
60. *ASJ* 82.
61. Coleman, *Songs of Heaven*, 45.
62. *IB* 469.

98:1; 99:9; and Isaiah 42:10. These songs may be "mystical songs unable to be learned by those who are not advanced in prayer," a reference to the saints who can "know" the songs of the angels as Job's daughters did (see *Testament of Job*).[63]

In Revelation 5:9 and 14:3 the descriptive word of song is καινός (*kainos*– "new"). This adjective refers to character and form implying the new form and character that the eschatological songs will consist of. The Song of Moses celebrated the deliverance of the Jews from the hands of their oppressor; the "new song of Christ" in Revelation celebrates the redemption of the once-for-all atoning work of Jesus Christ.[64] Καινός (*Kainos*) is "not new in time...but new as to [its] form or quality, of different nature from what is contrasted as old."[65] It is the Greek word νέος (neos) which "signifies (something) new in respect of time, that which is recent; it is used of the young."[66]

The writer of the Apocalypse "draws heavily upon the periods of the most active miraculous activity in the Old Testament." God's omnipotence, omniscience, and reality are recalled, and God's final victory is praised by the worshipers. "Visions and words of praise" recall God's previous deeds. But the doxological praise of Revelation does not end there. The Song of Moses is transformed into a new song. New acts of God are commemorated in new song.[67]

A "great chorus of believers" is pictured standing by a sea of glass (see Revelation 15:3– 4). In their hands are harps of gold which they played "to accent their songs of praise." The Song of Moses is transformed into the Song of the Lamb.[68] Just as Moses delivered his people from the hands of Pharaoh, so the resurrected Lamb delivers his people from the hands of eternal damnation.

TRUMPET CALL

Both the use of and the sound of the trumpet figure predominantly in the Apocalypse. The trumpet call is the foundation of trumpet melody, whether it be used as a royal fanfare or as a military signal.[69]

---

63. Ford, *Anchor Bible*, 233.
64. Vines, "New," 3:109.
65. Vines, "New," 3:109.
66. Vines, "New," 3:109.
67. Jenkins, *Old Testament*, 71.
68. Coleman, *Songs of Heaven*, 122–24.
69. *THM* 35.

Early Pagan

Many musical traditions of antiquity lay claim to having invented the trumpet. Altenburg hypothesizes a simple reason for this: a plethora of sizes, shapes, materials, and performance practices existed for this instrument.[70] The Jewish tradition claims that Jubal invented it; others say the Egyptians or the Etruscans created it. The second century historian Pliny wrote that Piseus, an Etruscan king, invented it in the year 2951 of the creation of the world (or the year 260 before the founding of Rome).[71] Tarr states that the trumpet (Greek is σάλπινχ [*salpinx*], and Roman is *lituus, tuba, buccina*, or *cornu*) was inherited from the Etruscans.[72]

The term trumpet comes from the Latin *tremor*, which literally means "a trembling or vibrating."[73] Tarr describes it as "a lip-vibrated aerophone."[74] The tone is produced via "a column of air" that becomes "excited (i.e., caused to be set in vibration. . .) by a player's lips."[75] The majority of ancient trumpets were "short, straight instruments of wood, bronze or silver and used for both military and ceremonial purposes."[76]

The Etruscans contributed the use of brass instruments for military purposes, and the Romans expanded this concept.[77] Sumerian straight trumpets were played by Assyrian soldiers.[78]

The Egyptian trumpet was made of a "yellow" metal. It was cone-shaped with a distinct mouthpiece and exhibited a "rather wide" bell. It was two feet in length and tuned similarly as the modern cornet.[79] Because the sound was so penetratingly loud and shattering, Egyptian police required that the trumpet could be played only in "barracks outside the city."[80] Plutarch commented that it sounded like an "ass's bray." An extant pictorial representation dated 1415 BCE shows that it was used by soldiers. It was also used in the sacred worship of the Egyptian god Osiris.[81]

---

70. *EIHM* 6.
71. *EIHM* 3–4.
72. Tarr, "Trumpet," *NGD* 19:214.
73. *HMI* 73.
74. Tarr, "Trumpet," *NGDMI* 3:639.
75. *MHBT* 21.
76. Tarr, "Trumpet," *NGD* 19:214.
77. Ulrich and Pisk, *History of Music*, 25; Miller, *History of Music*, 4.
78. *HMI* 73.
79. *HMI* 100.
80. Friedrich, "Σάλπινχ (Salpinx—'Trumpet')," 7:76.
81. *HMI* 100.

Extant Egyptian reliefs and paintings dating from the fifteenth century BCE have been confirmed by the finding of two trumpets in the tomb of King Tutankhamen. Both trumpets have short expanding tubes with a funnel bell. The longer trumpet (58 cm.) is made of silver, and the shorter trumpet (49.4 cm.) is constructed of sheet bronze with partial gold plating. The bells are both engraved with the King's name and also the emblems of various successful military units of the time.[82]

The Assyrians used a trumpet similar to that of the Egyptians. An example in a Sennacherib relief shows a pair of trumpeters. One is playing while the other is resting.[83]

Jewish

The Hebrew term for trumpet is *chazozrah*, not *jobel keren* (the Chaldean *shofar*). The shofar is variously translated to be a cornett, trombone, or a rams horn (which Jubal invented).[84]

The trumpet was known by the time of Moses (born ca. 2372 BCE). Yahweh commanded Moses (see Numbers 10:2) to construct two silver trumpets, and he gave one to each of Aaron's sons, Eleazar and lthamar. The sons of Aaron used them to lead solemn religious ceremonies out of doors. Moses taught that the trumpet was to be used for only sacred purposes and, consequently, it was to be played only by the priests. It was stored in the "hut" of either Moses or Aaron.[85]

While Moses was commanded to use only two silver trumpets, the dedication of the temple by Solomon witnessed a priestly ensemble of one hundred twenty trumpeters (see 2 Chronicles 5:12). Coupled with a song of praise, the trumpet ensemble signaled the moment when "the glory of God filled the house" (see 2 Chronicles 5:13).[86] Trumpets were depicted in the priestly insignia of the temple. Representations of trumpets can be seen on the Arch of Titus, and trumpets are mentioned frequently in the Dead Sea Scrolls.[87]

In addition to using the trumpet at festive occasions, the Jews used the trumpet in their cultic sacrificial rites. It was used at both the burnt offering and the peace offering (see Numbers 10:10). When the trumpet sounded

82. *BI* 53.
83. Tarr, "Trumpet," *NGDMI* 3:642.
84. *EIHM* 5.
85. *EIHM* 5.
86. Friedrich, "Σάλπινχ (Salpinx—'Trumpet')," 7:79.
87. Tarr, "Trumpet," *NGDMI* 3:642.

at the burnt offering, the worshipers cast themselves to the ground (see 2 Chronicles 29:27 and Sirach 50:16).[88]

Josephus described the *chazozrah* as an instrument "one ell long, chased [*sic*] from heavy metal, [an instrument] which expands gradually from the mouthpiece to the end in the form of a bell."[89]

According to Numbers 10:2, the trumpet was used by Moses to call the assembly together and "for the journeying of the camps" in the wilderness. In the temple, three trumpet blasts indicated the commencement of the morning sacrifice. Blasts were also used at the end of Levitical chant to signal the moment when the worshipers were to prostrate themselves in the temple. Thus, trumpet blasts or calls were used in Jewish practice to signal the beginnings of various events, whether in peacetime or in war.[90]

Greek

Trumpet is signified in the Greek language as σάλπινχ (*salpinx*). As a verb, σαλπίζο (*salpizo*) means "to produce a blast on the trumpet." The trumpet is not a typical Greek instrument. Homer was familiar with it, but it "does not seem" to have been utilized by the Greek military.[91] Due to the lack of information concerning Greek use of the trumpet, it can be conjectured that (1) its use was overshadowed by the use of the stringed (like κιθαρα [*kithara*— "harp"]) and wind αὐλός (*aulos*—"flute") instruments, or (2) the trumpet was used in a similar militaristic manner as the Romans used it. Oftentimes, music in the two cultures is labelled Graeco-Roman.

Roman

The Roman trumpet was an enlargement of the short trumpet. It was typically two cubits long and had a mouthpiece which was separate from the body of the instrument. The mouthpiece consisted of a cup, a choke, and a backbone made from bronze.[92]

Bate provides a more detailed picture of the Roman trumpet. He claims that four different trumpet types existed:

---

88. Friedrich, "Σάλπινχ (Salpinx—'Trumpet')," 7:79.
89. *EIHM* 5.
90. Tarr, "Trumpet," *NGDMI* 3:642.
91. Friedrich, "Σάλπινχ (Salpinx—'Trumpet')," 7:73.
92. *BI* 57.

1. *Lituus*—a cylindrical conically shaped instrument that was hooked like a letter "J." It was utilized by the calvary;
2. *Tuba*—a conically shaped instrument that measured forty-six inches in length. It was used by foot soldiers;
3. *Cornu*—a large horn that was gently tapered through eleven feet. It was coiled, about three-and-a-half feet across, and was more discriminately employed to sound fanfares at high-ranking military activities; and
4. *Buccina*—a simple bugle horn that was used "to mark the four watches of the night" in camp. It was also used to sound reveille.[93]

Flavius Josephus indicates that the instrument was as little as a cubit in length.[94] It disappeared from Europe after the fall of Rome but was later reintroduced during the time of the crusades.[95]

Early Church

The sound of the trumpet was used primarily to herald or announce the beginning of events. The use of the trumpet in the period of the early church is evidenced in Old Testament pseudepigraphal writings of the time. Examples of this are numerous. In *The Life of Adam and Eve* 22:1, the sound of the trumpet is used to mark the sayings of the Lord and to announce the Lord's coming into human presence. In *The Life of Adam and Eve* 37:1, the trumpet is used to indicate when the angels should stand: "While Seth was speaking to his mother, an angel sounded the trumpet and the angels who were lying on their faces stood up and cried out with a fearful voice, saying. . ."

Prophesying the birth of Jesus, *Apocalypse of Abraham* 31:1 says,

> And then I will sound the trumpet out of the air, and I will send my chosen one, having in him one measure of all my power, and he will summon my people, humiliated by the heathen.[96]

Speaking of eschatological events, *Apocalypse of Zephaniah* utilizes the trumpet to herald and announce several events.

1. Trumpets herald the seers' triumph over their accusers (see Revelation 9).

---

93. Bate, *Trumpet*, 90–103.
94. Josephus, *Antiquities*, 3.12.
95. Tarr, "Trumpet," *NGD* 19:214.
96. *OTP* 1:704–5.

2. Trumpets herald the opening of heaven (see Revelation 10).
3. Trumpets call the saints to intercessory prayer (see Revelation 11).
4. Trumpets introduce a discussion of the end-times (see Revelation 12).[97]

In the Book of Revelation

The verb σάλπιζο (*salpizo*—"to trumpet") occurs frequently in the book of Revelation. In 1 Corinthians 14:8, Paul refers to the military use of the trumpet metaphorically. He implies that if the use of tongues is not used in a clear manner, the effort will have no effect. It would be tantamount to an unclear militaristic trumpet call which does nothing to prepare the troops for battle.[98] The voice of Christ's angel sounds as a trumpet blast. The trumpet blast "had already acquired [a] Christian association" in earlier New Testament passages (see Matthew 24:31 and 1 Thessalonians 4:16).[99]

When the "sound of the trumpet" is used in Revelation 1:10 and 4:11, the sound is not akin to a militaristic trumpet blast. Rather, the sound refers to the "loudness and indescribability of the tone." This sound is not made by an angel (see Revelation 5:2; 17:1; and 21:9). Neither is this the sound of the voice of the Son of Man (see Revelation 1:15). Instead, it is the voice that is "surely that of God Himself" (see Revelation 16:1 and 17).[100]

Revelation 18:22 contains the only hint that the trumpet is to be used as a musical instrument. When the final judgment on Babylon is proclaimed, the silent trumpeters are grouped with the flautists, harpists, and other players.[101] The trumpet blast or call is primarily used as an introduction or an announcement of revelation.

SUMMARY

It is doubtful whether the trumpet was often used in the ancient world as a musical instrument. The Egyptian trumpets have "fundamentally only two notes, the basic and the tenth," though Kirby indicates a third tone two

---

97. *OTP* 1:498–99.
98. Friedrich, "Σάλπινχ (Salpinx—'Trumpet')," 7:86.
99. *ASJ* 13.
100. Friedrich, "Σάλπινχ (Salpinx—'Trumpet')," 7:86.
101. Friedrich, "Σάλπινχ (Salpinx—'Trumpet')," 7:88.

octaves above the basic.[102] Usage of the trumpet in the book of Revelation supports its usage as a heralding device. The trumpet was reserved for use to make signals and to set rhythms.

The trumpet is used eschatologically in a similar fashion by both Judaism and the early church.

1. The trumpet announces the great judgment at the end-time.
2. The loud trumpet blast is heard in all the corners of the earth. When it occurs, the angels will assemble the elect from all parts thereof (see Matthew 24:31).
3. The transforming of the living and the raising of the dead will occur at the sound of the trumpet.

The trumpet call is the eschatologically heraldic sound which will signal the end of the age. Friedreich believes that the sound which is made by the trumpet cannot be made by a human instrument.[103]

---

102. Friedrich, "Σάλπινχ (Salpinx—'Trumpet')," 7:75.
103. Friedrich, "Σάλπινχ (Salpinx—'Trumpet')," 7:87–88.

4

Performing Groups

WITHIN THE PAGES OF the Apocalypse both vocal and instrumental musicians are described performing in a variety of groupings. An analysis of the various groupings follows.

SOLOISTS AND A SMALL ENSEMBLE

While soloists do not figure prominently in the book of Revelation, a variety of vocal and instrumental ensembles are employed. Occasions for solo singing arise when solos are given to members of a larger ensemble. An example of this can be found in Revelation 6. Each of the four living creatures (ζώαν—*zoan*) in turn say in a thunderous voice, "Come!" Similarly, the ensemble of trumpeters mentioned in Revelation 8 are never heard playing together. While they are grouped together, each one individually heralds successive actions in turn.

A quartet comprises the smallest group of singers. The four living creatures (see Revelation 4:6, 8; 5:6, 8, 11, 14; 6:6; 14:3; and 15:7) are a blend of creatures, including cherubim (see Ezekiel) and seraphim (see Isaiah 6). Ezekiel's cherubim are of Babylonian origin and the seraphim are celestial beings, apparently of human form with six wings but of unknown origin. They are positioned near the throne and their function is to carry the platform of God's throne which is similar to a chariot.[1]

The Jewish mind sees the cherubim and seraphim together. In his vision of heaven (see 1 Enoch 71:7 and 14:23), Enoch sees the seraphim,

---

1. *IB* 12:403–4.

cherubim, and ophanim (the personification of the eyes on the wheels of the chariot of God's throne) protecting the throne of God. These creatures never sleep.[2]

In the Book of Revelation

In Revelation 4:8, perpetual music is heard around the throne. It is sung by the four living creatures who "never cease to sing." This is owing to the fact that "at a certain stage loyalty and love inevitably become lyrical, bursting into song." Although there may be different types of churches, "no church exists of perpetual silence." God has placed the four living creatures' "deathless melody" of eternal hope and life into the heart of every Christian.[3]

In Revelation 4:9–11, the four living creatures join with the twenty-four elders to sing antiphonally to the Creator God. This song assures humankind that God is in complete control over all of creation and that his power will soon be finally evident.[4]

Χορός (*Choros*—"Chorus")

One of the principal features of music or a music practice in the book of Revelation is the utilization of a chorus. Although the Greek word for chorus, χορός (*choros*), does not specifically appear in the book of Revelation, its implementation is implied. The first allusion to the chorus appears in chapter 4:10, 11:

> The twenty-four elders fall down before him who is seated on the throne and worship him who lives for ever and ever; they cast their crowns before the throne, singing, 'Worthy art thou, our Lord and God, To receive glory and honor and power, For thou didst create all things, And by thy will they existed and were created.' (RSV)

Early Pagan

Evidence of early pagan choirs is virtually nonexistent. The earliest organized choirs occurred in Davidic times in the Jewish tradition, but no information of surrounding cultures of that time is extant.

2. *IB* 12:404.
3. *IB* 12:403–4.
4. *IB* 12:405.

Jewish

Rabbinic sources have legends and visions which portray heavenly angelic choirs beginning their own songs of exultation in imitation of the Jewish community singing and praising God in the Kedusha and Exodus 15.[5]

The period of the kings of Israel and Judah finds the first signs of well-organized choral singing. In 1 Chronicles 15:16, three singers are found who were assigned the duty of signaling or leading the chorus. The use of cymbals and fourteen instrumentalists (playing eight psalteries and six harps) indicates that the singers were accompanied. This instrumentation became a standard for Jewish choral music accompaniment.[6] During Davidic times, twenty-four groups of twelve musicians (288 in all) whom Chenaniah had trained were appointed by the King. It is from these origins that a choir school was maintained by the successors of Chenaniah. This school continued training generation after generation of cantors and choristers. These Levitical choirs consisted primarily of men with boy apprentices but probably no women.[7]

By exilic times, vocal music likely lacked the accompaniment of instrumentalists owing partly to small financial resources and the lack of skilled players. However, the model of the temple choirs from earlier times still prevailed. Musical practice consisted of responsorial as well as antiphonal styles. Some of the psalms have superscriptions which can be interpreted to mean that they were performed by a soloist (cantor) with a responding choir. Nehemiah 12:31–39 illustrates the practice of antiphony. By the first century, Philo of Alexandria described congregational antiphony in his *De vita contemplativa*, paragraph 29:

> They rise up together and. . . form themselves into two choirs, one of men and one of women, the leader chosen from each being the most honored and most musical among them. They sing hymns to God composed of many measures and set to many melodies, sometimes chanting together, sometimes antiphonally. . . It is thus that the choir of the Therapeutae [a Jewish sect] of either sex—note in response to note and voice to voice, the deep-toned voices of the men blending with the shrill voices of the women. . . create a truly musical symphony.[8]

---

5. *TSB* 141.
6. Smith, "Chorus," 4:343. See also Kleinig, *Lord's Song*.
7. Smith, "Chorus," 4:343.
8. Smith, "Chorus," 4:343.

Greek

The χορός (*choros*) finds its greatest early utilization in Greek tragic drama. Modern knowledge of Greek drama is based on the extant plays of three fifth-century BCE Greek playwrights: Aeschylus, Sophocles, and Euripides. Of the more than one thousand plays written between 500–400 BCE, only thirty-one survive. The plays of Sophocles are considered to be the most skillfully conceived—*Oedipus Rex* being his greatest. The plays of Sophocles developed Greek music to its highest form. The typical play contained the following sections:

1. the prologue, which provides the background to the story;

2. the παραδος (*parados*), which provides the entrance for the χορός (*choros*). It relays the exposition and establishes the mood of the play;

3. a series of episodes—three to six episodes develop the story. They are separated by choral songs (στασιμα—*stasima*); and

4. the exodus, which provides the concluding scene in which the characters and χορός (*choros*) depart.[9]

The χορός (*choros*) served the dual purpose of singing and dancing and was commonly grouped in the following manner: (1) men, (2) women, (3) men and women, or (4) men and boys. The music which the χορός (*choros*) sang was characteristically monophonic in either a responsorial or antiphonal style. The singers were expected not only to sing but to dance as well. Choral music was performed in unison.[10] The χορός (*choros*) finds its Greek origins in the Periclean Age. It evolved from the religious and ceremonial performances of the six.th and fifth centuries B.C.E. The three principal types of choral dances found in Greek drama are as follows:

1. the *paean*—mentioned first in the *Iliad* (ca. 850 BCE). It is used as an invocation to Apollo who was the god of healing;

2. the *partheneia* (ca. 650 BCE)—was performed by a women's chorus of Spartan virgins; and

3. the *dithyramb* (ca. 600 BCE)—consisted of a choreographic display which told the story of the fertility god Dionysus. This form of the choral dance ultimately led to the Greek tragedies and dramas of the

---

9. Brockett, *History of the Theatre*, 13–14.
10. Anderson, *Ethos*, 2.

fifth and fourth centuries BCE.[11] The leader of the χορός (*choros*) was referred to as "a corporate commentator."[12]

The χορός (*choros*) in Greek tragic drama spoke for conventional society and assisted in enlightening the audience regarding the protagonist problems of the particular play. It is also described as a group of actors "who stood aside from the main action of the play and commented on it."[13]

The pre-dramatic choruses could be as large as six hundred, whereas the dithyrambic chorus normally consisted of approximately twelve to fifty boys and men who were arranged in a circle surrounding an *aulos* player. Comedies most often employed either twenty-four, fifty, or sixty in the χορός (*choros*), while the dramas commonly employed less. The early dramas of Aeschylus utilized twelve in the chorus, while Sophocles employed fifteen. A χορός (*choros*) of fifteen became the standard for the tragedies.[14]

Aeschylus's (525–456 BCE) use of the chorus as a dramatic resource within the storyline of the myth was employed to intensify the importance of the crisis within the episodes. But when Aeschylus introduced a second actor, he consequently reduced the role of the chorus. Sophocles (ca. 495–406 BCE) provided more balance between the actors and the chorus. The chorus in Sophocles's plays share the following characteristics:

1. it plays a small part in the action of the play;

2. its chief function was purely lyrical; and

3. it was employed between the histrionic scenes (which now became "acts") in order to carry the dramatic rhythm.[15]

Music and the χορός (*choros*) share the following characteristics by the time of Euripides (484–ca. 406 BCE):

1. the music and chorus were more emotional and coincided more closely with the realism and the pathos of the plots;

2. the chorus's role continued to diminish owing to the fact that the actors' roles were becoming more important. Non-tragic plots became more elaborate and important and resulted in the number of actors increasing to as many as eleven as seen in *Phoenician Women*; and

---

11. Smith, "Chorus," 4:341–42.
12. Smith, "Chorus," 4:342.
13. Hartnoll, *Theatre*, 176.
14. Smith, "Chorus," 4:342–43.
15. Hartnoll, *Theatre*, 404.

3. eventually the music of the chorus was reduced to merely decorative filler.[16]

Sophocles's plays represent the high point in tragic drama. Consequently, the characteristics inherent in his works are used as the standard in the analysis to follow.

Roman

Choral performances occurred in Rome on a grand scale. Roman theaters could seat as many as twelve thousand spectators. Seneca wrote that there were often more performers than audience at the plays of his day. Brass instruments were frequently placed in the audience because there was no room on or offstage for them.[17]

Early Church

In Colossians 3:16 and James 5:13, the early church gave approval to the use of music in church services. The early church functioned initially as a Jewish sect and attempted to follow the precedent of its Jewish forbears. However, it did not have the financial wherewithal nor the physical facilities which its Jewish counterparts enjoyed. Thus, most of the first-century Christian music consisted of congregational singing.[18]

Specific references to the early church's use of choirs is nonexistent. However, patristic writers indicate that choirs were common in their day. Eusebius (CE ca. 260–ca. 340), the Bishop of Caesarea, indicates in his *Historia ecclesiastica*, that antiphonal singing was "still" practiced by the Christians of his day.[19] It can only be conjectured that since choirs are common in Greek and Jewish practice up to and through the first century and subsequently are alluded to in writings after CE 100, that some form of choir existed during the first century in the Christian community.

Choral music in the modern sense was probably not employed by the early church owing to the fundamental concept of κοινωνία (koinonia—"fellowship"). Κοινωνία (koinonia) refers to the fellowship, the oneness, which the early church experienced. The early church consisted of slave and free persons. To raise up or lift up one group of a congregation by assigning

---

16. Hartnoll, *Theatre*, 404.
17. *MSR* 412.
18. Smith, "Chorus," 4:343.
19. Smith, "Chorus," 4:343.

them a special act in worship was outside of the concept of a unified fellowship. Thus, congregational singing, as normative choral singing, included all worshipers equally (see Acts 4:24–30; 1 Corinthians 14:15–16:26; Ephesians 5:19; and Colossians 3:16).[20] Ending the Lord's Supper with a song of jubilation, Jesus portrayed a powerful illustration of the κοινωνία (*koinonia*) of gathering in worship as an affront to the struggles that lie ahead. Empty, rote worship has no meaning and cannot compare with this type of refreshing and vital worship.[21]

Owing to Jewish influence, it is conjectured that antiphonal and responsorial singing originated in the early church in and around Jerusalem and, via the evangelical spreading of the Word, had been spread to the four corners of the then-known world by the fourth century. The patristic record indicates that opinion was divided on the use of instruments as accompanimental aids because of their association with pagan festivals. Clement of Alexandria (CE ca. 150–ca. 220) censored the use of instruments, but this practice was later repealed by Didymus of Alexandria (CE ca. 313–338) who wrote that a psalm is "a hymn which is sung to the instrument called either the psaltery or cithara."[22]

Summary

The chief characteristics of the chorus summarized from its origins follows.

1. In Jewish music practice, the chorus

    a. was well-organized;

    b. used instrumental accompaniment;

    c. consisted of trained and skilled musicians;

    d. used antiphonal and responsorial techniques which were chanted or sung;

    e. consisted of large groups (in excess of sixty members each), primarily men with boys, occasionally women; and

    f. sang hymns to God.

2. In Greek music practice, the chorus

    a. spoke for conventional society;

20. Smith, *Musical Aspects*, 29, 35.
21. *IB* 7:576.
22. *IB* 7:576.

b. commented on the action of the main plot;

  c. was twelve to sixty persons in size, primarily men or men and boys; and

  d. was lyrical and emotionally and physically dramatic.

3. In early church music practice, choral music

  a. consisted primarily of congregational singing;

  b. shows no extant record from the first century that choirs, other than "congregational choirs," existed; and

  c. was probably unaccompanied.

In the Book of Revelation

Three choruses are alluded to in the book of Revelation.[23]

A Chorus Consisting of the Twenty-Four Elders. This relatively small chorus is referred to in the following passages.

> *Revelation 4:10–11:*
>
> The twenty-four elders fall down before him who is seated on the throne and worship him who lives for ever and ever; they cast their crowns before the throne, singing, "Worthy art thou, our Lord and God, to receive glory and honor and power, for thou didst create all things, and by thy will they existed and were created." (RSV)
>
> *Revelation 5:8–9:*
>
> And when he had taken the scroll, the four living creatures and the twenty-four elders fell down before the Lamb, each holding a harp, and with golden bowls full of incense, which are the prayers of the saints; and they sang a new song, saying, "Worthy art thou to take the scroll and to open its seals, for thou wast slain and by thy blood didst ransom men for God from every tribe and tongue and people and nation, and hast made them a kingdom and priests to our God, and they shall reign on earth." (RSV)

---

23. A fourth choir is mentioned in Revelation 18 consisting of "kings of the earth who committed fornication and were wanton with her. . ." (see 18:9–10) and "the merchants of the earth [who] weep and mourn for her, since no one buys their cargo anymore" (see 18:11–20). But this choir is outside the scope of worship in the book of Revelation; consequently, it is outside the scope of the present study.

Revelation 11:16–18:

And the twenty-four elders who sit on their thrones before God fell on their faces and worshiped God, saying, "We give thanks to thee, Lord God Almighty, who art and who wast, that thou hast taken thy great power and begun to reign. The nations raged, but thy wrath came, and the time for the dead to be judged, for rewarding thy servants, the prophets and saints, and those who fear thy name, both small and great, and for destroying the destroyers of the earth."

Revelation 19:4:

And the twenty-four elders and the four living creatures fell down and worshiped God who is seated on the throne, saying, "Amen. Hallelujah!" (RSV)

The χορός (*choros*) of twenty-four elders borrows features of the Greek χορός (*choros*). It probably consisted of only men. Elements of Jewish chorus origins are evident in the organization, theatrics, and probable skill which the elders exhibit since they are robed similarly in white garments and golden crowns. Their actions appear to be choreographed, and it seems that they were able to play the harp. Thus, their singing was probably accompanied by musical instruments.[24] Just as Jewish chorus practice was directed primarily to a monotheistic god, Yahweh, so is this music directed to God the Father and Creator and to Jesus Christ, the Savior of the world.

A Second Chorus Numbering Thousands and Thousands in Heaven. This very large chorus consists of angels and the scriptural references to it are as follows:

[EXT] *Revelation 5:11–12:*

Then I looked, and I heard around the throne and the living creatures and the elders the voice of many angels, numbering myriads of myriads and thousands of thousands, saying with a loud voice, "Worthy is the Lamb who was slain, to receive power and wealth and wisdom and might and honor and glory and blessing!" (RSV)

Revelation 7:9–12:

After this I looked, and behold, a great multitude which no man could number, from every nation, from all tribes and peoples and tongues, standing before the throne and before the Lamb, clothed in white robes, with palm branches in their hands, and crying out with a loud voice, "Salvation belongs to our God who sits upon the throne, and to the Lamb!"

---

24. Quasten, *Music and Worship*, 72.

And all the angels stood round the throne and round the elders and the four living creatures, and they fell on their faces before the throne and worshiped God, saying, "Amen! Blessing and glory and wisdom and thanksgiving and honor and power and might be to our God for ever and ever! Amen." (RSV)

Revelation 14:2–3:

And I heard a voice from heaven like the sound of many waters and like the sound of loud thunder; the voice I heard was like the sound of harpers playing on their harps, and they sing a new song before the throne and before the four living creatures and before the elders. No one could learn that song except the hundred and forty-four thousand who had been redeemed from the earth. (RSV)

Revelation 19:1–3:

After this I heard what seemed to be the loud voice of a great multitude in heaven, crying, "Hallelujah! Salvation and glory and power belong to our God, for his judgments are true and just; he has judged the great harlot who corrupted the earth with her fornication, and he has avenged on her the blood of his servants." Once more they cried, "Hallelujah! The smoke from her goes up for ever and ever." (RSV)

Revelation 19:6–8:

Then I heard what seemed to be the voice of a great multitude, like the sound of many waters and like the sound of mighty thunderpeals, crying, "Hallelujah! For the Lord our God the Almighty reigns. Let us rejoice and exult and give him the glory, for the marriage of the Lamb has come, and his Bride has made herself ready; it was granted her to be clothed with fine linen, bright and pure" —for the fine linen is the righteous deeds of the saints. (RSV)

In Revelation 7:9–12, the heavenly choir of angels joins with the four living creatures and the twenty-four elders who fall on their faces before the throne worshiping God. They respond with a seven-fold doxology beginning and ending with "Amen." This counterpoint of praise represents "heaven's answer to earth's praise."[25]

The book of Revelation is often labelled a book of doom and gloom. However, as Blevins contrarily points out, it is a book of hope.[26] Every

---

25. *IB* 12:420.
26. *RD* 136.

generation of Christians from the early church has experienced persecution. The hope of every age is embodied within the spirit of the book of Revelation.

> In spite of all the tragedy which it [the book of Revelation] describes, it may be said to be one of the very happiest books ever written. The music of eternity sends its triumphant joy back into the life of time. The justification of glorious Christian music in this world is always justification by faith. . .The writings of Paul also have this characteristic of bursting into song. You can judge an interpretation of the Christian religion by its capacity to set men [sic] singing. There is something wrong about a theology which does not create triumphant music.[27]

In Revelation 14:2, the sound which the seer witnesses is "a voice like many waters and loud thunder heard in heaven." It is like "the sound of harpers playing upon their harps." The singers are not specifically identified in this passage, but if John considers the martyrs as being both in the heavenly and earthly Zion in this scene, then he could readily visualize the martyrs as the singers (see Revelation 7:10 and 2 Esdras 2:42).[28]

The "hallelujah" chorus (see Revelation 19:1–2, 3 and 6–8) is the expression of the great joy over the destruction of the wicked city of Rome. It is also heaven's rejoicing at the triumph over the final vestiges of evil on the earth. The term "hallelujah" (alleluia) comes from the Hebrew term *hallel* ("to praise"). When it is combined with Yahweh it means "to praise God."[29]

The writer of the Apocalypse indicates that this angelic choir is represented by "a single voice." The choir's performance indicates a total "harmony of emotion and feeling" (let alone musical excellence) as they corporately "lift their song in antiphonal praise."[30] The angelic choir is intoning a song of praise to the Lamb, and it is "quite liturgical in character." The number of angels is reminiscent of those mentioned in Daniel 7:10 and 1 Enoch 40:1; they are beyond human calculation.[31]

Evidence of Greek χορός (*choros*) practice is found in the positioning of this large choir "offstage" in heaven. Just as Greek choruses generally were not central to the onstage action, so is this χορός (*choros*) positioned outside of the mainstream of the action. The use of expression is indicated by the nature of their "loud" singing. The χορός (*choros*) appears to respond

27. IB 12:420.
28. IB 12:468–69.
29. IB 12:506–7, 309.
30. Coleman, *Songs of Heaven*, 55.
31. IB 12:409.

antiphonally to the χορός (*choros*) of elders who appear closer to the action of the principal characters, and the message of their singing provides commentary on the storyline. Similar to the χορός (*choros*) of twenty-four elders, this χορός (*choros*) of angels is accompanied by instrumentalists on harps and they focus their attention on the completed action which Jesus Christ has accomplished in history.

A Third Chorus Numbering Every Creature in Heaven and Earth. The size of this χορός (*choros*) appears to include all creatures ever created. The scriptural allusion to it follows.

> *Revelation 5:13:*
> And I heard every creature in heaven and on earth and under the earth and in the sea, and all therein, saying, "To him who sits upon the throne and to the Lamb be blessing and honor and glory and might for ever and ever!" (RSV)

When the angelic response to God and the Lamb is ended, all creatures in the universe join in this doxology to the Godhead. This mighty outburst of praise ascribes eternal "blessing and honor and glory and might" to the occupant of the throne and to the Lamb. The twenty-four elders prostrate themselves before the throne and the four living creatures end the doxology with an "Amen."

In Revelation 7:4–8, a choir of the redeemed is mentioned. This choir allegorically is numbered to contain 144,000; it is made up of twelve thousand from each of the twelve tribes of Israel. These twelve tribes are representative of all Christians who are the true Israel (see James 1:1 and 1 Peter 1:1).[32]

By literally becoming members of the kingdom of God, this χορός (*choros*) does not merely represent and speak for conventional society: it is the redeemed of conventional society. The size of the χορός (*choros*) has augmented the large choruses of Jewish tradition and performs the ultimate responsorial role. All of creation responds to the finished work of the Lamb. By the immense size of the χορός (*choros*), it is very likely that it is highly organized and consists of dedicated and skilled performers.

Summary

The choir appears to function primarily as a responding mechanism to others in the text, specifically to God the Creator and Jesus Christ the Lamb. God and Jesus Christ are represented at various points in the text as "the

---

32. *IB* 12:419.

voice of heaven" (see Revelation 10:8), "the voice of the temple" (see Revelation 16:1), and "the voice of the throne" (see Revelation 21:3).

A theological concept of the chorus in the book of Revelation contains the idea of corporate participation in response to the "revelation" expressed by the Godhead in either a responsorial or antiphonal style. This includes physical posturing, although this characteristic is prominent only in the smaller choruses. The chorus of twenty-four elders appear to lead the larger choirs as the action in the text builds in a mighty crescendo of participation and sound; it initiates with the chorus of twenty-four elders singing, followed by an antiphonal response of the creatures of heaven, and culminates when these antiphonal forces participate in a joined response with the remainder of creation, including the redeemed. Together they corporately direct their praise to the Godhead.

INSTRUMENTAL MUSIC

Bales states that "instrumental music in worship is not authorized in the New Testament."[33] However, the book of Revelation contains more instruments by name than the remainder of the New Testament and would consequently challenge Bales's assertion. The instruments are partly used in the Apocalypse in conjunction with the joyful celebrations revolving around Christ's ultimate victory over Satan.[34]

Small ensembles of instrumentalists are used at various times throughout the book of Revelation. The three specific groups are as follows:

1. a trumpet ensemble of seven (see Revelation 8 and 18:22);
2. a harp ensemble (see Revelation 5:8; 14:2; and 18:22); and
3. a flute ensemble (see Revelation 18:22).

These instruments are not intermingled in a mixed ensemble. The Greek musical style is maintained in order to express a single ethos.

The instrumental ensembles that fall within the realm of worship in the Apocalypse are the trumpet ensemble (see Revelation 8) and the use of harps by the twenty-four elders in Revelation 5:8. The other instrumental ensembles are not used in a conventional sense. Since the trumpet, flute, and harp ensembles mentioned in Revelation 18:22 are not utilized in worship, they are outside of the scope of this study.

33. Bales, *Instrumental Music*, 9.
34. Appleby, *Church Music*, 20.

Passages in Revelation 5:8–13, 14:3, and so on, portray a "heavenly celebration" which indicates that the author envisaged a highly ordered practice of music. The music of καθαρσις (*katharsis*) is taken for granted. The early church fathers were reluctant to allow instrumental music in their services because it "carried too many reminiscences" of pagan and Jewish temple cultic practices. The synagogue had banished all instrumental music because instrumental music partly represented mourning over the destruction of the temple.[35]

In the Jewish tradition it was common, however, for the instrumental musicians to serve in accompanimental roles or to play interludes. While admitting to no conclusive definition for the seventy odd occurrences of *selah* in the book of Psalms, Sendrey suggests the following interpretation as a possibility. When the singers came to the marking *selah* in the text, it may have been an indication for the musicians to enter loudly with trumpets and percussion instruments and for the voices to cease. Because the main task of doing the music in the temple services resided in the Levitical singers (1 Chr 16:37, 40), it was only natural that a period of rest and recovery occur frequently during a long service. The periods between text singing "might have caused the resorting to instrumental interludes" indicated by the marking *selah*. Sendrey submits the following example although there is no evidence to connect this with *selah*.

> Ben Arza clashed the cymbal and the Levites broke forth into singing. When they reached a break in the singing they blew upon the trumpets and the people prostrated themselves; at every break there was a blowing of the trumpet and at every blowing of the trumpet a prostration. This was the rite of the daily Whole-offering in the service of the House of our God.[36]

Instrumental solo or ensemble music carrying a melodic line is not specifically mentioned nor alluded to in the book of Revelation. Its use is reserved exclusively as a heralding device (see chapter 3 of this study) or as accompaniment to singing. Specific reference to accompanied song in worship occurs in Revelation 5:13. Accompanying the hymns, responses, doxologies, prayers, and *Tersanctus* are instrumental music, incense, and ritual movements.[37]

---

35. *TSB* 318.
36. *MAI* 150.
37. *IB* 12:410.

HARP ENSEMBLE

The generic name for harp-like instruments is chordophone. By definition, a chordophone exists when a "plane of strings is perpendicular to a soundboard."[38]

Early Pagan

Sumerian harps date from ca. 2800 BCE. The early Sumerian harp consisted of a plane of strings vertical to the soundboard with the body elongated at one end. The curved neck formed an arch. The boat-shaped resonators came in all sizes with up to six strings.[39]

The earliest extant harp from Mesopotamia dating ca. 2500 BCE was located in the Royal Cemetery at Ur.[40] From ca. 1850 BCE in Mesopotamia (the Old Babylonian period), the angular harp predominated and was played in two ways: when the strings were vertical the resonator rested against the player's body and both hands were used to pluck the strings. When the strings were horizontal to the resonator, the resonator was held under the left arm and the strings were strummed or picked by a plectrum by the right hand. The left hand was used to dampen the strings.[41]

The arched harp of the Old Kingdom in Egypt contained a resonator that was shaped like a spoon or a spade. Bas-reliefs in tombs surrounding the Giza pyramids illustrate this type of harp. It was customarily played by a kneeling man who was joined in accompanying a singer by a flautist and double-parallel pipe player. However, in the tomb of Mereruka at Saqqara (Dynasty 6, ca. 2345–2181 BCE), the Princess Seshseshat "plays to her husband on the harp and accompanies her own song."[42] A male ensemble of seven harpers can be viewed in the tomb of Ibi at Deir el-Gebrawi. By the time of the Egyptian Middle Kingdom, chamber groups tended to be smaller and contained more women. The resonator was deeper and more oval-shaped, like a ladle.[43]

The Egyptian New Kingdom harps illustrated the use of a wide variety of chordophones. They ranged from small portable harps with boat-shaped resonators that played on the shoulder to the giant harps. The giant harps

38. Griffiths et al., "Harp," 2:131.
39. Griffiths et al., "Harp," 2:133.
40. Griffiths et al., "Harp," 2:133.
41. Griffiths et al., "Harp," 2:133.
42. Griffiths et al., "Harp," 2:133.
43. Griffiths et al., "Harp," 2:133.

were played by standing male musicians. An example of this can be found in the tomb of Rameses III in the Valley of the Kings.[44]

The angular harp was so named because the body and the neck came together at an angle.[45] It appeared "schematically on a few later seals (after the third millennium) and on an incised stone of the second millennium from Megiddo of Palestine."[46] These were equivalent to the asymmetrical lyres used by the Jews from 2000 BCE.

Jewish

The Jewish harp was called a *kinnor*. It was similar to a lyre, called a κιθάρα (*kithara*) by the Greeks. It was made of wood, possibly cypress, and was shaped with curved outlines and horizontal crossbars. According to Flavius Josephus, the Jewish historian and Roman general born CE 37 in Jerusalem, it consisted of ten strings.[47] It was plucked with a plectron. It was tuned pentatonically without semitones through two octaves. It was not a solo instrument but was preferably used as a "tool for singing" (see 1 Chronicles 16:42). Thus, its role was one of an accompanimental nature, unlike the trumpet and cymbal. The melodies of the *kinnor* were of a gay, happy nature, and, consequently, were not used for lamentation.[48]

Greek

Greek musical practice did not mix instruments of different types within the same ensemble. To do this would be to confuse the ethos which the ensemble sought to portray.[49]

Sendrey found that in 283 BCE, Carinus produced a series of plays that utilized one hundred trumpet players. Other groups used one hundred horn players and two hundred χοραύλός (*choraulos*) and πιθαύλός (*pythaulos*) players. These plays, well received in their day, were considered to be highlights of the year.[50]

---

44. Griffiths et al., "Harp," 2:133.
45. *HMI* 79.
46. Griffiths et al., "Harp," 2:133.
47. Josephus, *Antiquities*, 7.12.3.
48. *HMI* 107–8.
49. *MSR* 412.
50. *MSR* 412.

Roman

Roman musical practice frequently mixed instruments of various types in performing ensembles.[51]

Early Church

Little information is available regarding the use of the harp in the early church. During that era the lyre

> remained comparatively unblemished by use in idol worship and was employed more frequently in private homes, while the flute, tambourine, cymbal, and all the other instruments were much more closely associated with pagan cults.[52]

However, no conclusive evidence exists to indicate that the lyre was used either as a solo instrument or an instrument for accompaniment in the early church, apart from its use in the book of Revelation.

In the Book of Revelation

In Revelation 5:13 and 18:22 appear the "harpers" (κιθάραδον [*kitharodon*]) who play on the harp (κιθάρα [*kithara*]). This term also appears in 1 Corinthians 14:7; Revelation 5:8; 14:2; and 15:2. Today's equivalent would be a harpist.[53]

In Revelation 5:13, the twenty-four elders are seen holding harps while they sing. While it is not explicitly indicated that the twenty-four elders played harps, their use as accompaniment to their song is implied. Used in this manner, the sound which they produced was presumably of a chordal nature, not a melodic one.

---

51. *MSR* 412.
52. Quasten, *Music and Worship*, 73.
53. Earle, *Word Meanings*, 460.

TRUMPET ENSEMBLE

Early Pagan[54]

The trumpet functioned primarily as a solo instrument.

Jewish

Numbers 10:1–2 and 9–10 contain the idea of "drawing Yahweh's attention towards his worshipers by a strong sound." The strong sound used by the Jews was that of the trumpet blast or call. Although this idea was primitive, the trumpet call was widely practiced in the early Jewish tradition. However, Elijah's later preaching refuted this concept theologically.[55] In 1 Kings 18:27 (RSV), Elijah shouted to the priests of Baal to "cry aloud: for he is a god; either he is talking, or he is pursuing, or he is in a journey, or per adventure he sleepeth and must be awakened."

The trumpet symbolically heralded the coming of the Lord (see Zephaniah 1:16; Zechariah 9:14; *Psalms of Solomon* 11:1; and *Apocalypse of Abraham* 31). And *Pseudo-Philo* 32:18 referred to singing accompanied by trumpets:

> And when Deborah made an end to her words, she along with the people went up to Shiloh, and they offered sacrifices and holocausts, and they sang to the accompaniment of the trumpets. And when they were singing and the sacrifices had been offered, Deborah said 'And this will be as a testimony of trumpets between the stars and their Lord.' And Deborah came down from there and judged Israel forty years.

From Aaron's day, the two original silver trumpets were the priestly instruments associated with sacrifices and used only near the tabernacle. By the time of the temple, trumpeters were separated from horn players who could only play outside the temple. Priestly trumpeters stood in front in battle and at the sacrificial altar in the temple stood on two pillars or stood near the ark of the covenant. The trumpeters' purposes were several: (1) to glorify God; (2) to show the Israelites were a holy people and soldiers of

---

54. See chapter 3 of this study for a discussion of the early history of the use of this instrument.

55. *HMI* 112.

Yahweh; (3) to encourage the soldiers; (4) to unite prayers with sonority; and (5) to remind the people of the presence of Yahweh.[56]

Greek

Chapter 3 contains a discussion of this instrument in the Greek culture.

Roman

Tibia players (*tibicines*) constituted one of the most ancient professional groups at Rome. Their music was used to "render inaudible any maleficent noises" which occurred during the Roman sacrificial rites. It was also used to "banish evil spirits and to summon up benevolent deities." Music was also used at funerals, other ceremonies, and at other sacrifices. While the music was occasionally accompanied by lyre players (*fidicines*), the tibia was the instrument traditionally used. The tibia was the national Roman religious instrument and originally consisted of "a bone pipe with three or four finger holes, and later, like the Greek aulos, [became] a double pipe reed instrument with two pipes made from ivory, silver or boxwood."[57]

Roman military music utilized trumpeters (*tubicines*) and horn players (*cornicines*). They originated as part of the constitutional reforms of the fifth century BCE and are attributed to Servius Tullius.[58]

The trumpeters provided signals to "sound the alarm, break camp, attack, or retreat." They also signaled changes of the watch and were played while on the march as well as at funerals and in triumphal and sacrificial processions. In battle, the combination of trumpet blasts and the "dark coarse noise of the horns" served to encourage the Roman army and to confuse the enemy.[59]

Early Church

No record of the use of the trumpet either as a solo or ensemble instrument can be found in the early church, apart from its use in the book of Revelation.

56. *EIHM* 18.
57. Fleischhauer, "Rome," 16:147.
58. Fleischhauer, "Rome," 16:148.
59. Fleischhauer, "Rome," 16:148.

In the Book of Revelation

Although the seven angels of Revelation 8 are given seven trumpets, they do not perform together as an ensemble. Rather, each one individually heralds the subsequent revelatory action in the text.

The two original silver trumpets were used exclusively near the tabernacle which housed the ark of the covenant. In the temple tradition, trumpeters were separated from horn players who were allowed to play outside of the temple only. The priestly trumpeters of the temple stood at the front in battle and during the sacrificial rite stood at the table on two pillars or near the ark of the covenant. Trumpets were used to glorify God, to show the Israelites they were a holy people and to show they were the soldiers of Yahweh, to encourage the soldiers in battle, to aid in prayer, and to remind the people of the presence of Yahweh.[60]

---

60. *EIHM* 18.

5

Performance Practice

THIS CHAPTER DEALS WITH the type of musical sounds made and the manner the sound is produced.

VOCAL

Reference to the types of sound made in the production of music in the Apocalypse are derived from the Greek word φωνή (*phone*). It is used throughout the book to represent both vocally and non-vocally produced sound. It can be literally translated to mean "a sound" or "a voice" and is often used to "address one by word of mouth."[1]

Early Pagan

Music is as old as civilization itself. At the earliest stages of development,

> music-making must have utilized, in a sing-song manner, sounds of different pitch. Out of such crude-sounding utterances came human song and even human speech which, according to some theories, developed from it laboriously over a long period of time.[2]

---

1. Moulton and Milligan, "φωνή," 680.
2. *MSR* 24.

The natural question arises: which came first, song or speech? Schneider believes that language came first.³ However, it is likely speech is a "watered-down" version of song. Anthropology informs us that humanity sought to imitate the sounds of nature first. This theory assumes that humanity sang before it spoke.⁴

The origin of vocal sounds by the human voice, either spoken or sung, consists of a wide variety of theories. An early theory put forth by Herbert Spencer suggests that speech and song appear to have originated from the same source.⁵ In summarizing Spencer's theory, Sendrey says,

> Singing was a primitive function of speech. The organs of speech, under the influence of emotion, create certain reflex actions, which manifest themselves in acts related to singing. The vocal peculiarities which indicate excited feeling, are those which especially distinguish song from ordinary speech.⁶

However, Spencer does admit that the distinctions between speech and song in early pagan times is still "hazy."⁷

Sendrey also summarized the opinions of Lombroso, Darwin, Buecher, and Sachs concerning the origins of singing. It is Lombroso's opinion that song originated in primitive dance.⁸ The onlookers, as well as the performers themselves, excited the dancers via collective vocal cheers. These cheers developed into a "sing-song pattern."⁹ From this earliest type of rhythmic chant came vocal sound production.¹⁰

Darwin attempted to relate the origin of singing with human courtship and mating. Buecher hypothesized that vocal music began early as a result of group-work activity.¹¹ To break the tedium of work, early pagan societies used "accompanying rhythmical devices."¹² This included singing.

Curt Sachs rejects all of these theories and other theories and concludes that their common mistake is their belief that music began from a single source.¹³ Sachs points out that

3. Schneider, "Primitive Music," 5.
4. Durant, *History*, 88.
5. Spencer, "Origin and Function of Music."
6. *MSR* 24.
7. *MSR* 24.
8. Lombroso, *Klinische*, 145; see also Leeuw, *Sacred and Profane*.
9. *MSR* 27.
10. *MSR* 27.
11. Buecher, *Arbeit*.
12. *MSR* 25–26.
13. Sachs, *Wellsprings*, 16–21.

music, bound to the motor impulses of our bodies to the vague images of our minds, and to our emotion in all its depth and width, eludes whatever attempt may be made to find a single formula.[14]

But he does agree that "music began with singing."[15]

Jewish

Traditional Jewish and Christian belief espouse a literal creation of the universe. When Adam and Eve were newly created by their Creator, it is assumed they could speak immediately. Likewise, as humankind was created in the image of God, just as God in Zephaniah 3:17 sang over creation, it is assumed that Adam and Eve could sing from the first day of their respective creation dates.

In the Jewish culture, ψωνή (*phone*) could be made by animals, nature, humankind, and the Godhead. Examples of its usage are numerous:

1. "noise," as in "claps of thunder" (Exod 9:23, 29, 33);
2. "roar" of great masses of water (Pss 42:7; 93:3);
3. "swish of rain" (1 Kgs 18:41);
4. "rolling of an earthquake" (Ezek 37:7);
5. "sound of steps" (Gen 3:8);
6. "trampling of horses" (Jer 4:29);
7. "rolling of wheels" (2 Kgs 7:6);
8. "whistling of whips" (Nah 3:2)
9. "tumult of a large and excited crowd" (1 Kgs 1:40) or "city" (1 Sam 4:14; Ezra 23:42);
10. "rustling of wings of the cherubim on the throne chariot of God" (Ezra 1:24; 3:13; 10:5);
11. "sound of musical instruments, especially the ram's horn" (Amos 2:2; Ezek 33:4; Exod 19:16; 20:18; 2 Sam 6:15; 15:10; 1 Kgs 1:41; Jer 4:21; 6:17; 42:14; Pss 47:5; 98:6; Job 39:24);
12. "sound of trumpets" (2 Chr 5:13);
13. "sound of zithers" (Ezra 26:13);

14. *MSR* 27.
15. *MSR* 27.

14. "sound of flutes" (Job 21:12);
15. "sound of the bells" on the upper garment of the high priest (Exod 26:13; Sirach 45:9);
16. "crying" (Isa 65:19; Ps 6:8);
17. "lamenting" (Isa 4:14; Jer 51:54);
18. "groaning" (Ps 102:6);
19. "jubilation" (Isa 48:20); and
20. God's revelation of himself (Ps 29).[16]

In Apocalyptic writings, φωνή (*phone*) is perceived as the following:

1. noise and sound, like the roaring of many waters;
2. the voice of man. "Man's faculty of speech is designed especially for the service of God's praise";
3. the voice of the angels. Their collective voice praises God with "one" voice (see Apocalypse of Abraham 18:2); and
4. the voice of God himself. Thunder is sent by God and is separate from the revelation of the Word. Lightning is a blessing or a curse from God. And the "voices of thunder" are under the control of the angels in heaven.[17]

In Rabbinic Judaism, φωνή (*phone*) never means "speech" or "word." Rather, it is translated as

1. noise and sound, similar to a door opening;
2. the human voice. The sound used by humans to communicate and considered to be an essential mark of the individual;
3. thunder. It comes from God as a universal declaration;
4. the voice of God at Sinai (Exod 19:16); and
5. an anonymous voice from heaven. Following the destruction of the second temple and the last prophets Haggai, Zechariah, and Malachi, Rabbinic Judaism believes that the Holy Spirit left Israel and substituted the voice of heaven in its place.[18]

---

16. Betz, "Φωνή (*Phone*)," 9:280–83.
17. Betz, "Φωνή (*Phone*)," 9:285–86.
18. Betz, "Φωνή (*Phone*)," 9:286–88.

Hellenistic Judaism interpreted the use of φωνή (*phone*) in the following manners.

1. Based on the Septuagint usage, φωνή (*phone*) was limited to the oral sounds of living creatures. The revelation of God only occurs by the Word.
2. Aristobulus (170–150 BCE) warns against an "anthropomorphic view of [the] divine voice." He claims that the voice of God should be comprehended by its operation, not the spoken word. He views it as it was described by Moses when Moses described the "works" Yahweh as "divine words."
3. Josephus uses the concept of God's voice to "express more clearly the distance between God and man."
4. Philo believes that among living creatures, only humankind has an articulate voice, and it should be used to serve praise to God.[19]

Greek

In Greek usage, the term φωνή (*phone*) is a sound "made by living creatures in the throat."[20] It could consequently be made by animals but was primarily an indication signifying the sound which humankind produced.[21]

Roman

No information can be found on the types of sound produced in the Roman world.

Early Church

In the early church, φωνή (*phone*) was construed to represent the following interpretations:

1. noise and sound. Similar to its usage in the Old Testament, φωνή (*phone*) can also denote the "melody" of a musical instrument.

---

19. Betz, "Φωνή (*Phone*)," 9:290–91.
20. Betz, "Φωνή (*Phone*)," 9:278.
21. Betz, "Φωνή (*Phone*)," 9:278.

Examples of this are flutes and zithers (1 Cor 14:7) and the signal of trumpets (1 Cor 14:8);

2. the human voice. The speech of human beings can make ψωνή (*phone*), which are "either agitated or moved by the Spirit" (Luke 23:23; Acts 7:57, 60; 26:24) and also which praise God (Luke 17:15; 19:37; Rev 7:10); and

3. the speech of angels, spirits, or bearers of the Spirit.[22]

In the Book of Revelation

The book of Revelation contains many occurrences of ψωνή (*phone*) which represent a wide variety of uses. In Revelation 1:10, 4:1, and 8:13, ψωνή (*phone*) implies the noise of the sound of trumpets. In Revelation 10:3, it is a "calling" that sounds like the roar of a lion.[23] In Revelation 7:10, ψωνή (*phone*) refers to the sound made by the human voice.[24]

Ψωνή (*Phone*) is produced by the speech of angels, spirits, or bearers of the Spirit as witnessed in Revelation 6:10. The souls of the martyrs cry out with a loud voice. It is their desire that God reign down retribution on those who have caused them pain and persecution (this is similar to the soul of Abel "lamenting in the realm of the dead").[25] Angels praise God in Revelation 5:12 in a way in which it will be heard on earth (see also Revelation 8:13; 14:7, 9, 18; and 18:2).[26]

In the Apocalypse, ψωνή (*phone*) can also represent the voice of God. In Revelation 10:3, the seven voices of thunder, which reply in speech to the cry of an angel, are not written down because they cannot be translated. The thunders represent the voice of God as witnessed in Psalm 29:3–9. However, the inarticulate thunder of God exists in the book of Revelation with the very understandable words of the Son of Man like the sound of the trumpet in Revelation 1:10–12. In eschatological fulfillment, God's speaking through nature and angelic creatures is replaced by the directives of the Son of Man "in plerophorous [a variety of] expressions the signs of the theophany at Sinai are transferred to the world-shaking catastrophe of the last judgment."[27]

---

22. Betz, "Ψωνή (*Phone*)," 9:292–93.
23. Betz, "Ψωνή (*Phone*)," 9:292–93.
24. Betz, "Ψωνή (*Phone*)," 9:292–93.
25. Betz, "Ψωνή (*Phone*)," 9:293.
26. Betz, "Ψωνή (*Phone*)," 9:293.
27. Betz, "Ψωνή (*Phone*)," 9:296.

The ψωνή (*phone*—"sounds and voices") produced by the participants in musical worship in the book of Revelation are made by two groups. The first group is comprised of the Godhead or agents thereof, principally the angels. The type of sound produced by this group can be called revelatory. The second group consists of all creatures of creation who recognize the Godhead. Their primary musical and worship activity is response to their God. This group is comprised of the martyrs, the four living creatures (who represent all of creation), the twenty-four elders, and the angels of heaven (see Appendix). Notice that only the angels can serve in both categories.

Voice (as revelation—see Revelation 1:12). The voice from heaven is often anonymous.[28] The heavenly voice "seldom gives revelation or elucidation."[29] Most often this voice provides the following:

1. imperatives or commands to its hearers (see Revelation 1:11; 10:4, 8; 14:13);
2. instructions to the angels as to the next action which they need to undertake in the "heavenly drama" (Revelation 9:13; 16:1); or
3. the final assertion to the completion of the eschatological act (Revelation 11:15; 12:10; 16:17; 21:3).[30]

Voice (ψωνή [*phone*]) *of a sound of many waters* (as revelation—see Revelation 1:15 and 14:2; as response—see Revelation 19:6). In Revelation 1:15, this sound is reminiscent of the sound of God's voice in Ezekiel 43:2.[31] The voice portrays the radiant glory of God.

Great loud voice of an angel (as revelation—see Revelation 5:2; 7:2; 10:3; 14:7; 14:9; 14:15; 14:18; and 19:17). This sound is made by a strong angel. Perhaps this angel was one among the celestial order of angels. Ford conjectures that this angel might be Gabriel whose name means "God is my strength."[32] This sound conveys the paramount importance of the message of God.[33] The authority to wield such a weighty message could only be given by the Godhead.[34]

Great loud voices of angels, four living creatures and twenty-four elders (as response—see Revelation 5:11). These corporate voices create a

---

28. Betz, "Ψωνή (*Phone*)," 9:282.
29. Betz, "Ψωνή (*Phone*)," 9:296.
30. Betz, "Ψωνή (*Phone*)," 9:296.
31. *IB* 12:376.
32. Ford, *Anchor Bible*, 85.
33. Kiddle, *Revelation*, 96.
34. Ford, *Anchor Bible*, 117.

"blending of divine, human, and angelic sounds in response to the crowning glory of the Godhead."[35]

Voice in the midst (as revelation—see Revelation 6:6). Swete asserts that "from the midst of the [ζῶα] zoa" comes "what sounds like a voice, the protest of Nature against the horrors of famine."[36]

Great loud voice of martyrs (as response—see Revelation 6:10). The cry of the martyrs is for God to avenge their blood. They petition God to perform just judgment. It is also a cry of haste. It is imploring the speedy coming of eschatological fulfillment. This type of cry of the righteous sufferers has frequently been sent up to heaven throughout time.[37] Every generation of martyrs since the first century has "called aloud for judgement [sic] on the pagan world" for their sacrificed lives.[38]

Great loud voice of all creation (as response—see Revelation 7:10). Gelineau suggests that

> when the book of Revelation describes the many groups which sing Amen, Alleluia, Holy (presumably the *Sanctus* found in Isaiah 6), and the other hymns to God and the Lamb, the author is using his own experience as a model for the practice of heaven. The canticles in the opening chapters of Luke, and those passages of Paul which are definitely hymns, witness to the creativity of the early Christian communities. It is quite by chance that we learn that Paul and Silas, when in prison at Philippi, spent the night hours "praying and singing hymns to God" (see Acts 16:25).[39]

Swete describes their response as "the polyglott [sic] [multi-lingualed] multitude shout[ing] its praises as with one voice."[40] To cry in this way is equal to giving an Emperor, such as Caesar Domitian, one's loyalty.[41]

Great loud voice out of heaven (as revelation—see Revelation 9:13; 10:4; 10:7; 10:8; 11:2; 11:15; 12:10; 14:13; and 18:4). This voice is a single, set apart voice which seems to proceed from the horns of the golden altar mentioned in Revelation 8:3. It is perhaps the voice of an angel standing above the altar with a golden censer or the voice could represent the saints' prayers. This

---

35. Ford, *Anchor Bible*, 233.
36. *ASJ* 87.
37. Beckwith, *Apocalypse*, 526.
38. *ASJ* 90.
39. Gelineau, "Music and Singing," 498.
40. *ASJ* 101.
41. *ASJ* 101.

solitary voice declares the desire of the Church throughout all the ages.[42] It is difficult to pinpoint the author of this voice out of heaven. In Revelation 11:15, this same great loud voice in heaven may belong to the ζῶα (zoa) who represents all of creation. Revelation 12:10 does not attribute the great loud voice to either the angels or the ζῶα (zoa). Swete believes it to be the voice of one of the elders. But in Revelation 18:4, the great loud voice is either the voice of God himself or the voice of one of the angels representing him.[43]

Great loud voice as a lion roars (as revelation—see Revelation 10:3). The lion is a recurring symbol in the Graeco-Roman world. It represented a sun deity who ruled the world, put an end to evil, and placed the dead into the security of the next world. For the Jewish mind, the lion represented Yahweh's power and the power of the Torah.[44] Consequently, the type of sound produced was one which was very authoritative and powerful.

Great loud voice out of the shrine (as revelation—see Revelation 16:1). This voice also illustrates the strength of God's voice. Yet, a parallel reference, in Deuteronomy 28, speaks of a "mystical voice coming out of the high heavens."[45]

Great loud voice from the throne (as revelation—see Revelation 16:17; 19:5; and 21:3). When the classical prophets received the Word of God, they ordinarily did not mention that the specific voice of God spoke to them. This was due to the fact that the prophets perceived themselves to be God's voice.[46]

Great loud voice of a crowd in heaven (as response—see Revelation 19:1). Swete believes that these shouts of triumph are from a crowd in heaven. He believes that the crowd consisted of an angelic host (*ochlos polus*).[47] Contrarily, Beckwith calls this an "anticipative chorus" with all of the heavenly hosts doxologically praising their God because he has visited justice to the beast and the "slayer of the saints."[48] This antiphonal response is expressed by the four living creatures, the twenty-four elders and "all the orders of heavenly beings ranged before and round about the Almighty." Both the "higher and lower orders" of creation sing antiphonally.[49]

---

42. *ASJ* 120.
43. *ASJ* 141, 154, 228.
44. Ford, *Anchor Bible*, 88.
45. Ford, *Anchor Bible*, 260.
46. Betz, "Ψωνή (Phone)," 9:283.
47. *ASJ* 242.
48. Beckwith, *Apocalypse*, 720–21.
49. Beckwith, *Apocalypse*, 720–21.

Summary

The Godhead, as Creator, relates in a discernably audible manner to Creation via a lowly, human mechanism called φωνή (*phone*). Vocal φωνή (*phone*) can only be produced by air passing through a throat. Characteristic of revelatory vocal φωνή (*phone*) is the empowered strength and clarity of its tone. While prophets in the Old Testament were able to "speak" for Yahweh, only angels will be able to be sanctioned to carry the Godhead's message in eschatological time.

Responsorial vocal φωνή (*phone*) can be expressed by groups as small as a quartet on the one hand and by legions upon legions of all types of creatures on the other. Yet, the type of φωνή (*phone*) that they collectively declare is heard as a single voice. Even multi-lingual responses sounded simultaneously will be discerned as a single, unified voice.

NON-VOCAL (INCLUDING INSTRUMENTAL)

In the Book of Revelation

The types of non-vocal φωνή (*phone*) produced in the Revelation can be categorized into two groups. One group consists of the sounds of nature and the other group are sounds produced by musical instruments. The musical instruments utilized in the Apocalypse in worship are the harp and the trumpet.

Great loud voice as a trumpet (as revelation—see Revelation 1:10–11). This great loud voice rings out as "clear and incisive as a trumpet note." The sound thus produced is "clear, thrilling and ominous."[50] At Sinai, God broke the silence with the voice like a trumpet, and it was excruciatingly loud. At the morning rite, the great door of the Jewish temple was opened by the signal of a trumpet. The year of Jubilee was ushered in by the call of a silver trumpet. Similarly, the trumpet blast in Revelation will herald the "Apocalypse of our Savior."[51]

Voice as of a trumpet (as revelation—see Revelation 4:1). Interestingly, the seer first hears the voice, as a far-off voice, and then sees the one speaking.[52] This sound is like that which is mentioned in 1 Corinthians 14:8, 1

---

50. Kiddle, *Revelation*, 11, 80.
51. Seiss, *Apocalypse*, 2:70.
52. *IB* 12:54.

Thessalonians 4:16, and Hebrews 12:19. It is a Sinai motif taken from Exodus 19:16–19 and 20:18.[53]

Out of the throne came forth lightnings and voices and thunders (as revelation—see Revelation 4:5). Similar phenomenon accompanies other theophanies (see Exodus 19:16; Ezekiel 1:13; Apocalypse of Abraham 17; and 1 Enoch 14:11, 17) as in this passage. The sound emanates from the throne and displays the "awesome majesty of God."[54] A loud voice or other great noise often occurs with Christophanies as well.[55]

In Revelation 4:5, the Greek word ψωνή (*phone*) is used to represent a type of sound in nature called βροντή (*bronte*). In this context it means "thunder." In the plural it could mean "peals of thunder."[56] In this passage it means "sounds" or "rumblings."[57]

In Psalm 29, thunder is not merely a natural phenomenon. Rather, it serves as the "rumbling, majestic voice of God."[58] According to Betz, in Apocalyptic literature, the "sound, size, and color" of claps of thunder are typically exaggerated. Psalm 29 describes the voice of God as does the theophany of thunder at Sinai (see Exodus 20:18; Hebrews 12:18).[59] The display of lightnings, voices, and thunders from the throne illustrate the Creator's power to "destroy the creation which denied his laws."[60]

These sounds indicate that the throne is a throne of judgment and that God's wrath will proceed from it. Similar to Yahweh preparing to visit Egypt's sins on her, he "sent thunder (voices), and hail, and fire ran along upon the ground" (see Exodus 19:16 RSV).[61] When Yahweh's wrath was kindled against the Philistines, he "thundered with a great thunder on that day. . ., and discomfited them, and they were smitten before Israel" (1 Sam 7:10 RSV).[62]

In John 12:28–29, when a voice from heaven spoke to Jesus, some in the crowd thought that it had either thundered or an angel had spoken to Jesus.[63]

---

53. *IB* 12:70.
54. *IB* 12:403
55. *IB* 12:374.
56. Earle, *Word Meanings*, 460.
57. Earle, *Word Meanings*, 460.
58. Betz, "Ψωνή (*Phone*)," 9:283.
59. Ford, *Anchor Bible*, 97.
60. Kiddle, *Revelation*, 85.
61. Seiss, *Apocalypse*, 1:245.
62. Seiss, *Apocalypse*, 1:245.
63. Ford, *Anchor Bible*, 159.

Sound as of harpers (as response—see Revelation 5:8; 15:2). Just as incense is associated with the office of the priest, similarly the harp is associated with the prophets. In 1 Samuel 10:5 (RSV), Samuel relayed to Saul that "thou shalt meet a company of prophets coming down from the high place, with a psaltery and a tabret, and a pipe, and a harp before them, and they shall prophesy." Similarly, the six sons of Jeduthun prophesied with a harp (see 1 Chronicles 25:3). In Psalm 49:4 (RSV), David says "I will open my dark sayings upon the harp."[64] In Revelation 5, the prophetic harps and prayers of incense are held and performed by the worshipers of the Lamb. They remind the Lamb of all the prayers, songs, and prophesies which have come before. When the Lamb takes up the Book of Life, he seals the pledge of the Godhead to save them and consequently assures the Redeemed of their long-awaited reward.[65] The type of sound produced by the κιθάρα (*kithara*) are accompanimental.

Great loud voice of an eagle (as revelation—see Revelation 8:13). This proclamation of a highly dramatic nature is rendered by a bird of bad omen. This is verifiable in both the Scriptures and cultural superstitions.[66] The type of sound produced by the bird captures the attention of all who hear it.

Sound of thunders (βροντής [*brontes*]) (as revelation—see Revelation 14:2; as response—see Revelation 19:6). The sounds of Revelation 14:2 are not made by the 144,000, but by a heavenly crowd.

In contrast to the angelic host of Revelation 19:1, the voice in Revelation 19:6 is the voice of the "Universal Church" (see Revelation 7:9).[67] These "sound[s] of the collective praise of the Church" in the writer's ears are like "the din of a vast concourse, the roar of a cataract [waterfall or flood]" (see Revelation 1:15; 14:2), or the roll of thunder (see Revelation 6:1; 10:3).[68] The words are discernable. This hallelujah, the fourth one sung in chapter 19, is thanksgiving to God because he has set up his kingdom.[69]

Summary

Revelatory sounds in the book of Revelation are made by the trumpet and nature. The types of sounds which the trumpet and nature make are majestic, articulate, authoritative, and powerful. In contrast to these decidedly

---

64. Seiss, *Apocalypse*, 1:290.
65. Seiss, *Apocalypse*, 1:290.
66. Kiddle, *Revelation*, 153.
67. *ASJ* 177.
68. *ASJ* 177.
69. *ASJ* 177.

punctuated sounds are the non-vocal sounds produced by those who respond. These accompanimental, non-vocal sounds blend well and are harmonious with the vocal sounds made by the worshipers.

PERFORMANCE PRACTICE—MANNER SOUND IS PRODUCED

This section will analyze how the vocal and non-vocal sounds are produced.

Vocal

Ψωνή (*Phone*) can be performed by the human voice in a variety of ways. It can be

1. "uttered" (Amos 1:2; Prov 2:3; 8:1);
2. "called aloud" (Jer 4:16; 12:8; 22:20);
3. "lilied up" (Jubal 9:7);
4. "lilied up in joy and rejoicing" (Isa 24:14);
5. "Raised" (Gen 39:15, 18; Isa 13:2); and
6. a "great loud" voice (Gen 39:14; 1 Sam 28:12; 2 Sam 15:23; 19:5; 1 Kgs 8:55; 18:27; 2 Kgs 18:28; Isa 36:13; Ezek 8:18; 11:13; Prov 27:14; Ezra 3:12; 10:12; Neh 9:4; 2 Chr 32:18).[70]

When ψωνή (*phone*) is used in the above ways it helps the reader to identify the speaker. It signifies the manner of dealings between the Godhead and creation. In Psalm 19:2, the ψωνή (*phone*) declares the glory of God. But Isaiah 6:3 indicates that humankind cannot hear the cries of the seraphim as they never cease to praise God. Yet, the ψωνή (*phone*) of the seraphim are "so loud that they cause the lintels of the temple to shake."[71]

The strength of the ψωνή (*phone*) of angels is similar to Yahweh's use of angels in the Old Testament:

1. the roaring of a lion (Rev 10:3; Amos 1:2; Hos 11:10); and
2. the noise of many waters (Rev 1:15; 14:2; 19:6; Ezek 1:24; 43:2).[72]

---

70. Betz, "Ψωνή (*Phone*)," 9:281.
71. Betz, "Ψωνή (*Phone*)," 9:282.
72. Betz, "Ψωνή (*Phone*)," 9:294.

The voice of heaven can be regarded as "angelic speech" by some and as a "clap of thunder" by others.[73] Singing, as the response of humankind, has a unique role in the Christian liturgy because it combines pure music with the Word which has been revealed. The revealed Word is the worshiper's "confession of faith in Christ" that "all music can indeed be religious or sacred, but only that music is specifically Christian which articulates the Christian faith."[74]

Wainwright reports that B. Fischer believes that the early church did not sing the psalms. Rather, they read them as though they were only scriptural lessons. This conclusion is disputed by J. D. Crichton in *Christian Celebration: The Prayer of the Church*.[75] Crichton points out that the Hebrew and Greek languages do not have separate words in their respective vocabularies for "music," per se. The distinction between singing and speaking was far less wide in the ancient world than it is today in the present century. From the earliest times, when speech turned into poetry in a public setting, rhythm and melody were naturally incorporated.[76] Gelineau illustrates the continuum which exists in vocal ψωνή (*phone*) from speech to chant to song:

The continuum from word to music is as follows:

1. ordinary speech;
2. proclamation (cantillation);
3. meditation (psalmody);
4. chant;
5. hymn (lied);
6. acclamation (develops from the human cry);
7. vocalise or jubilus (including the use of melodic instruments).[77]

As previously discussed, both views are correct according to recent scholarship. In the synagogue, psalms were not sung but only taught and read. In early church worship—following the example of the worship in the temple—psalms were sung.

Two characteristics of singing in the early church were that one must be filled with the Holy Spirit, and the singing must be the expression of

---

73. Betz, "Ψωνή (*Phone*)," 9:294.
74. Gelineau, "Music and Singing," 443; Crichton, *Christian Celebration*, 59–61.
75. *DOX* 211.
76. Gelineau, "Music and Singing," 444.
77. Gelineau, "Music and Singing," 450–54.

a conscious faith.[78] All musical action in a liturgical context consists of a "significant" human act, a symbolic and ritual context, and a given musical form.

The main characteristic of singing in Christian worship is "to act as a support for the words."[79] That is, the music, as a means, should serve the text (the end). The term that defines this role of music is logogenic as opposed to pathogenic.[80] The actual performance should look for real human and religious dimensions which provide "significance to the musical activity" in question.[81]

In the Book of Revelation

Say (λέγω [*lego*]) (as revelation—see Revelation 1:11, 17; 4:1; 6:6; 7:2; 9:14; 10:4, 8; 11:12, 15; 12:10; 14:7, 8, 9, 13, 18; 16:1, 5, 17; 18:4; 19:5, 17; 21:3; as response—see Revelation 4:8, 10; 5:5, 9, 11, 13, 14; 6:1, 3, 5, 7, 10; 7:10, 12; 11:16; 15:3; 19:1, 4, 6).

λέγω (*Lego*) can be translated in a variety of ways:

1. "I say or speak";
2. "I speak of";
3. "I mean";
4. "I tell"; and
5. "I command."[82]

In Revelation 2:1 and 8, λέγω (*lego*) is also used as a "formal and solemn phrase to introduce the edicts of emperors and magistrates" (see also Matthew 5:34, 39; and Romans 2:22).[83] When λέγω (*lego*) is used as revelation via the voice of the Godhead or an agent thereof, it is used in the imperative and implies a command. This use can be seen in Revelation 10:8 when the voice commands the seer to take the scroll from the angel.[84] In Revelation 11:15, a loud voice proclaims that which was previously hidden

---

78. Gelineau, "Music and Singing," 445.
79. Gelineau, "Music and Singing," 450.
80. Pathogenic music describes the situation that exists in melismatic music in which the text is delivered in a highly florid, emotional manner.
81. Gelineau, "Music and Singing," 450.
82. Moulton and Milligan, "λέγω," 372.
83. Moulton and Milligan, "λέγω," 372.
84. Kiddle, *Revelation*, 173.

in the silence after the opening of the last seal. And in Revelation 12:10, the voice is sounded in a proleptic (anticipated) manner.[85]

The doxological praise of the twenty-four elders in Revelation 4:10–11 is different from the praise ascribed to the Godhead by the four living creatures. The twenty-four elders address God, and the praise is based on God's work in creation. The ζῶα (zoa) praise God for his divine attributes. Later in Revelation 5, the twenty-four elders will praise the Lamb for his work in redemption.[86]

Sing (αδω [ado]) (as response—see Revelation 5:9; 14:3; and 15:3). The Greek word αδω (ado) literally means "to sing" or "to celebrate" something.[87] In the period of the early church, αδω (ado) could dually represent both the spoken word and song. The era did not differentiate between the two: the distinction between them was "fluid."[88]

In Revelation 5:9, 14:3, and 15:3 appears the phrase αδειν οδαν (adein odan—"to sing songs"). This same language appears in Colossians 3:16 and Ephesians 5:19. Both Ephesians 5:19 and Revelation 5:13 include the word λαλειν (lalein—"to say"). Revelation 5:9 reads αδουσιν οδαν καιναν λεγοντες (adousin odan kainan legontes—"they sing song a new saying"). This verse contains both the verbs "sing" and "say." However, λέγω (lego) appears most frequently without αδω (ado) throughout the remainder of the book of Revelation. Because the construction of the formula of Revelation 5:9 is similar to that of the other λέγω (lego) passages in Revelation, it can be conjectured that λέγω (lego), broadly defined, can include the act of singing.[89] The practice of chant refers to the process of furnishing words and sentences with "the most phonetic inflexion."[90] Three types exist:

1. plain recitation (spoken);
2. echonesis (semi-musical recitative); and
3. cantillation (regular musical chant).[91]

Consequently, λέγω (lego) can be interpreted broadly to include "to sing."

---

85. Kiddle, *Revelation*, 207, 233.
86. Mounce, *Book of Revelation*, 139, 147.
87. Schlier, "Ἀδω (Ado)," 1:163–64.
88. Schlier, "Ἀδω (Ado)," 1:163–64.
89. Schlier, "Ἀδω (Ado)," 1:164.
90. *TSB* 104.
91. *TSB* 104.

A preference for the high voice can be found in the ecclesiastical chant which was essentially carried over from the synagogue tradition where the cantor had "an almost monopolistic influence."[92] The high voice was desired because it was "flexible and capable of the elegant delivery of melismatic lines."[93] The musicians who performed classical Greek music developed a "speech melody" (λογοδες μελός [*logodes melos*]) which consisted of a "system of tonic accent distinguished by actual variations in pitch. Among the symbols devised by Alexandrian scholars, the acute accent mark indicates an original heightening, the grave accent a lowering, and the circumflex a combined rise and fall."[94] Consequently, pitch accent may have had a part in shaping melodic lines.

Proclaim (καρυσσο [*karusso*]) (as revelation—see Revelation 5:2). The common usage of καρυσσο (*karusso*) in the period of the early church was "to announce" as in a public announcement.[95]

Cry (εκραζό [*ekrazo*]) (as revelation—see Revelation 7:2; 10:3; 14:14; 18:2; and 19:17; as response—see Revelation 7:10). In Romans 9:27, this same word was used for the crying of the prophet Isaiah. It was also used in conjunction with the "fervent prayer of the Spirit in the hearts of men" (see Galatians 4:6).[96]

Spoke (ελαλεο [*elaleo*]) or uttered (as revelation—see Revelation 10:3, 4). This sound is "a low sound, like the lowing of an ox" (see Job 6:5 and 1 Kings 6:12) or the "growl of thunder."[97] Coupled with this low or deep voice is the fact that it is extremely loud in volume. The sound probably does not convey understandable words.[98] This sound is not a cry of fear or distress but a "shout of power."[99] Its sound draws the awe-inspiring attention of its hearers. It serves in this passage as a signal. No words were uttered, although a reply was at once forthcoming.[100]

Rejoice (Χαιρόυσεο [*Chairouseo*]). . . *and are glad* (ευθραινεο [*euthraineo*]) (as response—see Revelation 11:10). The root, χαιρό (*chairo*), means "to rejoice" and is a very common opening in letters from the period

---

92. Jander, "Singing," 17:339.
93. Jander, "Singing," 17:339.
94. Anderson, *Ethos*, 3.
95. Moulton and Milligan, "καρυσσο," 343.
96. Ford, *Anchor Bible*, 99.
97. Ford, *Anchor Bible*, 158–59.
98. Ford, *Anchor Bible*, 158–59.
99. Seiss, *Apocalypse*, 2:129.
100. *ASJ* 127.

of the early church (see Acts 15:23; 23:26; James 1:1).[101] It is used as a "mutual greeting" as in the following example: "Greeting (χαιρό [*chairo*]), my Lord Apion."[102]

Responsory (as response—see Revelation 5:9–14; 11:15–18; 16:4–7; 19:5–8). The simple idea of expressing a common thought through repetition by a large group of people occurred from the earliest times in the Jewish culture as well as other ancient groups, primarily the Orientals. The Babylonian-Assyrian liturgy contained formulas of acclamation which were likely sung and were used as an introduction to various ceremonies. The oft-repeated refrains in Assyrian hymns were likely sung responsorially by a priest as the precentor and answered by a choir.[103]

Responsorial and antiphonal singing met the sociological needs for groups of people to bond.

> This trend. . . is manifest wherever religiously bent people are grouped together in a common social environment. If religion is to be considered one of the strongest cementing powers of collective life and communal consciousness, singing in joint religious manifestations must be adjudged the same binding force.[104]

The role of music in Egyptian religious cultic practice was of the highest significance. Soloists intoned hymns to which choirs answered responsorially.[105] Babylonian hymns and psalms were sung responsorially by priests and congregations. They heavily influenced the Jewish psalm writers. When the Jews were deported from Babylon by King Nebuchadnezzar (see Nehemiah 7:67), they continued the Babylonian practice of responsorial singing as well as the singing of psalms and lamentations.[106]

As much as it appears that pagan influences weighed heavily on the formulation of a Jewish musical tradition, it should not be over-emphasized. The religious institutions of the other ancient peoples were markedly very dissimilar to the patriarchal religion of the chosen people of Yahweh.[107]

In the realm of Jewish music, responsorial psalmody can be defined as "the chanting of a psalm by alternation between a soloist (cantor), who sings a verse or verses, and a chorus (congregation or choir), who sing a refrain

---

101. Moulton and Milligan, "χαιρό," 682.
102. Moulton and Milligan, "χαιρό," 682.
103. *MSR* 166–67.
104. Lietner, *Der gottesdienstliche*, 38.
105. *MSR* 41.
106. *MSR* 53.
107. *MSR* 138.

("respond").[108] It was both a style of performance and a formal structure. An example of responsorial music occurred at the Exodus. Following the Israelites crossing of the Red Sea, the responsive singing of the Jewish women and the Song of Moses praised Yahweh for his mighty salvatory deliverance. This act of responsorial singing was heavily influenced by the Egyptian culture.[109]

The psalmody referred to in the Talmud was responsorial in character as opposed to antiphonal. Present-day scholarship has recently established that the psalms were originally composed for a cultic purpose—"the response of a group to a leader in prayer is a fundamental and universal manner of worship."[110]

Early Christian writers, like Tertullian and Egeria, mention the use of responsorial music in their respective worship practices. From their comments, it can be conjectured that perhaps "a natural continuity of responsorial psalmody" originated from Jewish tradition.[111] Logically, in time it likely passed through the first-century early church to later Christian liturgical use.[112]

Antiphony (as response—see Revelation 4:8–11; 5:9–14; 7:9–17; 19:1–4). Antiphonal singing was the dominating musical force at Egyptian festivals. It was performed by choral groups which consisted of dancing men and women. Frequently, young men marched in procession and sang songs until, "possessed by the spirit," they began to prophesy in honor of their bull-shaped god Apis.[113] Sacred music was performed by a special guild of temple singers and musicians. The tradition was passed orally and was revered because of its "effect upon the human soul."[114] The Assyrians performed hymns antiphonally and illustrate well the fact that both antiphonal music and responsorial music were used long before it was recorded in the Old Testament Jewish culture.[115]

Although no precise reference alludes to antiphony in the Old Testament, antiphonal psalmody is implied in Exodus 15:21, Numbers 10:35 and 21:17,[116] 1 Samuel 18:7, Ezra 3:10–11, and Nehemiah 12:31–42. Antiphonal psalmody consists of the "chanting of a psalm by two choirs or

---

108. Connolly, "Responsorial Psalmody," 15:759.
109. *MSR* 87.
110. Connolly, "Responsorial Psalmody," 15:759.
111. Connolly, "Responsorial Psalmody," 15:759.
112. Connolly, "Responsorial Psalmody," 15:759.
113. *MAI* 40.
114. *MAI* 40.
115. *MAI* 46.
116. Martin, *Worship in the Early Church*, 40.

half-choirs in alternation, commonly with an added refrain-like text called an antiphon."[117]

Antiphonal singing was part of the original official liturgy in the temple and became an oft-used form in sacred musical performances. Antiphonal singing was also mentioned in connection with funeral observances (see 2 Samuel 1:19, 25, 27; 2 Chronicles 35:25).[118] Antiphonal singing was the Jewish tradition's greatest early contribution to the development of music.

Summary

The use of λέγω (lego) in the Apocalypse contains the spectrum of vocal sound production, from declamatory speech to sung song. Λέγω (Lego—"to say"), χαρυσσο (karusso—"to proclaim"), εκαζό (ekrazo—"to cry"), and ελαλεό (elaleo—"to speak or utter") are manners in which revelatory vocal ψωνή (phone) are produced in the book of Revelation.

Eschatological fulfillment, as witnessed in the book of Revelation, indicates that responsive creation replies to the acts of the Godhead via a more mannered speech, i.e., song. The singing in the time of the early church could be expressed by αδω (ado—"to sing") as well as λέγω (lego—"to say"). In contrasting balance to the declamatory ψωνή (phone) of the Godhead, the praise of creation will be responsorial and antiphonal singing given in a spirit of glad χαιρουσεο (chairouseo—"rejoicing").

Non-vocal (including instrumental)

Instruments have been kept out of the church throughout the ages largely on socio-historical grounds. But Gelineau proposes that "a balanced attitude to instrumental music sees the instrument as an extension of the human voice and body."[119] When people accompany their singing or perform pure instrumental music, it widens their capacity for song.[120] An analysis of non-vocal music in the book of Revelation follows.

Having harps (presumably to play them) (as response—see Revelation 5:8; 15:2). In Revelation 5:8, the harps, which the twenty-four elders play, serve as a pacifying accompanimental force which blends harmoniously

---

117. Connolly, "Antiphonal Psalmody," 1:481.
118. *MAI* 168.
119. Gelineau, "Music and Singing," 444.
120. Gelineau, "Music and Singing," 444.

with their song. The harps are "held" to the players' breast by the left hand. The strings are strummed by the right hand.

When the martyrs acquire harps in Revelation 15:2, it can be conjectured that the harps are played in a similar manner. The martyrs' harps, however, could be played in a different manner because they are called God's harps and accompany the song which "no one else can learn." Kiddle suggests that "the celestial harmony is now complete, [with] the diapason closing full on [Redeemed] man."[121]

. . . *In order that they might trumpet* (σάλπιζο—*salpizo*) (as revelation—see Revelation 8:1, 6). No two of the trumpets are alike and "there is a gradual rising" from the first until the last.

> One touches the ground, the trees, and the green grass. Another touches the sea, the ships, and the creatures of the sea. A third touches the rivers and the springs of water. A fourth touches the sun, moon, and stars. A fifth breaks open the door of separation between earth and hell. A sixth unlooses the dreadful army of horses and horsemen, the seven thunders, and the mighty struggle and murder of the two witnesses. And the last brings on "the battle of the great day of God Almighty."[122]

This description illustrates a great deal of order and forethought. When the Scripture says, "They prepared themselves that they might trumpet," it is not referring to mere technical performance practice. It is referring to the "deliberate adjustment among themselves [the angels] of the place and subject which each one was to take in the work" of the end-times.[123] The sounds made in succession are not "haphazard" sounds. Ετοιμαζο (*Etoimazo*—"readymaking") is used to imply the "pre-determinations" of actions which follow the necessary rehearsals before the action is to take place.[124]

The voice of the trumpet is the most significant voice mentioned in the Scriptures. In early Old Testament times, it was described as a strong and loud cry which was sounded only for special events. In Revelation 8, the number of trumpets is seven: a complete and perfect ensemble. These trumpets are not mere copies of those that came before throughout history. The trumpets in the book of Revelation are the prototypes. The Old Testament trumpets are copies of the heavenly trumpets that the seer witnessed in his vision.[125]

121. Kiddle, *Revelation*, 266.
122. Seiss, *Apocalypse*, 2:40.
123. Seiss, *Apocalypse*, 2:40.
124. Seiss, *Apocalypse*, 2:42.
125. Seiss, *Apocalypse*, 2:22–25.

Trumpeted (as revelation—see Revelation 8:2, 7, 8, 10, 12; 9:1, 13; 11:15). In Revelation 8:2, 6, 7, 8, 10, 12, and 13, 9:1 and 14, 10:7, and 11:15, the trumpet stands "by itself, separate and complete."[126] It is used in Scripture because of its "loud, piercing, and far-reaching sound." The purpose of the trumpet blast is "to demand the attention of all men [sic] in view of a matter of urgent importance."[127]

In Revelation 8:7 appears the word "sounded" (Greek verb is σάλπιζο [salpizo]) which comes from the noun σάλπινχ (salpinx), which means "trumpet." In this passage, sounded means "to sound a trumpet."[128]

According to the account of Plutarch, "certain Egyptian delta towns" disliked the sound of the trumpet because it sounded like an "ass's bray."[129] Baines conjectures that the sound consisted of "a series of powerful blasts on a pitch roughly corresponding to the lower sound" of a trumpet.[130]

The angels which perform the trumpet calls are seven in number. Ford supposes them to include the following:

1. Uriel—the "fire of God";
2. Raphael—"God has healed";
3. Raguel—the "friend of God";
4. Michael—"Who is like God";
5. Sariel—the "prince of God";
6. Gabriel—"God is my strength"; and
7. Remiel—the "thunder of God" or the "height of God."[131]

Being about to trumpet (as revelation—see Revelation 8:13; 10:7). The trumpet was primarily used to sound an alarm, but in later centuries, in Christian liturgical use the trumpet came to be a priestly instrument. In the book of Revelation, it serves primarily as a heralding instrument.[132] In this passage, the trumpet introduces the "acts of God," which are "cosmic disturbances uncontrollable by man. . ."[133]

---

126. *IB* 266.
127. *IB* 266.
128. Earle, *Word Meanings*, 460.
129. *BI* 56.
130. *BI* 56.
131. Ford, *Anchor Bible*, 130.
132. Ford, *Anchor Bible*, 132.
133. Ford, *Anchor Bible*, 146.

Summary

The sounds of both the harp and the trumpet are likely produced according to commonly accepted earthly practice. The harp is strummed, and the trumpet is played with pursed lips by blowing air through a narrow shaft. Due to the nature, however, of the song that "no one can learn," it is possible that the martyrs' accompanimental harps are played in a completely unknown way. Because the present age has no clue as to the physical nature of their "heavenly bodies," it is impossible to conjecture as to the manner in which the martyrs' harps might be played.

Seiss makes a point of stressing the "readiness" with which the angels prepare to trumpet. Eschatological fulfillment requires a meticulously worked out plan. So, too, does the music that accompanies it.

POSTURES OF PERFORMANCE

An important element in the production of the types of sounds recorded in the book of Revelation is the physical posture from which they are made. Unfortunately, little research has been done in this area.

In the Book of Revelation

Sitting (as response—see Revelation 4:4; 11:16). The twenty-four elders are angelic kings, "a rank in the heavenly hierarchy."[134] They are kings owing to the fact that they are wearing robes and crowns and they are sitting on thrones about the throne of God.[135]

Before [facing] *the throne* (and round the throne) (as response—see Revelation 4:6; 5:11; 14:3). "In the midst" of the throne connotes an orchestral circular area which is reminiscent of a Greek amphitheater.[136] In the Greek theater, the speaking place of the gods was situated on the perimeter of the stage, whereas in the book of Revelation, it dominates the center of the stage. Surrounding it are stone seats which serve as small thrones. They were carved out of stone and reserved for important personalities.[137] In the book of Revelation these seats are occupied by the twenty-four elders. Throughout the drama of heavenly worship, the twenty-four elders assume standing, sitting, and kneeling positions.

134. Beckwith, *Apocalypse*, 498.
135. Beckwith, *Apocalypse*, 498.
136. Ford, *Anchor Bible*, 70.
137. Ford, *Anchor Bible*, 70.

The martyrs or redeemed mentioned in Revelation 7 are seen facing the throne. While they are not "joined to the throne," they are in its presence. Consequently, they occupy a place near the throne,[138] perhaps even nearer than the angels.[139]

Fall before (as response—see Revelation 4:10; 5:8, 14; 11:16; 19:4). The twenty-four elders prostrate themselves before the throne, cast their crowns before the throne, and praise the Godhead.[140] Owing to the fact that the elders are holding harps, it is highly unlikely that when they "fell down" to worship they prostrated to their bellies. Rather, it is perhaps more likely that they went to their knees and bowed. This would provide them with the freedom to accompany themselves on the harp.

Standing (as response—see Revelation 5:6). A literal translation of the text indicates that the angels stood in a circle around the throne. No mention is made of a standing posture of the four living creatures, the twenty-four elders, nor the martyrs.

Summary

Very little material concerns itself with the physical posturing of the responsorial groups around the throne in the book of Revelation. While it is typical to sit or stand erect in order to play the trumpet and to sing, little instruction is provided in the text of Revelation regarding this. The most notable inference regards the playing of the harp. In Revelation 5:8, while holding harps, the twenty-four elders "fall down" and worship before the Lamb. They clearly cannot prostrate themselves on the ground and accompany their singing with the harp. It is more likely that they bowed on their knees.

---

138. Seiss, *Apocalypse*, 1:448.
139. Seiss, *Apocalypse*, 1:448.
140. Mounce, *Book of Revelation*, 139.

6

A Theology of Music for Worship

THIS CHAPTER SETS FORTH a theology of music for worship derived from the book of Revelation. In order to accomplish this task, this chapter will synthesize the purely musical elements found in worship in the book of Revelation and provide a manner in which to deal with the music from both a theological and worship context.

BACKGROUND—THEOLOGY BECOMES RITUAL

The six dimensions of the religious experience advanced by Ninian Smart are as follows:

1. ritual;
2. mythological;
3. doctrinal or theological;
4. ethical;
5. social; and
6. experiential.[1]

In the development of religions, what was done via ritual probably occurred before it was determined what was said (myth). But ritual and myth are linked because it can be supposed that "the myth is already implicit in

---

1. Smart, *Religious Experience*, 7–12.

the ritual."[2] Wainwright agrees and adds that worship in a Christian context is

> the point of concentration at which the whole of the Christian life comes to ritual focus... Into the liturgy (of the ritual) the people bring their entire existence so that it may be gathered up in praise.[3]

Wainwright includes in his definition of worship both Smart's ritual and myth.[4] Theology typically is developed following ritual and myth in order to describe those activities.

Theology is the discipline which "investigates and systematizes knowledge concerning the phenomenon of God."[5] Systematic theology seeks an orderly progression of this knowledge and thereby approaches a scientific study. However, in a true sense "theology can never be a science because it does not recognize the supreme law of science, namely reason as the final arbiter."[6]

Theology relies ultimately on faith. Zerbe agrees with Brunner's assessment and purports that theology, whether systematic, polemical, or other, "is neither historical, biblical, polemical and dialectic."[7] Unfortunately, in order for polemical theology to refute reason, it must employ reason to do it.[8] Theology spreads the vision of the Christian community by articulating its message, and the vision of theology experiences a singular consummating objective in worship.[9]

As this study was begun, this writer had concluded that the type of theology of music that would result would be entirely systematically reasoned. But, as the study progressed, he has found it to be systematic also in a "practical" sense. This study has identified the music for worship in the book of Revelation and analyzed it according to: (1) the forms of music; (2) the performing groups; (3) the types of sounds the performers make; and (4) how they make those sounds. This analysis is essentially practical but does not imply a "pragmatic" study as defined by Smart. Smart refers to pragmatic theology as theology or ritual aimed at "the attainment of certain

---

2. MacQuarrie, *God-Talk*, 19.
3. *DOX* 8
4. *DOX* 9
5. *ATM* v.
6. Zerbe, *Karl Barth*, 244.
7. Zerbe, *Karl Barth*, 244.
8. Zerbe, *Karl Barth*, 244.
9. *DOX* 9.

experiences" via human response.[10] This is in contradistinction to "sacred ritual," which he describes as being "directed toward a holy being, such as God."[11] The practical theology that follows can be aligned with the doing of sacred ritual. It is directed solely toward the Godhead. Also, while this "theology" is derived from the book of Revelation, this "theology" is rooted in and relies on the entire biblical record—Genesis to Revelation. Christian theology must be placed in its full historical continuum.

All the great religions developed through theophanies. In Judaism, Moses witnessed the presence of God at Mt. Sinai. Elijah was able to challenge the priests of Baal at Mount Carmel when he called down Yahweh's fire from heaven. Even in Jesus's day, his followers witnessed many of his signs and miracles. But in the following current age, it seems that a "non-religious secularized environment" has taken hold wherein the supernatural has been limited to indwelling finite believers.[12] In the future eschatological time of final judgment, which the book of Revelation deals with, supernatural manifestations again reappear.

Zerbe asserts that both Barth and Brunner believe that religious education cannot begin with what people do in practicing their faith. Rather, religious education must be approached from the perspective of what the Godhead has done, is doing, or will do;[13] or, perhaps, it must be approached through what the Godhead allows humankind to do in religion. In the book of Revelation, the visions that the writer unveils to the reader are glimpses of what the Godhead allows all of creation, including humankind, to do in terms of eschatological worship. The place of music in worship can be summarized as follows:

> Music is in some strange and mystical way a credential of God. We come into some place where sacred songs fall upon our spirits, and a transformation begins within us. We do not argue. We seek no syllogism. But there comes a sense of God, a consciousness of his holy presence. What does this? . . . Is it the inevitable creed of music, recited in the temple of the soul? Is it the confession of faith, set in the harmony of God's own making? The theologian, without being dogmatic, will not hesitate to reply affirmatively, and to declare that the song of God is an evidence of the God of song.
>
> . . . Music can have no higher function than this—of taking its large and persuasive place in the program of God's holy

10. Smart, *Religious Experience*, 7.
11. Smart, *Religious Experience*, 7.
12. MacQuarrie, *God-Talk*, 19.
13. Zerbe, *Karl Barth*, 267.

temple and of thus preparing us for that city in which the seer beholds "no sanctuary" simply because the habit of worship has so trained the heart that all the world becomes "Bethel," the house of God.[14]

While it presupposes submission to God, worship, in its highest sense, is not supplication for needs, or even thanksgiving for blessings, but "the occupation of the soul with God himself."[15]

A THEOLOGY OF MUSIC FOR WORSHIP

A summary listing of the chief characteristics of music in worship derived from the book of Revelation forms the basis of a proposed theology of music. They are:

(1) A continuum of vocal sound ranges from declamatory speech to sung word as revelation and response mechanisms.

"Liturgical music serves one purpose—to support the text."[16] Similarly, the music of the book of Revelation serves to support the eschatological worship of God. Revelation of the Godhead is generally expressed by declamatory speech in the book of Revelation, whereas the worshipers' responses appear to consist of the continuum from declamation to singing.

(2) A mandate exists for the saints to continue the *Imago Dei* process by creatively composing new songs of praise.

Through the end of the age, humankind is exhorted to fulfill the process of creation. For the use of music in worship, this means that worshipers are to continue to create new musical compositions. Although the work of Christ was completed at Calvary, the saints are to persevere to the end of time. Characteristic of the martyred saints in the book of Revelation is the utilization of their own "new" songs as they doxologically praise the Godhead. These fresh examples of song imply that the martyred saints are continuing to grow in their responses to the near-completed eschatological work of the Godhead.

(3) Instrumental accompaniments (specifically, timbres which blend with the human voice) are used to aid in the vocal response to the Godhead.

---

14. Zerbe, *Karl Barth*, 68.
15. Coleman, *Songs of Heaven*, 58.
16. ATM 11.

The book of Revelation assumes that the Godhead is most satisfied with the vocal sounds produced by the creaturely device known as "speech" (including song). But the worshipers, whether they are the saints or the twenty-four elders, are allowed to augment their utterance of praise via non-vocal means. In the Apocalypse, the distinctive timbre of the harp in worship blends harmoniously with the worshipers' collective voices. It should be noted that the instrumental support does not supplant the importance of the words of the text, nor does it contain a mixture of diverse instruments. The instrumental ensemble contains a singular type of instrument which blends with the voice. This supports the Greek idea of ethos. The careless mixing of instrumental timbres could destroy the single affection of the moment. Also, only the worshipers as responders use instrumental accompaniment, and the instruments are presumably the handiwork of their own invention.

(4) Instrumental heralding (specifically, the trumpet call) is used to announce the revelation of the Godhead.

Only the angels, as agents of the Godhead, are called upon to play the trumpet. Used in a priestly context, trumpets are symbols of the Godhead. As heralding revelatory devices, trumpets appear in an ensemble but are not used in the ensemble in a conventional manner. Rather, they are used singly in succession. The natural question arises, "Why could not a single angel blow the same trumpet seven times?" This study has shown that the angels appear most frequently as a group, perhaps to provide a well-balanced and unified social order. Just as the church is made up of many members who need to band together, so too, the angels, as agents of the Godhead, can function in a more balanced and complete manner as a group.

(5) The exhibition of emotion in the performance of the music exists owing to the use of a variety of Greek verbs such as "say," "sing," "rejoice," "cry," and a variety of sounds from nature. Examples of the sounds of nature are the sound of many waters and the sounds of thunder.

Dramatic expression is conveyed throughout the various dialogues in the book of Revelation. The Godhead expresses Godself through an assortment of voices, primarily of nature. God employs the human "cry" in only one passage. Although these voices are understood by the hearers, some of whom are human, the respective voices' characteristic timbres are basically taken from animate and inanimate nature. Contrarily, the responses of the worshipers are primarily manifest via the sound and timbre of the human voice. But even in that, the continuum of vocal human sound from declamation to sung song is evident.

Human beings exist of two components: mind and emotion within the *Imago Dei*. To separate them would detract from the balance which God intended. It is important that each exists in order to provide balance.[17] This is true not only for contemporary worshipers, but it will continue to be important for eschatological worshipers. Eschatological worshipers, as evidenced in the Apocalypse, display a dramatic excitement in their doxological praise of the Godhead.

(6) The postures for the performance of music in worship involve more than just sitting and standing.

Just as singing, speech, and sounds of this old earth seem to continue on in the seer's glimpse into the future, so apparently, our "new" physical bodies display characteristics of our "old" bodies. The worshipers appear around the throne in a variety of human postures: sitting, standing, kneeling, and falling down. These physical postures represent the worshipers' attitudes before and around the throne. Coupled with these positions is the idea of facing and coming before the throne. It seems important for the worshipers visibly to be able to see the object of their worship. Consequently, the "new" body will be able to withstand the "blinding" glory and splendor of the Godhead. So too, it appears, our new "personhood," perhaps, will be subject to the gravitational forces of the New Jerusalem.

(7) The music of worship includes the use of the sounds of nature from all creation, both animate and inanimate.

The revelation of the Godhead utilized the entire gamut of vocal and non-vocal sounds known to all of creation. Coupled with the theophanies of thunder, et al., is the anthropomorphism of the angel's, as agents for the Godhead, exclusive use of a human being's "cry." Based on evidence in the book of Revelation, only expressions of revelation by the Godhead, or its agents, can be accompanied by all animate and inanimate sounds of nature from all creation. The worshipers of the Apocalypse express themselves via the primary means of vocal production. Only instrumental accompaniment is optional for these worshipers. Instrumental solos as a response are not found in this eschatological worship.

(8) A sense of unity (κοινώνια [*koinonia*]) is perceived via the dynamics of antiphonal and responsorial response by the various groups.

---

17. Johansson, *Music and Ministry*, 64–65.

The use of a variety of choirs and ensembles in the Apocalypse portrays the responsorial creatures assembled in like-kind groupings. They respond in an orderly and balanced manner which witnesses the totally complete, uncompromising unity of all of the Godhead's creation. Worship in the Apocalypse is "genuinely congregational" and inclusively unites variegated levels of creation into a sea of doxological praise to the Godhead.[18]

The assorted musical ensembles are well-organized, well-rehearsed and, consequently, well-prepared. And the preparedness extends beyond mere musical considerations; the ensembles are wellchoreographed also.

(9) Old προσκυνέο (*proskuneo*), motivated by reverential fear of a vertical master-to-slave nature, merges with a new προσκυνέο (*proskuneo*), motivated by love of a horizontal host-toguest nature. Theology becomes doxology as the solemn act of worship.

The master/slave mentality of the relationship between Yahweh and his chosen people loses primacy. It is superseded by the host/guest relationship which Jesus displayed between himself and his followers. The deemphasis of physical prostration in the new προσκυνέο (*proskuneo*) allows for ἀγάπη (*agape*) love to be manifest as the primary motivator of the doxological praise of the Godhead. This overriding characteristic of spiritual love predominates the worship of the Godhead. It is supported by the full spectrum of humankind attributes: emotive musical expression, the social unity of musical ensembles, the mental assertion of the musically creative will, and the physical actions of human posturings in musical performance. The gamut of eschatological worship is in perfect doxological balance as the worshipers respond to the consummated actions of the Godhead in history.

(10) Music dramatically involves all the senses of humanity and all the collective resources available in all creation.

The music in worship found in the Apocalypse illustrates well the counterpoint of all the forces of creation: humankind versus the heavenly hosts versus all other living creatures; the redeemed of humankind versus the unbelievers; the new earth versus the old; and the new music versus the old music. Ritual ties "speech, gesture, rhythm and agreed ceremonial" into the activity of humankind worship.[19] It results in uniting humankind's physical, mental, and emotional components in a socially unifying response to its focus.[20] Within this entirely balanced system exists music that appeals

18. Underhill, *Worship*, 98.
19. Underhill, *Worship*, 37.
20. Underhill, *Worship*, 37.

to all the senses of all creation. To all creation this "new" music appeals to all levels of animate and inanimate consciousness: mental, emotional, physical, social, and spiritual and others which humanity cannot presently fathom.

The music for worship in the book of Revelation is a means whereby the worshipers lose themselves in the total adoration of the Godhead. To "lose themselves in worship" does not imply a loss of the worshipers' relational position to the Godhead. Rather, it implies that any of the worshipers' wrong motivations for worship are suppressed entirely. The highest form of the worshipers' spiritual love is poured out to the Godhead in doxological praise.

SYNTHESIZING A THEOLOGY OF MUSIC FOR WORSHIP

According to Adey, there are three primary types of hymns.[21] They are

1. objective, which "offers praise or beseeches mercy for all. . . [or] conveys teaching to believers."[22] Humanity is invited to shed all its worldly distinctions and concerns in favor of adoration to the Godhead. Objective hymnody consists primarily of songs of praise.

2. subjective, which contains a "core of objective assertions" and is typically sung in the first person.[23] Gospel hymnody is basically embodied in this category.

3. reflexive, which lends itself to idolatry because it "hovers on the edge of ecclesiology."[24] This type of hymnody is evidenced textually by phraseologies that speak of the actions of the worshipers. Reflexive texts that survive from long ago are those that are able to detach their message from contemporary issues.[25]

The above categorizations regarding hymns can be generally applied to worship encounters. One can experience worship in the following three ways: (1) actually "doing" worship (objective), as in doxologically praising the Godhead; (2) personalizing worship (subjective); and (3) talking about what the worshiper does in worship (reflexive).

---

21. Adey, *Hymns*, 7; Adey, *Class*. In his two books, Adey enumerates a total of fifteen types, of which the three mentioned here are primary.
22. Adey, *Hymns*, 7; Adey, *Class*.
23. Adey, *Hymns*, 7; Adey, *Class*.
24. Adey, *Hymns*, 7; Adey, *Class*.
25. Adey, *Hymns*, 7.

Θεός (*Theos*) is God; "ology" (λογος—*logos*) in "theology" connotes a reflection or a study, as in the study of a science. Thus, "theology" is the study or science of knowing God. But theology was not originally intended to be a reflexive study. Rather, just as the term mythology originally meant the actual doing or recital of myth, so too, theology was first practiced as the "solemn utterance about God himself."[26] So, it was not at first reflexive. Theology originally consisted of the act of knowing God and thus, in reverence, bowing before God.

Before theology was developed, ritual and myth were the actual recital of worship to a deity based on oral tradition. From this foundation, theology evolved to interpret and codify the actual practices. Through the ages, an aspect of theology has reflexively become the study of the recital of worship. Liturgical theology is rooted in thought. And thought is perhaps tertiary, subsequent to the primary action and secondary vocalization of it.[27] The actions of humankind's doing something has historically occurred prior to their reflection upon the same. Gerhard van der Leeuw says,

> There is no basis for doing what theology might perhaps wish to do and give words an exclusive or even a preferred position in the relationship of man to the 'other', in the religious sense... Words do not even represent the original form of human expression. For the first work was a gesture... Gesture is not only... an elucidation of the word, but is its predecessor... The words are secondary.[28]

The history of music in worship from Genesis leading up to the Apocalypse has come full circle and reverts to ritual and myth once again. And in the context of the book of Revelation, this theology of music for worship becomes a doxological worship, the highest form of sacred ritual. The music in worship in the Apocalypse is always objective. It is a proto-typical expression of actually doing worship. Consequently, a theology of music for worship set in the doxological context of the Apocalypse must in the end not be a study, as this study has been, but must become, paradoxically, the actual doing of music in worship. The glimpse into eschatological time does not tell us what our future will bring but actually shows us what it is.

The Cappodician theologians of the patristic period sought to contemporize the experiences of eschatology. In the fourth century a group of three theologians, Saint Basil, his brother Saint Gregory of Nyssa, and their friend Saint Gregory of Nazianzus, formulated Orthodox Christian doctrine and

26. Staehlin, "The Church Hymn," 26.
27. Hoon, *Integrity of Worship*, 87.
28. Leeuw, *Sacred and Profane*, 124.

were known as the Cappadocian theologians. All three were educated in secular disciplines yet are more well remembered today for their mystical Christian doctrines. St. Gregory of Nyssa inherited the mysticism of Origen, which was based on the Alexandrian Jewish-Christian traditions of Philo, Clement, and Plutinos.[29] St. Gregory of Nyssa's theology was "dynamic and progressive; it is [was] set on an endless journey."[30] For the Cappadocian theologians, theology was not a reflexive study; rather, it consisted of actually "travelling towards the infinite, towards the vision of the divine, which ancient sages and modern-day contemplators have both sought after."[31] The doing of theology consists of "the ascent or perpetual growth of the soul" and is bound up in επεκτασις (*epektasis*)—which literally means "the tension, extension, and stretching out towards the Immovable."[32]

This way of looking at theology is consistent with Old Testament theology. Old Testament theology does not consist of a reflexive study of the Israelites knowing Yahweh. Rather, Yahweh dealt with the Old Testament Jews in a linear manner, which is rooted in historical encounters. Although Israel was tied to the cyclical course of nature, she was bound up with specific historical events with Yahweh. As successive generations remembered these prior historical encounters, they represented more than mere reflection. These past dealings literally became actualized in each new generation. Only as the assembled community recited its festive rituals did Israel, as Yahweh's chosen people, come into being. Each commemoration placed the contemporary Jewish nation into the historic situation to which the festival in question was related. When Israel ate the Passover, she "was doing more than merely remembering the Exodus; she was entering into the saving event of the Exodus itself and participating in it in a quite 'actual' way. . ."[33]

Just as the contemporary Jew brings the "past" to the "present," Christians are exhorted by Christ to remember the Last Supper by taking the "present" back to the "past" (αναμνεσις—*anamnesis*). Why, then, should one not use the music of the "future" as found in the book of Revelation in the "present" age?

This concept of theology aligns with Pike's theology of music. If music is "a product of the mind in time, embodying in material form the fluctuating spiritual states of the soul," then it needs to be used as a positive means

---

29. Gregory of Nyssa, *Commentary on Song of Songs*, 7.

30. Gregory of Nyssa, *Commentary on Song of Songs*, 1–3.

31. Gregory of Nyssa, *Commentary on Song of Songs*, 3.

32. Gregory of Nyssa, *Commentary on Song of Songs*, 13. See also Hopko, *All the Fulness*

33. Von Rad, *Old Testament Theology*, 104.

to assist finite humanity in reaching his or her unattainable "perfection" in this life.[34] In its pure state, the mind seeks the unification of all the disparities of life. The mind seeks an ordered whole. Music provides the mind an ordered microcosm of life.[35]

The Godhead is both the "First Cause" and the "Final End" of the past, present and future.[36] Pike indicates that

> his [God's] plans will evolve regardless. To those who chose to willingly participate, progress will be easier. Man [sic] can use his mind to praise and contemplate God, but he can also use this same faculty for trivial and even obscene things.[37]

As an ordered microcosm of life, music has "more undeveloped potentialiary [sic] for spiritua l expression than any other art."[38] Christians have been given the attitude of prayer which assists them in contemplating the multitudinous aspects of the Godhead. The church's use of music seeks to relay these thoughts: "music is the was [sic] we should like life to be, a glimpse of that world where all strife ends."[39] In approaching that eschatological journey in this lifetime, the worshiper can transcend not only his or her finiteness but even the music itself. Pike states that music is purposeful only if it serves as a means of knowing the Godhead. The primary purpose and function of music in worship in the book of Revelation is to know God.[40]

But how then do music and worship interrelate? Music is "an expression of life" or a form of life, whereas worship is a "celebration of life" or a dramatization of life.[41] Music and worship share several characteristics. They both contain the idea of moving forward. This involves flow and movement. Music is more suggestive; it acts as a stimulant. Both possess inherent spiritual qualities. While music is an "autonomous" art, worship is primarily an end in itself.[42] The common end that both music and worship seek is the doing of worship itself. The medium of music and worship becomes worship itself. The medium of music and worship becomes the worshipers' own offering. The meaning of music is spiritual, whereas the meaning of

34. *ATM* 48.
35. *ATM* 69.
36. *ATM* 88.
37. *ATM* 88.
38. *ATM* 94.
39. *ATM* 94.
40. *ATM* 94.
41. Taken from a summary of music and worship by LeRoy Evert Wright. Wright, "Place of Music," 329–43.
42. Wright, "Place of Music," 329–43.

worship lies in "an awareness of and reverence for the Ultimate Reality in a universe which is fundamentally spiritual."[43] The ultimate purpose for both music and worship is communion between person and God. This is accomplished through the social characteristics of music and the intensely "corporate" character of worship.[44]

Following Wright's ideas, Smart says of worship that it

1. is a relational activity;

2. expresses the superiority of the Focus (the Godhead) to the worshiper via ritual;

3. "performatively sustains" or is part of the power of the Focus;

4. is an experience which is expressed by the numinous and the object of worship is then perceived to be awe-inspiring.

5. involves a Focus which is transcendent, or unseen;

6. displays the superiority of the Focus over the worshiper. This gap of power is infinite wherein the worshiper has no relative merit apart from that which the Focus ascribes; and

7. involves praise by the worshiper which is addressed directly to the Focus.[45]

This study has shown biblically that Smart's concept of worship has been met.

Although this study has shown that non-vocal, non-texted music is not used in the Apocalypse's worship as a responsive mechanism, the early church, including the patristic period, utilized a Christian theology that consisted of all types of praise and liturgy.[46] The following legend illustrates the relationship between liturgy and theology: Fra Egidio, of the order of St. Francis, was cornered one day by a "most learned theologian with an array of profound propositions." The theologian's logical arguments never seemed to cease. Brother Egidio waited to reply until he was sure his opponent was through. "Then, taking a flute from the fold of his robe, he played out his theological answer in song!"[47]

In the totality of humanity's responsive efforts to the Godhead, Wainwright shows the interrelationships between the sacred and secular life

---

43. Wright, "Place of Music," 329–43.
44. Wright, "Place of Music," 329–43.
45. Smart, *Concept of Worship*, 26, 41, 44, 51, 75.
46. Leclercq, "Theology and Prayer," 62.
47. Hoon, *Integrity of Worship*, 90–91.

experiences. He focuses on three themes: life, doctrine, and worship.[48] Wainwright is able to divide our very existence into these tight little bundles because of the great disparity which can separate them this side of eternity. The book of Revelation, however, shows how all three can and will be fused together eschatologically. We should not assume a fatalistic attitude because of our inability totally to fuse them all now. Rather, our spirits should contrarily gain energy as we seek and try to serve God doxologically in worship for the hope which shall one day be.

The corporate expression of worship, including music in worship, represents the "total orientation of life towards God," and it is expressed via "stylized liturgical action and spontaneous common praise."[49] The book of Revelation portrays an idealized form of Christian worship wherein all of the "sensible accompaniments of an ordered cultus—music, song, incense, ritual movements, and prostrations—are all there and already taken for granted."[50] The picture of eschatological worship "stretches back to the very beginnings of... worship" and consequently links the past with the future.[51] For "doxology is at the beginning (in the past and in the present) and at the end (in the future) of all striving for unity."[52]

---

48. *DOX* 217.
49. Underhill, *Worship*, 84.
50. Underhill, *Worship*, 92.
51. Underhill, *Worship*, 92.
52. *DOX* 290.

7

Implications for Today's Church Musicians and Worship Leaders

Is THE MUSIC FOR worship that the writer of the Apocalypse portrays a true glimpse into eschatological music for worship? Was the music that humanity had fashioned up to the time of the Revelation actually so similar to what the seer foresaw? Was the couching of it in terms of the past and present the only way in which the seer could relate his visions to finite humanity? How do we interpret apocalyptic music for use today? This chapter seeks to begin to answer these queries by setting forth some applications and considerations for the contemporary church musician and worship leader based on the present study of the music utilized in the eschatological worship of the book of Revelation.

Admittedly, the music in the book of Revelation is performed eschatologically by redeemed and perfect humankind, as well as the other sinless creatures of heaven and earth. How could it be possible to develop a theology of music for worship from it in order to enlighten or assist church professionals in the present century? The music cannot be matched in human standards this side of eternity. Yet, the music of the contemporary church is rooted historically primarily in the Jewish and pagan traditions, music traditions that sometimes had very high standards and abysmal standards at other times. Additionally, the contemporary church is musically richer by the blending of Catholic and Protestant traditions. With this rich past on the one hand and the high ideals of music in worship which the book of Revelation portrays eschatologically on the other, how can the contemporary church musician sit idly by and say that neither affects him or her?

Regardless of whether one believes in the Jewish concept of a chosen people's encounter with its Creator in linear time, the Greek world's encounter with everyday life in a cyclical pattern, or even the spiral progression of Christianity in this period of grace, contemporary Christianity is historically tied to its past and eschatologically pulled into its future.[1] The recorded lessons that the contemporary church has experienced in the past and the eschatological glimpses it has received of the future must be analyzed, codified, and then utilized, if possible.

Should earthly music of the present time strive for the heavenly sound as portrayed in the Apocalypse? The writer of the Apocalypse heard from heaven music that was perfect, complete, and at best a wishful dream for human beings. But the writer also knew that "the heavenly music can so sing in human hearts that all the world is changed."[2] Christianity's quest to follow the Master's command to "be holy" demands nothing less of all Christians than willfully to strive for perfection in this life. This is true within the realm of music in worship, too. A key to advancing church music rests in the worshipers' individual and collective attitudes. The moment that worshipers even think of snubbing either their own, or more likely, another's music in worship, they have destroyed the act of worship. Fortunately, each new day that the Lord provides in this life gives a fresh opportunity to "better it" the next time.

Historical Christian worship is couched in terms of an "eschatological tension."[3] The fourth-century church sought to worship via its credal dictum of "one holy, catholic, and apostolic church." Christians have sought to fashion their lifestyles after the words of the Bible for two thousand years. But when it has come to finding guidelines for the doing of music in worship, few have found substantial assistance from the New Testament, especially from the last book of the New Testament. Church musicians and worship leaders throughout the history of the church have bemoaned the fact that the New Testament has so little to say concerning the use of music in worship. These leaders have set varying degrees of high standards for the use of music in worship based often on non-scriptural bases. Coincidentally, many of these same standards have been the highest standards for secular music as well.

This study has sought to analyze the use of music in worship in a bona fide book of the New Testament. For contemporary church music and worship to aspire to this "perfect" representation is not entirely out of the reach

1. Blevins, *Revelation*, 7–8.
2. *IB* 12:405.
3. *DOX* 121–22.

of the contemporary worshiper. Perhaps the Godhead allowed this glimpse of eschatological perfection in the music of worship specifically for us to seek after. While music can create barriers within the church, music has the ability to break down denominational, racial, and ethnic barriers. Perhaps the Godhead provided the church with this glimpse of eschatological music to aid the Holy Spirit in assembling an ecumenical community. A key to ecumenicity could be found in the church's musical doxology in corporate worship.

The ten points of musical theology for worship derived from the book of Revelation as summarized and synthesized in chapter 6 of this study are discussed in a contemporary context, as follows. This chapter is a think-piece stemming from the prior chapter's "decalogue" of music for worship characteristics in the book of Revelation; the following discussion suggests a beginning springboard of ideas that hopefully the reader will be able to continue in future thought, dialogue, and studies. Placing eschatological music and worship standards in our "sights" can provide a measuring stick of where we are in the present age and point us to a direction for the future.

1. A continuum of vocal sound ranges, from declamatory speech to sung song, as revelation and response mechanisms—logogenic versus pathogenic music.

As a responsive mechanism, music in the church today is performed typically in only one manner: lyrical singing. However, music in the Apocalypse is probably performed in ways ranging from singing to chanting to declamation. Perhaps the church today could broaden its concept of performance practice by encouraging its composers to provide a wider repertoire of non-sung vocal music and perhaps an opportunity to "rediscover" lost non-lyrical repertoire. Examples of non-sung vocal music consist of works performed by declaiming or chanting ensembles.

Only the words of the music of Revelation survive today. Perhaps this fact bears witness to the fact that the music from the first century is primarily logogenic. Otherwise, if the actual music had been of critical importance for worship, would not the church leaders have sought some sure long-term way of preserving it, even though it appears to have been beyond their means? Or would not the Godhead have seen to its being maintained through some other way? A lesson in this for the contemporary church worship leader is that the music utilized in revelatory and responsive worship should be primarily logogenic. Music should be a means, not an end, to relate the revealed Λόγος (*Logos*), i.e., Jesus Christ, in worship.

This argument, however, suggests that there is perhaps something inherently suspect in pathogenic music. But does not pathogenic music allow the responder in worship the opportunity to transcend his or her finiteness for a moment of mystical and emotional worship? Is not this perhaps one way in which our spirits groan in unutterable doxology to the Godhead? In order for pathogenic music to be viable in worship, perhaps the worshiper has to have potentially reached a certain "level" in his or her pure worship pilgrimage. Otherwise, pathogenically driven music as response invariably could be judged according to its aesthetic merit and thereby be limited as a means to worship.

Can the musical adoration that worshipers lift up to the Godhead "pass over the linguistic horizon into silence."[4] Music begins and ends with silence; on silence is layered patterned or unpatterned sound. Perhaps church musicians could give more thought to the idea of offering up worshipful silence to the Godhead. The words that we cannot utter, which only the Spirit knows, perchance could be given more purposeful direction and import in the musical expressions of praise that we lift up each week.

2. A mandate exists for the saints to continue the *Imago Dei* process by creatively composing new songs of praise.

Christians are commanded to "grow in grace" (2 Pet 3:18). How can one grow in grace when presumably the total grace of God is showered on a Christian from his or her conversion? The answer can be found from the Christian's perspective. Growing in grace is partly quenching the Holy Spirit less on a moment-by-moment basis. When a Christian actively seeks to quench the Holy Spirit less each moment, he or she grows in his or her perception of an increasing amount of grace from the Godhead. When a Christian actively seeks to quench the Holy Spirit less, he or she can experience a long-term growth that culminates in his or her passing from this world into the next. The climb would be ever upward in seeking to follow the command to be "holy," as Christ is holy (1 Pet 1:15–16). John Wesley said that church music, specifically hymns, could assist the worshiper "as a means of raising or quickening the spirit of devotion; of confirming his faith; of enlivening his hope and of kindling and increasing his love to God and man."[5]

A certain way to grow in grace is to incarnate the *Imago Dei* principle pointed out by Johansson.[6] An application of this concept for the Christian

---

4. *DOX* 39.
5. Wesley, *A Collection of Hymns*, preface.
6. Johansson, *Music and Ministry*, 21–27.

community of every age is to exhort its composers to continue to create new music for worship. The mandate is clearly supported by evidence found in the book of Revelation. The saints of God are singing new songs which no one else can learn or discern apart from the Holy Spirit's understanding. Johansson tells the contemporary church that "the church music program needs to take active steps to widen and deepen the church's scope of influence in the artistic realm."[7]

But Johansson goes on to caution the church that not all "new" music can or should be acceptable. His criterion of acceptable "new" music is that

> 'new' means nothing if it is not creative (that which breaks new ground imaginatively and with integrity). Much of the religious 'new' is a commercialized variety of afterthought, a warmed-over version of pop music's last frontier, the wake of everchanging fads, a copy of its nonchurch counterpart. Often, so-called contemporary religious music has not the slightest relationship to biblical creativity.[8]

Today's church music composer can do nothing less than to pursue his or her calling to compose fresh, ever-new praise for worship. Part of the creative artistic process falls on the performer of the music also. As interpreters of the musical score, church musicians, as performers, are actively carrying forward the λόγος (*logos*) by means of fresh, creative energy, which seeks to put forth both the Creator's and the creator's wishes.

Creating new songs should not be limited, however, to thoroughly written-out musical compositions. Well thought-out spontaneity can occur regularly within the context of church music for worship. The four living creatures, which represent all living creatures, never cease to give praise to the Godhead. This possibly implies that newly improvised songs are being composed alongside their learned, wellrehearsed praise.

The emphasis that music schools place on the performance of the memorized "classics" needs to be balanced with church musicians who are able to express extemporaneous musical thoughts effectively as well. Examples of well-thought-out spontaneity can be found primarily in today's charismatic and Afro-American churches. Often, time is provided for the congregation to share testimonies intermingled with spontaneous outbursts of song. The worship leader moves on with the service when he or she "feels moved by the Spirit" to do so. Church music schools can devote class time to experiential worship practices that incorporate spontaneous as well as

---

7. Johansson, *Music and Ministry*, 19.
8. Johansson, *Music and Ministry*, 19.

memorized choruses and other music within the context of the greater whole of worship.

3. Instrumental accompaniments (specifically, timbres that blend with the human voice) are used to aid in the vocal response to the Godhead.

The use of instrumental accompaniment is possible in today's church based on its use in the book of Revelation. However, it is used within three very specific guidelines: (1) The worshiper must utilize the accompaniment without even the slightest thought of its secular connotation. Is this possible in today's world? Can we so condition our minds and spirits so as to totally to suppress worldly connotations? Although the rhetorical answer to this question is "no," another question needs to be asked. What worshiper can cleanse totally his or her heart in order to worship at all? Because the answer to this is a decided "none," the question begs to be asked "why should Calvinistic thinking prevail regarding the use of instrumental accompaniment in worship?"; (2) Instrumental accompanimental music in the book of Revelation is composed of a single timbre. This implies a single affection. Is there room in church music for orchestral accompaniments with mixed timbres? Can contemporary orchestral accompaniment relay a single affection?; and (3) Evidence in the book of Revelation suggests that instrumental accompaniment is desirable if it does not dominate the text. Accompaniment acts in a manner that supports the logogenic character of the music.

4. Instrumental heralding (specifically, the trumpet call) is used to announce the revelation of the Godhead.

Instrumental heralding is used in the book of Revelation as an announcement of pending revelation. So, too, it can be used in the church today in a similar manner. The use of an instrumental ensemble or a soloist before a revelatory event can be recommended based on its usage in the book of Revelation. But the question arises "Can revelatory instrumental heralding, as evidenced in the Apocalypse, be employed in worship in the contemporary church as a non-heralding responsive mechanism?" Although the book of Revelation does not allow for the responsive use of "pure" music, the Christian experience historically supports its practice in many traditions.

5. The exhibition of emotion in the performance of the music exists owing to the use of a variety of Greek verbs such as "say," "sing," "rejoice," "cry," and a variety of sounds from nature. Examples of the sounds of nature are many waters and the sounds of thunder.

The music of Revelation is full of emotion. The worshipers are actively desiring to express their heart-felt, nay, life-felt, gratitude to the near-completed work of the Godhead. The saints have endured so much pain and sorrow throughout the cyclical course of history that they lose themselves in worship. But this ecstatic adulation of the Godhead is not entirely without order. Evidence in the book of Revelation indicates that it is and can be well-planned, well-rehearsed, and well-performed. This is spoken of in Proverbs 16:1–3, which exhorts humankind to devise a plan, commit it to God, and have faith that God will bless it.

But alongside well-planned order exists, perhaps, spontaneity. Raymond Bailey speaks of four manners of praying:

1. entirely spontaneous praying;
2. planned spontaneous praying;
3. well thought-out praying, which is not spontaneous except in its conception; and
4. written out prayers.[9]

These manners of praying can be directly applied to the performance practice of music for worship. Music for worship can range from spontaneity, on the one hand, to entirely written-out compositions on the other. Most churches across Christendom display a tendency for one or perhaps two of the above characteristics. But how many churches actively seek for a consistent balance of this continuum within their services?

Many Christians' experience of music in worship could basically be categorized almost exclusively as "well-thought-out." No room for spontaneity is desired, let alone considered. Consequently, the music tends to be performed generally in a mechanical manner. Perhaps a lesson can be learned from "charismatic" brothers and sisters who display a wide range of physically vocal emotions in their services. Why can the church not literally "shout" spontaneously in worship? Why can the church not literally "whisper" spontaneously in worship? At the other end of the spectrum, why can the church not write out a musical liturgy to be used by the people? Does it have to bore one's spirit? The music that is used in worship needs to cover the range of emotions that we experience in everyday living. If it does not, perhaps we have limited our potential for worship.

Worship is a celebration of life. As a microcosm of life, then, it should contain the full gamut of all the good that makes up life. This includes the wide range of emotions that humanity experiences. Until worshipers can

---

9. Bailey, "Four Manners of Praying."

couple this range of emotions with the added preparatory experiences (ranging from spontaneity to fully written-out types of music in worship), perhaps they cannot hope to experience the freedom that comprises the doxological worship evidenced in the book of Revelation.

6. The postures for the performance of music worship involve more than just sitting and standing.

A clear mandate is provided the church musician to employ all human postures in worship: from sitting to standing to kneeling to lying prostrate on the floor. Worship demands the total range of all human posture, including interpretive or liturgical dance. Restrictively sitting or standing alone inhibits worshipers from experiencing the total spectrum of worshipful encounters. The actions of the participants and revelers in worship are not haphazard, but quite planned and orderly. In the book of Revelation, these posturings tend to be choreographed.

Religious ritual contains the idea that the Godhead is hidden to the worshiper's eyes. In primitive pagan thought, it was believed that if one was seen by another, the one seen would lose his or her power. In historic Christianity, God is hidden (*Deus absconditus*).[10] But not so in the book of Revelation. In eschatological fulfillment, all of the redeemed of creation shall come before the very face of the Godhead in worship. However, on this side of eternity, perhaps the only revealed face of the Godhead that we can see are those we rub shoulders with in the choir, in the church, and in the remainder of creation during the week.

The creaturely posturings that we employ in worship should betray the expectation of the continuing revelation of the Godhead. How dare worshipers slouch! How can one expect to be worshipfully responsive, spiritually fed, mentally stimulated, emotionally restored, and socially responsible if one is physically lackadaisical in his or her musical posture in the worship experience?

The concept of coming round the throne also carries the idea of symmetry in worship. Worship in heaven will not consist of responsive creatures lined up in pews. Eschatological worship will perhaps exhibit the neo-classic posturing or positioning of the orchestra around the conductor who led from the harpsichord in the midst. This circular concept of posturing in worship also will perhaps not only be twodimensional; it may be three-dimensional!

7. The music of worship includes the use of the sounds of nature from all Creation, both animate and inanimate.

10. *DOX* 33.

Revelation is expressed audibly in the sounds made by all of creation. The divine Λόγος (*Logos*) is not limited to mere human speech. Its production and timbre can be couched in all types of the sounds of human-made instruments and of nature, too. Why not utilize the sound of thunder in worship? It could accompany the revealed Λόγος (*Logos*) or even speak revelation apart from the Word. The sermon, Scripture reading, and revelatory music could be accompanied by a variety of sounds and sights from nature, like lightning, the roar of a lion, or of a waterfall. Even technological laser light shows could be used! Ascribing the classification of musical keys or modes to certain smells might have merit. Maybe the Dorian mode could best be described by the smell of cinnamon. A "smell" study could parallel Scriabin's and Rimsky-Korsakov's independent colorization of the major and minor modes in Western music. Synchronizing musical "colors" with the colors of the church year is a possibility. This could be broadened into a general study of the use of the other non-musical senses, i.e., taste, touch, and sight, in the practice of worship in the Apocalypse or worship in general, which has roots in the "higher" traditions of the church.

Part of the job description of humanity is the task of using the natural creation properly.[11] Although natural creation is "used" in a revelatory manner in the book of Revelation, humankind should not lose sight of the fact that humanity is charged with the stewardship of creation. When Christians care for creation, they are responding by "fulfilling a priestly function on behalf of creation" and "when they give God thanks and praise [for it], they are [also] fulfilling a priestly function on behalf of creation."[12] Consequently, humanity needs to assume the lead in "assisting" creation in responding to the Godhead. In worship, this can be seen through the Eucharist. Wainwright states that participation by the saints in the communion meal presupposes a commitment to "the proper use of the earth's resources."[13] But this does not necessarily pertain to the sounds of nature unless one hears the cracking in the fraction of "the breaking of the bread" and the liquid sounds in "the pouring of the blood."

8. A sense of unity is perceived via the dynamics of antiphonal and responsorial responses by the various groups. Is music ever divisive? Is it always unified in the book of Revelation?

Choirs are disappearing from many churches today. Robert Hayburn reports that "everyone is making music in the church, except trained

---

11. *DOX* 23–24.
12. *DOX* 25.
13. *DOX* 32.

musicians."[14] Many churches today exclusively use the congregational choir in worship. This trend runs counter to the biblical norm found in Revelation. Evidence in the book of Revelation does not support the absence of smaller choral ensembles from worship. Rather, this study has shown a balance in the use of congregational groups and large and small choral ensembles in worship.

The choirs of eschatology are very well organized. The early historical mandate for this is found in the choirs of the Jewish temple. Today's choirs can be no less planned for, rehearsed, nor seasoned in performance.

The church musician in the present century is exhorted via the evidence of the book of Revelation to use music responsorially and antiphonally. By and large, high traditions, charismatic and AfroAmerican churches implement these styles more consistently than their small, average church-size counterparts. Even though the average church is only two hundred members strong, with an average choir attendance of five to fifteen percent of the congregation, antiphonal singing is possible. If a single church's choir is small, why not sing antiphonally with the congregation as a choir or join with another church in antiphony? Why should local congregations in the same region, or even across the country, not become acquainted? It is already possible and is being done via large-screen teleconferencing.

An inherent characteristic of the use of choirs in the book of Revelation is the fellowship and community that they enjoy. Although potentially divergent groups join together, they can and do so in "perfect" harmony. The eschatological choir shares a fraternity that the contemporary choir can emulate. Just as the Christian sacraments are enjoyed corporately, so too, the choir in the church cannot exist apart from considering themselves and performing as a cohesive, unified team in concert "with," "to," and sometimes "for" one another.[15]

Music has the ability to break down all types of barriers, not the least of which are racial, ethnic, and denominational. Utilization of church music in worship is a positive means by which to evangelize an unsaved world and a positive way for Christians of all traditions to unify. Just as Wainwright states that the "implied vocation of the church is to catholicity," so too should our choirs be a blending-pot of the diversity of our congregations and churches.[16] The choirs in the church should be a microcosm, a cross-section of the local and universal congregation, just as the eschatological choirs will be very diverse, yet unified in their purpose and mission.

14. Hayburn, *Papal Legislation*, 408.
15. *DOX* 142.
16. *DOX* 133.

9. Old προσκυνέο (*proskuneo*), motivated by reverential fear of a vertical God-to-slave nature, is merged with a new προσκυνέο (*proskuneo*), motivated by love of a horizontal host-to guest nature. Theology becomes doxology as the solemn action of worship.

Many Christians were "saved" or converted at an early age in a "fire and brimstone" atmosphere owing to a guilty conscience and the fear that he or she might "go directly to hell" should he or she die without knowing Jesus. Although the Apostle Paul does not encourage this means of salvation in Philippians 1:15–18, he does come to the conclusion that "at least they are saved." But Paul does imply that coming to know the Lord with the principal motivation of genuine heartfelt love is to be desired. So, too, should our music in worship be motivated by this ἀγάρη (*agape*) love. The music of our worship should be able to lift us up into a spiritual love in order that we might become lost in doxological praise of the Godhead's work in all of eternity, both historical and eschatological.

The highest form of doxological praise is objective in character: it is not subjective nor reflexive. It is admittedly impossible for the church this side of eternity to practice only the objective form of worship. This is partly owing to the fact that as finite growing human beings, persons are often striving for more educatively. Consequently, worship of the Godhead will necessarily at times be reflexive. While objective worship in its highest doxological sense cannot be practiced by mere "saved" mortals this side of eternity, the contemporary church must constantly seek this unattainable goal. To avoid futility in this quest, the church must firmly rest in its eschatological hope in the completed work of the Godhead.

Matthew 22:37–40 provides us Jesus's summarization of the law:

> And he said to him, "You shall love the Lord your God with all your heart, and with all your soul, and with all your mind. This is the great and first commandment. And a second is like it, you shall love your neighbor as yourself. On these two commandments depend all the law and the prophets." (RSV)

Certainly, the obviously necessary element in Christan worship is to vertically praise the Godhead for its revealed and promised mighty acts in history. But perhaps those of us able-bodied saints who claim to be able to worship "quite well, thank you" week after week by watching their favorite televangelist are missing out on the fullness of Christian worship. "The second (commandment) is like unto the first"; equal to the vertical praise with which worshipers respond to the Godhead is the horizontal "rubbing of shoulders" with those in the pew. Part of the fullness of Christian worship is the responsibility of Christians to encourage those in and out of the faith to want to seek to praise the Godhead. By showing up to corporate worship regularly Christians can minister to "the least of all." Insofar as we exhort and encourage our fellow brothers and sisters to praise God, we have done it unto the Godhead, and thus we are fulfilling the full vision of προσκυνέο (*proskuneo*) spoken of by the writer of the Apocalypse.

10. Music dramatically involves all the senses of humanity and all the collective resources available in all creation.

The Creator and redeemed creation commune in a relational activity called worship. And true worship expresses life as a whole.[17] Many times church musicians are handicapped by the limited musical resources available in the local church. But the book of Revelation exhorts us to break those bonds that cloud our view and rise up to grab hold of every human, spiritual, emotional, physical, financial, and natural resource that is available in order to assist our music to serve its worship goal. The church professional must realize that all creation is the music of life. To restrict one's choir to only sing songs in four balanced parts accompanied by a pipe organ or a Steinway piano is not all that there is to music. Music is more. It is much more. It is the energy of all of creation! It is perhaps that bridge that will in part carry finite, physical creation to its final destiny with the Godhead. The music of our worship and worship itself should drive us through all of life. Wainwright argues that "the ethical acknowledgment of Christ's sovereignty in everyday living is secondary to the religiously primary acknowledgment of Christ as Lord in the context of worship."[18]

One reason that our church choirs may often appear apathetic and unmotivated is because its leaders have failed to provide balance in the music program. Granted, the Scriptures have often been neglected and thus had little to say concerning music in worship in past times. However, contemporary church musicians and worship scholars are providing more Scripture-based tangibles that we dare not ignore any longer.

The doing of worship should be driven by the sacrificial love that the worshipers purposefully return to the Godhead. The old adage, "the Spirit is willing, but the flesh is weak" should no longer be an allowable excuse. Individuals need willfully to be more responsible; they need to comprehend consciously that they will be held individually responsible for their actions or inactions in worship as in life.

17. *DOX* 16–20.
18. *DOX* 48.

Perhaps until one encounters dramatic balance in worship, one cannot be transformed by the worship. Part of becoming lost in worship is not just "knowing" the Godhead but "conforming" to the image of the Godhead. This will not change our relational position before the Godhead but will free us from the shackles of our finiteness. Doxological worship, rooted in the motion of Christianity's most characteristic rituals, is transforming in character.[19]

Christianity's personhood is as much spiritual as physical. Yet Christianity is often consumed with its seemingly sole attention on its physical state. Contemporary church music has the potential, as it is empowered by the Holy Spirit, to take Christianity's mind off its physical condition and vivify its spiritual souls. Although this appears to be possible only on an eschatological level, finite humanity has been provided a model for music in worship in the end-times. Christianity was perhaps given this glimpse of future worship so that it may imitate it this side of eternity. Granted, this imitation may be only for fleeting moments in periodic worship; Christians may only transcend their physicality for short-lived moments in time as they hope for their final eschatological consummation as true members of the church—the bride of Christ. But that is realized eschatology whereby each worshiper is being transformed little by little into his or her individual and collective fullest dimensions as the *Imago Dei* is played out in doxological praise.

---

19. *DOX* 121.

8

Regulative Principles in the Book of Revelation

THIS CHAPTER PRESENTS SYNOPTICALLY a summary of the text augmented from 1990 to today and includes additional thoughts and wisdom gained from further study and from others during presentations of this material to worship leaders in churches and at worship conferences.

Piper states that

> there is very little in the New Testament about the forms and style and content of corporate worship. . . and that God must mean to leave the matter for form and style and content to the judgment of our spiritual wisdom—not to our whim or our tradition, but to prayerful, thoughtful, culturally alert, self-critical, Bible-saturated, God-centered, Christ-exalting reflection driven by a passion to be filled with all the fullness of God. I assume this will be an ongoing process, not a one-time effort.[1]

I disagree that the New Testament has little to say about the forms and style and content of corporate worship. While it is a given that the Old Testament has much to say about music in our worship today, Bible scholars decry so little to be found in the New Testament about music in worship. Yet, I contend that the New Testament has much to say in a bonafide book of the New Testament—the book of Revelation—but everyone ignores it. Why? Because we cannot replicate it this side of eternity? I disagree and

---

1. John Piper, "Thoughts on Worship and Culture."

purport that, if it has been recorded in the Apocalypse as inspired by the Holy Spirit, why cannot we seek to emulate it today?

You might ask how it can be possible to contemporize eschatological thought? Rabbis today tell their adherents to picture the Passover happening today—thus, bringing the past to the present. Christians are exhorted by Jesus to remember (*anamnesis*) the first Lord's Supper in the upper room—thus, taking the present back to the past. So, why can we not bring the future to the present, mindful that the past, present, and future in this age are merely separated by two nano-seconds (2×10^{-9}) in time? Also, please consider what the Cappadocian theologians practiced in the fourth century as they sought to contemporize eschatological thought as inspired by the book of Revelation as well as many of the Psalms and other songs and prayers in the Bible. Not only were they and all Christians grateful and mindful for the acts of God in history, but were and are collectively grateful with hopeful expectation of that which God will do in the future.

I have shown that the book of Revelation is full of regulative principles that historically tie us to our past and how they pertain to the doing of music in our worship as the eschatological glue or tractor beam pulling all Christians to their heavenly home as their citizenship is there already.

According to Smith, "Authorities are rather well-agreed that the music of ancient Israel, especially the vocal, was solo or unison rather than harmonized."[2] As to the use of a choir in worship, "choirs were not found in the synagogue although they were found in the temple. . . as they would have been a violation of *koinonia* ("fellowship"), which is the concept of *una voce dicentes* ("with one voice"). But, they will emerge within the church by the time of monasticism and the *schola cantorum* ("singing school")."[3]

The book of Revelation has much to inform us of our "doing of music" in worship that can be categorized as regulative principles. Regulative principles are manners of doing worship based on what the Bible says. But so many delimit what the book of Revelation has to say about worship because it is eschatological and thereby unattainable by Christians this side of eternity. But how dare we not try!

Calvin (1509–1564) himself never called "the rule of worship" the "regulative principles" (to do only that which is recorded in scripture).[4] Yet, it is commonly attributed to him today in contradistinction to Luther's normative principles. Luther's normative principle suggests that what is not

---

2. Smith, *Musical Aspects of the New Testament*, 9.

3. Smith, *Musical Aspects of the New Testament*, 35.

4. R. Scott Clark, "Calvin's Principle of Worship," in ed. David Hall, *Tributes to John Calvin: A Celebration of his Quincentenary* (Phillipsburg: P&R Publishing, 2010). 247–69.

specifically prohibited in the Bible is open to use in worship. Calvin was particularly opposed to the use of instruments in worship in his day. The Belgic Confession (1561; BC) states that it is not permissible to use something that is not explicitly taught in Scripture. (BC7). Both the Heidelberg Catechism (1563; HC) and Westminster Confession of Faith (1647), written about eighty years after the death of Calvin, have the same sentiment. The Westminster Confession of Faith (1647; WCF) says

> But the acceptable way of worshiping the true God is instituted by Himself, and so limited by His own revealed will, that He may not be worshiped according to the imaginations and devices of men, or the suggestion of Satan, under any visible representation, or any other way not prescribed in the holy Scriptures. (WCF 21.1)[5]

Why do we ignore worship as displayed in the book of Revelation? The ten regulative principles identified in my dissertation in 1990 and in my book in 1995 are repeated and further elaborated here.

THE PLACEMENT OF MUSIC IN CHRISTIAN WORSHIP

In order to begin to understand music in worship in the book of Revelation, one must review the Greek verbs that imply the process of Christian worship in the New Testament. They are as follows:

1. ἐθελοθρησκεία (*ethelothreskeia*)—as a noun describes "whom one wills to worship";
2. εὐσεβής (*eusebes*)—as a verb means "to act piously towards one" whom one worships;
3. λατρεία (*latreia*)—as a verb is "the service rendered by priests" as a "sacred service";
4. προσκυνέω (*proskuneo*)—as a verb is the act of prostration by "kissing one's feet" in order "to show homage by kneeling or physical prostration";
5. σέβασμα (*sebasma*)—as a noun refers "to the object of one's worship";

---

5. Juliette Colunga, "The Reformation, The Regulative Principle, and the Modern Church: Examining Calvin's Dedication to Purity in Worship (Part I)" in the Heidelblog, July 30, 2025; see also MacPherson, *The Westminster Confession of Faith*, 21.1; see also Ursinus, "The Heidelberg Catechism," Q&A 96.

6. σέβομαι (*sebomai*)—as a verb appears "to revere whom one awes";

7. σεβάζομαι (*sebazomai*)—as a verb implies the process of "worshipping cultically" and "to honor religiously";

8. θρησκκεία (*threskeia*)—as a noun suggesting the doing of worship with "religious fanaticism" as in a "religious ceremony."[6]

In a Christian context, all of these words for worship often allude to one's response to the revelation of the Lord and Maker of Creation by the completed work on the cross and resurrection of our Lord and Savior Jesus Christ in and by the power of the Holy Spirit.

A ninth word, λειτουργία (*leitourgia*), is technically not a word for worship but is the word from which we derive liturgy, which can be described as "doing the work of service."[7] As a work of the laity, a thought-provoking visual of this can be found in the practice of many churches over the centuries to hang a sign above the entrance to their sanctuary reading, "Enter to Serve in Worship." Upon departing the sanctuary after the worship service, congregants would read on an opposite side of the entryway, "Depart to Worship in Service" or "You are Now Entering the Mission Field."

Of these words for worship in the New Testament, the most common in the New Testament are 1) σέβομαι (*sebomai*), 2) λατρεία (*latriea*), 3) λειτουργία (*leitourgia*), and 4) προσκυνέω (*proskuneo*). Of these, only προσκυνέω (*proskuneo*) appears in the book of Revelation and it appears fifty-eight times. Breaking προσκυνέω (*proskuneo*) down, προσ (*pros*) means to direct "towards" and κυνέο (*kuneo*) means "to kiss." Its Old Testament precursor is the Hebrew word *shetachavah*, whereby one literally prostrated oneself physically before someone or something whom one 1) highly respected, 2) a king or a queen, or 3) a deity. This very much signified a vertical relationship as from a slave to his or her master, lord, or deity.

In the New Testament, according to John Burkhart, προσκυνέω (*proskuneo*) takes on a new dimension in meaning. When Jesus meets the Samaritan women at the well in John 4:20–24, προσκυνέω (*proskuneo*) seems to imply a wholly new sense of worshipping "in the Spirit and in truth." Thus, this purely physical act as an outside gesture, which is physically bound in place and gesture in the Old Testament, is elevated to a new dimension, ushering in the concept that maybe there is no longer an exclusive physical place of worship of Jesus Christ on this planet Earth. Burkhart rather

---

6. Bertram, "ἔθνος," 2:364–69; Grundman, "εὔσημος," 2:770; Strathmann, "λατρεία," 4:58–65; Greeven, "προσκυνέω," 6:763–66; Foerster, "σέβομαι," 7:174–75, 169–74; Schmidt, "θρησκεία," 3:155–59.

7. Strathmann, "λειτουργία," 4:215–22.

suggests a spiritual prostration of one's heart.[8] Jack concurs and suggests that, while it entails a response to God that beforehand included bowing before him literally, now it is more figurative, honoring him in a spirit of reverence and submission from the heart, as exhibited by a holy kiss,[9] and more relationally as host and friend. Leaver insightfully suggests that music in worship moves us from the mind to the heart:

> ... Just as theology prevents music from becoming an end in itself by pointing man to its origins. In the doxology of creation, music prevents theology from becoming a purely intellectual matter by moving the heart of man to consider its ultimate purpose...[10]

Interestingly, just as Yahweh God suffered to allow King David to build for him a temple in Jerusalem on the same geographical place that Abraham sought to offer up his son Isaac as an offering on Mount Moriah, God did not want to be bound to a geographical location on the earth. Yahweh God much preferred wandering with his people in the tabernacle, and in this age of grace, each believer now has the temple of God within their person, according to 1 Corinthians 3:16.

Reicke observes that "nowhere in the New Testament does προσκυνέο (*proskuneo*) mean technical worship performed by Christians on this earth." Thus, those who "prostrated themselves to Jesus during His lifetime suddenly had no place toward which to turn after Jesus's final ascent to heaven." Yet, at Pentecost, God gave us the Holy Spirit to indwell each of his believers. But God also gave us what else at Pentecost? God gave us each other—the church—and perhaps God sat back and chuckled and rhetorically thought, "I am going to make them work together." The church was started this side of eternity to commemorate Jesus's resurrection from the dead, which the early church did on what they called "the Lord's Day," the 8th Day. The second Adam, Jesus, was crucified on the 6th Day—the day humanity was created—and this second Adam, Jesus the Christ, rose from the dead on the 8th Day.

Sadly, owing to the pandemic of 2020, church goers in some states across America and globally were prohibited from gathering at Church and were relegated to "participating in Church worship" from their "caves" at home. Owing to having passed through the pandemic recently, unfortunately, even after our churches were "re-opened," this led to many simply

---

8. Leaver and Litton, *Duty and Delight*, 19.
9. Chris Jack, "The *Proskuneo* Myth," 8–9.
10. Leaver and Litton, *Duty and Delight*, 19.

worshiping on the Lord's Day from the comfort of their streaming services at home.

Many today eschew attending church because of the hypocrites they find there, and they worship God by either going out into nature on a hike, by playing golf, or by staying at home and watching their favorite preacher on cable or live streaming. Owing to the near elimination of Blue Laws on Sundays (the closing of retail stores on Sundays, except for today's Chick-fil-A and Hobby Lobby), many like to shop on Sundays and enjoy little league games with their children or grandchildren. But I contend that Christians will not experience the fullness of corporate Christian worship until and unless believers regularly rub shoulders horizontally with the oft "hypocrites in the pews" of the church as we are exhorted to in Hebrews 10:24–25 "And let us consider how we may spur one another on toward love and good deeds, not giving up meeting together. . ." We, as the church, are the bride of Christ. We, the church, need each other for *koinonia*, love, unity, evangelism, discipleship, and accountability, owing to our perichoretic nature, for we are a social community, similar as is the Trinity.

Also, we have the responsibility to glorify God, not only in our private devotions, family devotions, corporate worship, and periodic celebrative worship,[11] but we also must point all persons by our words and actions to saving faith in Jesus Christ as Lord and Savior by the power of the Holy Spirit, allow the Holy Spirit to do the work of the conviction of one's heart, and then to disciple one another so as to create spiritual giants.[12] Having worked vocationally as a consultant to entrepreneurial businesses, not-for-profits, and church entities throughout my career, I have always sought for the lead entrepreneur to risk being "the dumbest person" on the staff because he or she created spiritual and business giants around him or herself. By this means, the legacy created by the entrepreneurial leader has its best chance to endure. This responsibility likewise applies to all Christians. They are to disciple one another and to spread the good news of the gospel to all peoples based on the Great Commission, as found in Matthew 28:19–20.

The transformation of the Hebrew *shetachavah* (physical prostration) in the Old Testament to the Greek *proskuneo* (spiritual prostration of the heart) in the New Testament, finds that Yahweh God appears to be the "conquering hero" in the Old Testament. But, there is a move from being only the conquering hero simultaneously toward that of being our generous host, Jesus, in the New Testament. Thus, the Old Testament master-slave orientation (↑) is transformed to include our New Testament host-guest

---

11. Brooks, *Worship Quest*, 64.
12. Brooks, *Worship Quest*, 64.

relationship (↔). United then, the vertical abasement now includes no less than a figurative horizontal "holy kiss" or (↔ ↕). The most basic practice of Christian worship involves the believer's daily individual, familial, and periodic corporate (including celebrative) response in "Spirit and in truth" to God's revelation of himself in Jesus Christ by the power the Holy Spirit.

MUSIC FORMS FOUND IN THE BOOK OF REVELATION

Music in worship in the book of Revelation falls into the following categories: 1) the musical forms, 2) the performing groups, 3) their performance practice, including sounds they made, and 4) their postures, including the emotions evoked. In order to place this eschatological exercise into a biblical and historical context, this study has discussed each of these musical aspects through early pagan, Jewish, Greek, Roman, early church times, and then they are applied over the past two millennia.

The only music forms discernable in the book of Revelation are the 1) ᾠδή (*oda*— "song") and 2) the σάλπιγξ (*salpinx*—"the trumpet call") and its verb σαλπίζω (*salpixo*—"to trumpet").

Psalms, hymns, and spiritual songs are mentioned in passages such as Colossians 3:16, which states, "Let the message of Christ dwell among you richly as you teach and admonish one another with all wisdom through psalms, hymns, and songs from the Spirit, singing to God with gratitude in your hearts," as well as Ephesians 5:19, which encourages believers to address "speaking to one another with psalms, hymns, and songs from the Spirit. Sing and make music from your heart to the Lord. . ." What is interesting here is that when each of the over thirty song texts in the book of Revelation are referred to in the book of Revelation, they are not called psalms, hymns, or spiritual songs; rather, they are all referred to as *oda*. What does this mean? Is it possible that by the late first century psalms, hymns, and spiritual songs have congealed into *oda*? Or, is the writer of the Apocalypse not versed in the differences between psalms, hymns, and spiritual songs? Regardless, as prompted by the Holy Spirit, the writer used this singular term, "*oda*."

What is the most important *oda* in corporate worship? It is not a solo or ensemble sung or performed during the service. Many pastors over the years have told me that the most important song in corporate worship is the solo before the sermon. The pastor needed the right song in order set the tone for his sermon. Many have said that the choral anthem sung by a choir is the most important song in worship. Yet, the most important response in worship in the book of Revelation is congregational song, sung as a single voice that belies total unity of the congregants.

This song is always logogenic ("text dominated"). It is a time when together the gathered congregation adores God in φωνή (*phone*—"one voice"). Sadly, much of Christian corporate worship has lost this today with its bent for the praise team performing a concert on stage with songs often unknown to the congregation. This is not the fulness of corporate worship and is not a regulative principle as found in the book of Revelation. The congregation is not the audience, as Soren Kirkegaard pointed out in the nineteenth-century; rather, the primary responders to God in worship are individual members of the congregation gathered in unity. There is room in worship for soloists and ensembles including adults, youth, children, and seniors, but they should not dominate corporate worship. In the New Testament, the song of worship sung by the congregation is conceived as "a form of sacrifice unto God."[13]

The two primary activities of worship are that God reveals Himself (as revelation) followed by believers who respond (as response) to the past, present, and future acts of God in Jesus Christ by the power of the Holy Spirit.

Worship as revelation is performed 1) vocally, by means of the sermon, Scripture reading, the children's corner, and so on, 2) by pathogenic non-texted music, such as pure instrumental music, and 3) by the sounds of nature according to the book of Revelation. A good example of pathogenic music as revelation is the trumpet call as it calls the congregation together in corporate worship. Pathogenic music (non-texted instrumental pure music) and the sounds of nature reveal God in worship. Thirty-six years ago, when this author was researching this topic, I had many occasions to speak to church organists, which have largely disappeared in our worship services today. When they were asked about their rendering of an offertory solo on the organ, were they responding to God on behalf of the congregation or revealing God to the congregation? Their most often response was they, as likely the most-trained musician in the church, were responding to God on behalf of the congregation. Based on evidence in the book of Revelation, this is exactly wrong. Pure instrumental music in corporate worship serves as God's revelation of Himself, as can be the use of the sounds from nature, but not as response.

---

13. Smith, *Musical Aspects of the New Testament*, 163.

Performing Groups in the book of Revelation.

Many choirs are included in the book of Revelation, whose congregations crescendo in size and sound as they respond. They are: 1) a chorus of twenty-four elders; 2) the chorus numbering thousands and thousands in heaven including the four living creatures, the twenty-four elders, the angels. all of the redeemed including the Jewish descendants of Abraham in Revelation 7 and those redeemed by the blood of Jesus Christ in Revelation 14; and 3) the assembled choir of all of creation. They are each heard antiphonally and responsorially as one *phone* (voice); thus, their collective articulation is immaculate and always discernable.

REGULATIVE PRINCIPLES OF MUSIC FOUND IN THE BOOK OF REVELATION

Ten regulative principles of music in worship in the book of Revelation identified in 1990 are restated here with additional learnings and insights gained over the past thirty-five years.

1. A mandate exists for the saints to continue the *Imago Dei* process by creatively composing new songs of praise alongside the seasoned songs of prior generations. The most recent worship wars over the past 50 years have largely subsided although there are some churches today who still only sing their old hymns and other churches that sing nothing but Christian contemporary music. Blended music is more apropos; that is, suitable worship music from many generations is more desired to match the demographics of the congregation in the local church. Composers and arrangers over the years have been able to reset many of the older hymns and songs with a contemporary feel, primarily through the use of harmonies and rhythms. This is supported in the book of Revelation because the idea of "new" music contains two distinctive meanings: 1) νέος (*neos*) is used to distinguish newly created music, thus the use of newly composed contemporary music that must be biblically sound, and 2) καινός (*kainos*) is used to distinguish older music—not new in time but new in quality. While all music decays over time, once we attain heaven, the old will no longer decay but will continually become new.

Is it possible to perform each piece of music, especially the "old" music in worship, as though it was not decaying, as though believers are singing it for the first time? Believers are encouraged to participate in corporate worship week-to-week regularly in order to better fulfill the command of II

Peter 3:18 "to grow in the grace. . ." Thus, to play out the *Imago Dei* in our worship requires fresh expressions of praise, alongside historical expressions of praise, as the Holy Spirit informs our worship. The old hymns and songs have become the church's oral tradition and, whether good or bad, many congregations know more of their songs and hymn texts by memory than beloved Scripture passages.

In my twenties, I became consumed with the idea presented in II Peter 3:18 of seeking to "grow in the grace and knowledge of our Lord and Savior Jesus Christ. . ." (RSV). In an interview to teach MBA/Arts classes for a Christian university in the 1990s, I was asked to relate a business principle to the Christian walk. I chose to illustrate it by paralleling "growing in grace" to a real estate amortization chart as follows.

When one takes out a mortgage to buy one's residential home, the bank or lending institution will make a fully amortized loan as the first mortgage. What this means is that while the homeowner will make equal payments monthly over the typical thirty-year life of the loan, the interest paid in year one is as much as 95 percent of the monthly payment with only 5 percent going towards paying down the principal loan amount.

Throughout the life of the loan, the interest amount decreases monthly over time and the principal amount grows each month. This was done in order to reward returning GIs from World War II as it gave them the ability to own a home by allowing the interest on the loan to be written off on Schedule A of one's annual federal and state income tax filing. Thus, by the time the last of thirty years of payments is made, as much as 95 percent of the payment is principal and only 5 percent comprises interest.

When one accepts Jesus Christ as one's Lord and Savior after repenting of one's sins and being baptized, the amount of God's justifying grace imparted at that moment, prevenient grace aside, is no less than one hundred percent, and this will not change over time. One hundred percent of God's sanctifying grace (including the Holy Spirit living within) is evident in one's life. But early in the believer's walk, the believer is continually fighting with the old sinful nature. As one dies to self daily, the interest of the fully amortized bank loan represents one's ego and decreases over time. Then the willful obedience to our Savior on a moment-by-moment basis based on Romans 12:1 of "offering our bodies as a living sacrifice" can evidence the growth of the Holy Spirit from within. The principal amount represents the moment-by-moment filling of the Holy Spirit's sanctifying grace in one's life, which grows with one's growth in discipleship, thus representing "growing in grace." Believers must never stop being discipled.

We are on the verge of becoming more bionic than flesh, owing to all of the artificial body parts some of us now have. I have been suggesting to pastors for a number of years that when they are presiding over the burial of a loved one, instead of saying, "ashes to ashes, dust to dust," they may need to start saying, "ashes to ashes, rust to rust." For one day soon many of us will be more bionic than flesh. And of course, the bionic body parts will not rust, as they are generally made of platinum and other non-oxidizing metals and materials. And owing to you being genetically right sized often to a parent, the healthcare community may deny paying for your new bionics. They may suggest to you to harvest artificial body parts from your parents when their faith becomes sight as their bionic parts have more useful life capacity and can be used for you as you age. Of course, it would not be long before a secondary market in used body parts would spring up. So, then to the extreme, if we are on the verge of becoming fully bionic, how much flesh do we need to have in our body to keep our spirit, our *Imago Dei*? Because if we lose our spirit, then we become robots?

We are on the verge of cloning human beings. Can a human being clone be saved and offer up praise to God? It depends on whether God will bless a human being clone with His spirit as the *Imago Dei* of God is embedded within natural-born human beings. I have spoken to tens of attorneys, pastors, ethicists, and even Harvard bio-ethicists. The Harvard professors countered with ". . .a soul?. . .a spirit? Human beings have no spirit." Scientific thought was originated by the Church during the Renaissance to scientifically prove the existence of God. The first fifteen hundred universities in America were all started under God, but today are leading with humanism. In the nineteenth century, evolutionary theory postulated that animals evolve upwards to mankind. An argument against evolutionary theory is the idea of entropy where all matter goes from order to disorder over time, not randomly from disorder to order. This is the Second Law of Thermodynamics, but it has been potentially debunked owing to it only being able to occur in a closed system. But, another argument against evolutionary theory is when and how does an evolved animal obtain the *Imago Dei* (spirit of God)? The *Imago Dei* was uniquely imbedded in humanity from Day 6 of Creation in Adam. This is what sets humanity apart from the animal kingdom. Yet, a Kentucky Bar Association president of years past commented that if forty souls or spirits were on a plane, five of them being human clones, and the plane crashed and all perished, the legal community would likely conclude that forty souls or spirits were lost because, in their estimation, the clones looked and acted no different than their normal human being counterparts. Contrarily, if we conclude that human clones have no *Imago Dei* (spirit of God), then if one is killed, it would not be a capital offense of murder but rather a matter for the ASPCA.

So then, when does one gain the *Imago Dei* (spirit of God)? Tertullian (ca. 155–ca. 220), an early Church father, is of a mind that when the egg meets the sperm in human conception that God, *ex nihilo*, imparts a newly created spirit as the *Imago Dei* of Creator God to the newly formed fetus. This is contrary to Egyptian religion and Mormonism who purport that a pre-existent pool of souls or spirits exists and that God moves one over to the newly fertilized fetus. If we take Tertullian's thought as a given, then the *Imago Dei* (spirit of God) begins at conception, although others may disagree. If Tertullian is correct, does that prohibit a human being clone from receiving the *Imago Dei* of God? I have many Jewish friends who share a variety of views. An orthodox Jewish acquaintance suggests that a soul is imparted to a person not at conception but when the baby takes its first breath (πνεῦμα - *pneuma*) outside of the womb. All of this to say, will God impart His *Imago Dei* to a human clone? If not, do we then conclude that a human clone cannot be saved, nor be able to praise God, nor experience eternal life with God?

2. A continuum of vocal sound ranges from declamatory speech to sung song as revelation and response mechanisms. Our worship is twofold, in which the faithful respond to God's revelation of himself. In the book of Revelation, all response is logogenic (word-dominated) which means it is text-dominated and is never pathogenic (non-texted pure instrumental music and the sounds of nature), and it is always heard as one *phone* (voice). Revelation, on the other hand, is often logogenic, comprised of a sermon, children's corner, Scripture reading, and the like, but it can also include non-texted pure instrumental music and the sounds of nature. When I first wrote my dissertation in 1990, the idea for the church to use sounds of nature in corporate Christian worship was anathema because it sounded like New Age thinking. But that fad has largely passed as of this writing. There is a prominent top ten-sized American church in the Louisville, Kentucky, area that employs the sound of a waterfall during their baptisms and has done so for over twenty years. Can we respectfully use the sounds of nature as revelation, such as the roar of a lion, a clap of thunder, or the sound of rushing water in our worship if it fits the character or nature of our worship on any given corporate worship day?

The prevailing Greek verb in the New Testament for "to sing" is ἀδώ (*ado*). It is used importantly in the Pauline writings of the New Testament in Ephesians and Colossians. But just as psalms, hymns, and spiritual songs have congealed by the writing of the Apocalypse into *oda* by the end of the first century in the writing of the book of Revelation, so *ado* gives way in the final book of the New Testament to the Greek word λέγω (*lego*— "to say").

Lego is the exclusive Greek verb in the book of Revelation to introduce the thirty some odd *oda*. And, as we know, Handel used much of the *oda* in the book of Revelation as song texts in his oratorio, *Messiah*. Further study on the etymology of *ado* and *lego* is provided, as per Gelineau, in Jones's *The Study of Liturgy*, in which it is shown that a fluid continuum exists from the spoken word to music whether chanted, sung, acclaimed, or as jubilus, as follows:

a. ordinary speech;

b. proclamation (cantillation);

c. meditation (psalmody);

d. chant;

e. hymn, including *lied*;

f. acclamation (evidenced by the human cry); and

g. vocalise or jubilus (see footnote 77 in Chapter 5).

Thus, *lego* can introduce any of these forms of human vocalization as musical texts and appears to include the sung song of *ado*.

Calvin eschewed singing in parts and accompaniment in worship of his day, and it continues in many Reformed churches today. Calvin believed that all congregational singing should be in unison. Based on singing in one *phone* as response in the book of Revelation, this seems entirely appropriate and reasonable.

In the book of Revelation, vocal response is heard as one voice (*phone*). Does that mean all worshippers are singing the same melodic line in unison? This side of eternity, this regulative principle is not possible with men and women and children in a mixed-age demographic in corporate worship. Singing in unison this side of eternity is only possible with children's choirs before puberty and with altos and tenors as adults where the very same note can be sung by those men and women. But, when one adds in adult soprano and bass voices, a true unison is not possible, as the pure unison will be augmented an octave apart. Will our vocal ranges in heaven give us the ability for redeemed men and women to sing in true unison on the same pitch in the same *tessitura* (vocal range)? Thus, is this regulative principle of singing in one voice possible this side of eternity?

Contemporary Christian songs tend to be sung more in this type of imperfect unison rather than harmonized. So, is true unison in a congregation possible on this side of eternity in our corporate worship? While Calvin suggested the same, the answer this side of eternity is, musicologically, "No";

thus, it cannot be a regulative principle but a normative one in accordance with Luther. So, will we have expanded *tessituras* (vocal ranges) in our heavenly voices one day in eternity so that all can sing in pure and perfect unison? That is implied by the use of "singing in one *phone*" in the book of Revelation.

Also, what about part singing? Again, no allusion to it is made in the book of Revelation. Thus, the move over the past fifty years to primarily congregational singing via contemporary Christian music in our imperfect unison is closer to a more regulative practice based on the book of Revelation. Yet so many retired baby boomer Christians, who spent a lifetime singing parts in the choir that are largely missing in corporate worship today, feel like Christian refugees in their own church. While part singing produces a wonderful sound, too many times the performers must focus and concentrate so much on singing their part that they lose the primary focus of singing praise to the Godhead.

When I was growing up in the 1960s, one of the hymns continually sung in Sunday School was "Trust and Obey." Children readily find that they can trust anyone easily but over the years we have had to caution them about trusting strangers. But, at least half of the children cannot seem to obey as they are constantly seeking to stretch boundaries that parents or society seek to set. Leading a Sunday night song service 40 years ago with adults as we sang "Trust and Obey," the idea of trust and obey flipped for me. It dawned on me that adults typically can obey the laws of the church and society, but they struggle with trusting God as so many adults become control freaks even to the extreme of "helicopter"-ing their adult children. I am hoping that one of the lessons Christians learned from the pandemic is that we need to trust God more. God is in control. The point is that adult Christians need to approach God regularly in worship as "little children" as expressed in Matthew 19:14 when "Jesus said, 'Let the children come to me, and do not hinder them; for to such belongs in the kingdom of heaven.'" Congregational singing in one voice can simplify our praise of God in worship as we hopefully are able to become lost in worship continually.

Since no later than the 1950s, America has been living in an age of affluence resulting in boredom. This boredom in our lives is being accelerated by Artificial Intelligence (AI) age that we are now entering into that will cause so much societal change that the reason to attend school could become virtually obsolete at least academically beyond rudimentary learning. Knowing where to find the answers through AI will be all we need to know. Bloom's Taxonomy may largely become irrelevant on no less than the cognitive domain of intellectual processing. Schooling then may be relegated to only needing to teach socialization skills including etiquette and discipline which are encompassed in the affective domain (emotional responses and attitudes) and the psychomotor domain (physical skills and abilities).[14] With more of the toil of human work "by the sweat of our brow" potentially decreasing, will it give God's faithful literally additional time to worship God more deeply and to disciple others more frequently and with greater fervor? Could AI be no less than a blessing to Christianity?

3. Instrumental accompaniments, specifically timbres that blend with the human voice, are used to aid in the vocal response to the Godhead. Based on evidence in the book of Revelation, response can be accompanied by instrumental music, but only a single timbre is used, not a mixed timbre based on the Greek *Doctrine of Affections.*

The writer of the Apocalypse was Jewish who lived for as many as fifty years in likely the most multi-cultural cities in the first-century, Ephesus. Thus, the writer was likely very familiar with the Greek ethos that permeated the Roman and pagan cultures of the times. In these blended cultures, vocal accompaniment used an instrumental timbre that complimented the vocal text, such as wind or string instruments only. Neither brass nor percussion were used, and this is consonant with what one finds in the book of Revelation. Vocal accompaniment never dominates the text (*logos*); thus, the vocal response is considered to be and must be logogenic where the text is always readily understood. If the text is poorly articulated or drowned out by the accompaniment, it is not regulative as per its practice in the book of Revelation.

While mixed-timbre accompaniment in worship is evident in the Old Testament, it simply does not occur in the book of Revelation. Why? Over two millennia ago, pagan rites often found children and virgins being sacrificed on altars. In order to drown out the screams and wails of those being violated, practitioners often played a variety of percussion instruments, such as cymbals and tambourines, and likely also included the playing of brass instruments. By so doing, the ones performing these sacrificial, killing rituals would not be haunted by the screams of those being violated. This practice continues to this day in some parts of the world. Prior to the 1970s, percussion instruments were basically not found in weekly corporate worship services within the Western church, owing largely to this negative association of use. But, owing to the influence of Rock music evolving since the 1940s, it appears that both mixed instrumental accompaniments, including the use of percussion, have become regulative based on Old Testament practice, but no evidence of this is found in the book of Revelation. So, does

---

14. Charlotte Ruhl, "Bloom's Taxonomy of Learning" in SimplyPsychology, March 11, 2025.

the use of a praise team or church orchestra (or "churchestra"), comprised of divergent timbres, create a single-blended timbre that is satisfactory in corporate worship as a regulative practice? Based on evidence in the book of Revelation, the answer is "no."

Owing to current technology, sound teams can ensure that this accompaniment stays soft enough so that the logogenic text can easily and readily be understood. For if the accompaniment drowns out the logos or if the words of the *logos* are mumbled and not articulated well, why are we singing? My first life verse that I received at age nine when I accepted Jesus Christ as my personal Lord and Savior and repented of my sins, was Colossians 3:23— "whatsoever your task, work heartily as serving the Lord and not man" (RSV). When I attended my first choir rehearsal with a prominent downtown church in Louisville, Kentucky, which aired on live television weekly, I asked the choir to sing their favorite anthem so that I could hear them performing well and at their best. They chose "Total Praise" by Richard Smallwood and often sung by the Brooklyn Tabernacle Choir. They sang it very well, but I could not quite make out the song text on page seven. I said to them that if they mumble or do not articulate their text clearly, why are they singing? It would be just like mumbling my life verse, which could sound like "whatsoever your task, work hardly as serving the Lord and not man." Not articulating sung response well nor the use of accompaniment drowning out the words as response in worship is simply not biblical based on evidence in the book of Revelation.

4. Instrumental heralding by use of the trumpet call is used to announce pending revelation of the Godhead. While one finds seven angels holding seven trumpets throughout the book of Revelation, they never play as an ensemble but only singly. In heaven, will we need multiple trumpets to announce pending revelation or will a single trumpet sounding alone be sufficient for all to hear? Owing to current sound technology today, can we achieve this through amplification? A mixed instrumental music timbre is not regulative in the book of Revelation, although it is regulative in the Old Testament. Because the Apocalypse reveals our future music as citizens in heaven, does it trump the mixed-use timbre of the Old Testament and of today's praise teams and churchestras?

In America of the past fifty years, education for the masses has been dumbing down every bit of subject matter so much that we have reduced all learning to a ninth-grade level or less. Perhaps this is a good thing, as Jesus compels mature born-again Christians to approach him as though they are children. Interestingly, the book of Revelation seems to strip away all the complex harmonies and timbres of music so that we can move past that sound to simply focus on and worship the Godhead in spirit and in truth.

5. The exhibition of emotion in the performance of music exists with great passion by the participants. The favorite and only response in worship in the book of Revelation appears to be vocal and can be aided through the sounds of single-timbre instrumental accompaniment while revelation can be expressed through the voice, pure instrumental music, or by the sounds of nature.

The writer of the Apocalypse, assumedly the Apostle John, was a Jew and thus was mindful of Jewish customs. After Christ's ascension, John migrated to Ephesus. The church at Ephesus was the most multi-cultural church of its time, comprised of the greatest number of people-group factions of the first-century. In Ephesians, Paul stressed the unity of such a divergent congregation. Thus, John, a Jew, lived in the Roman world of his day in the most multi-cultural city of its time, and was deeply influenced by Greek thought and other pagan thought. The Greeks had codified ethical characters of musical scales, although they were not yet tempered. The exhibition of emotion was evidenced in the tone. Semi-tone scales, such as the Dorian scale (D to D) from the white notes on today's tempered western scale, denoted "manliness and strength." The Phrygian mode from E to E represented the emotion that was "ecstatic and passionate." The Lydian mode from F to F displayed "femininity and lasciviousness," while the Mixolydian mode from G to G was "sad and mournful." These "ethical" characters of pitch level carried over to the Medieval era and into the church modes. Prior to creating the twelve-semitones, tempered music scales between the octave during the Baroque era from 1600 to 1750, micro-tones also existed, as described by Boethius (470–525 AD) and were evident dating back to the time of the Greeks before Christ was born beginning in the time of Euripides (ca. 480–406 BCE).[15] And, before the tempered scale was created by the time of the Baroque Era, as an example, the pitch of D-sharp and E-flat were not the same pitch, although now, in the tempered scale, they are enharmonic. From the time of the Greeks up to and including the Medieval era, pitch levels of music displayed various emotions. But by the time of the Baroque era, pitch-level association appears to have become largely divorced from western music.

Today, conventional Western church music exists only in the tempered major and minor scales. An example of major key emotions is described by Schubart as described below: [16]

15. Percy A. Scholes, "Notation and Nomenclature," 87.
16. Schubart. *A History of Key Characteristics.*

1. C major—completely pure;
2. D major—the key of triumph;
3. E major—noisy shouts of joy;
4. F major—complaisance and calm;
5. G major—every gentle and peaceful emotion of the heart;
6. A major—declarations of innocent love and trust in God; and
7. B major—wildly passionate displaying anger, rage, jealousy, fury, and despair.

Additionally, Russian composer Alexander Scriabin (1872–1915) in the early twentieth-century placed light waves onto sound waves in his color wheel. The colors were placed in a clockwise direction on a clock face, going around the circle of fifths, as follows: [17]

1. 12:00 (C major—red);
2. 1:00 (G major—orange);
3. 2:00 (D major—yellow);
4. 3:00 (A major—green);
5. 4:00 (E major—turquoise);
6. 5:00 (B major—light blue);
7. 6:00 (F-Sharp/G-Flat major—blue);
8. 7:00 (D Flat major—indigo);
9. 8:00 (A-Flat major—purple);
10. 9:00 (E-Flat major—mauve);
11. 10:00 (B-Flat major—pink); and
12. 11:00 (F major—maroon).

Do any church musicians or composers today place their music in musical keys that align the text or intent of the music to one's natural emotions or affections by sound, pitch, and color? If not, why not? As a graduate fellow for a New Testament professor at the Southern Baptist Theological Seminary while studying for a Doctor of Musical Arts degree, I aided in the production of the book of Revelation as a seven-act Greek Tragic Drama. Interpretating the Apocalypse as a literary work in this way had nothing to do with end-time speculation of pre-, post-, or a-millennial views. I

17. Wolfman, "Scriabin's Color Symbolism in Music."

suggested that we begin each of the seven acts with an *oda* pitched in one of the original modes that matched the affection of each act, thus setting the stage for each of the seven acts. By performing the Apocalypse on stage aloud, as suggested in Revelation 1:3, "Blessed is he who reads aloud the words of the prophesy, and blessed are those who hear, and who keep what is written therein. . .", students gained the ability to seek to understand the thematic storyline from beginning to end in a way that at the least was able to give the listener an overview of the content. This is such a good way to conceptualize the entire Apocalypse before a preacher then sermonizes on it. Interestingly, so many pastors I have heard preach on Revelation over the years stop after chapter 5 because they have little understanding of the content or they do not wish to be too judgmental. For that matter, from my experiences since the 1960s, many pastors simply have avoided speaking on the topics of sin, hell, or money because they do not wish to offend their congregation. This appears in recent years to be changing.

Part of the reason of not placing *oda* into the appropriately affectionate mode or key is that this side of eternity, men and women are delimited in their respective vocal ranges. Worship leaders need to know the song *tessitura* (vocal range) of their respective congregations. The typical vocal range for woman is A below middle C to D a ninth above middle C. For men, it is basically an octave lower. If a congregational song goes above or below this range, many will simply stop singing or jump an octave to continue singing. Once we attain heaven, this author purports that one's vocal *tessitura* will likely be much broader and the ability to sing as one *phone* ("voice") in perfect unison and thereby unity will be possible.

Also, to be expressive in our worship, one must consistently be willing to employ a range of dynamics from very, very soft, *ppp* (*pianississimo*) to very, very, loud, *FFF* (*fortississimo*). Too much of today's music in worship is performed at *FFF* and in the same tempo. Boring! Sustaining this level of sound for a thirty to forty-five minutes-long song service is seldom musical, edifying, glorifying, nor aesthetically beautiful. Singing every song in the same tempo is likewise not musical nor edifying nor potentially glorifying to God. In Revelation 8, thirty minutes of silence is utilized, implying that silence in worship is relevant, akin broadly to an extended *agogic* accent.

In Leonard Sweet's *Soul Café*, we are reminded that at the base of all of God's creation are vibrations that create not only sound waves (as well as light waves for the color of our senses) but also creates our ability to relationally communicate, which then drives our heartfelt worship both as revelation and response.[18] Our vision of Christ is not seen through our eyes,

---

18. Sweet, *A Cup of Coffee*.

which take us into the world, but through our ears, which brings the world into us. Just as "faith comes from what is heard, and what is heard comes by the preaching of Christ" (Rom 10:17 RSV), so our use of music in worship has the ability to increase our faith when we use music in our worship today. And this will continue throughout the whole lifetime of a believer.

Interestingly, in Revelation 8:1, σιγάω (*sigao*—"silence") is "heard" in heaven for half an hour. If this is silence at absolute zero where zero degrees Kelvin equals -273.15 Celsius, then vibrations of the entire universe stop almost altogether. Is this what is implied here in the book Revelation? Or it is simply the absence of sounds that human beings experience? Either way, purposeful and planned silence is a genuine part of our worship. Where in worship can this be intentionally used? Live streaming services eschew the use of silence as they do not want to waste precious seconds of airtime. But, if properly introduced into worship, this can be valuable so as to slow one down from the rush of today's busyness. Silence can be used in many ways such as during one's participation in the communion (Lord's Supper or Eucharist). Biblical "silence" often signified "reverence, stunned conviction, interior reflection, or orderly restraint" in the New Testament. But it also signifies that one should be a believer filled with awe, obedience, and anticipated proclamation.[19] And, what better way to be ready to hear the "still small voice of God?"

Serving as the worship leader at a church that was live on television every Sunday, I worked with the production team to ensure that all actions and words were *segued* tightly. No room was allowed for unnecessary gaps during a worship service. Yet, sometimes the gaps, either planned or serendipitous, actually enhanced the worship experience. A *cappella* (unaccompanied vocal music) is also an option not commonly used in worship today, outside of strictly Calvinistic churches. Musical volume levels require a tech team in the sound booth who have been sensitized and trained to understand how to use a variety of sound levels that are entirely subjective for every worship service as led by the Holy Spirit.

So, a hypothetical question follows that, if we were able to align our five senses (hearing, seeing, tasting, smelling, and touching) "harmonically" in worship, could we worship God in Jesus Christ by the power of the Holy Spirit at a deeper level? Granted, the Holy Spirit can take us deeper of his own volition at any time, but if we could harmonize the key or pitch or sound level of our *oda* with the light spectrum of color and then aligned it with the taste, feel, and smell of our communion elements, could we

---

19. Thayer, "Silence." Thayer's Greek Lexicon, Biblesoft.com electronic database, 2011.

worship at a deeper level naturally for God's greater glory and one another's greater edification, and thereby possibly go deeper still?

6. The postures for the performance of music in worship involves more than just physically sitting, kneeling, and standing. Will there be a gravitational force that would allow the redeemed to physically sit, kneel, and stand? Or is our rightful posture simply a bowing of one's heart and soul spiritually? In eschatological fulfillment, all of the redeemed of creation shall come before the very face of the Godhead in worship, although neither Moses in his day nor we in this age are able to do so. While now God is hidden (*Deus Absconditus*) from us, yet perhaps the face of God we experience this side of eternity is in those we rub shoulders with inside and outside the church today, for all of humanity has been created in the *Imago Dei* of our perichoretic trinitarian Creator in three persons.

To be rightly postured in corporate worship suggests that we be prepared beforehand. Do our postures of expectation in worship betray the continuing revelation of the Godhead? How attentive to our loving God are we when we attend worship? I wish that we could remove the backs of our comfortable pews and chairs in the sanctuary so that we would sit up and forward with our hands faceup in our laps. This would physically convey that we are in an attitude of expectation. So many times over the years of teaching the youth, I found so many of them almost fully reclined in their Sunday school classes, sipping on their can of soda, in an entirely bored manner. When asked why they were at church that day, they would respond that their parents required them to be there. In order to help them think more deeply about the gravity of this issue, I reminded them that, based on what the Bible had to say, they were wasting their time if the most important reason for their attendance wasn't the hope of the resurrection in Jesus Christ (I Pet 1:3).

Having spent fifteen summers, a month at a time, in Madeira Beach, Florida at my grandparents' island home, I began college as a chemistry major intent on pursuing further degrees in oceanography. But God had other plans that led me to majoring in music as a pianist. While working on a master's degree in piano performance, God opened up an opportunity to teach chemistry and physics alongside band and choir at a Christian high school. Later, having obtained an MBA, I served as a consultant in CFO and treasurer roles, overseeing finance, human resources, and IT in a number of small businesses, non-profits, and churches throughout my career, including a top thirty-sized foundation with almost $2 billion as its investment officer. After earning an MBA in Entrepreneurial Studies and working with a team that created the "Nano-Technological Drug Delivery Patch" business plan, this team represented the University in five international business plan competitions, including the Moot Corp. Competition at the University of Texas in Austin. Thus, I can be considered a nerd.

Although computers are routinely doing the complex work of thousands of human laborers in a fraction of the time, ultimately, computers are very simple. They are programmed simply in a binary format: 0 or 1, or "yes" or "no".

As an example, *Star Trek: The Motion Picture*, released in 1979, found Star Fleet Command pulling Kirk and Spock out of retirement and sending them in the newly refurbished Enterprise on a mission to destroy that which was destroying everything in its path on its way to planet Earth. They landed on it and found that its name was "V-ger." They determined that it was the middle twentieth-century satellite, Voyager, sent on a one-way trip away from planet Earth in order to determine the size of the universe. The movie, taking place in the middle twenty-second-century, found that Vger's artificial intelligence (AI) evolved over some two hundred years to such a high degree that it determined its highest priority in its AI-ness was not to return to planet Earth to destroy it but to be re-united with its creator, NASA. And in its haste, it destroyed everything in its bee-line path.

Having taught youth and nerds throughout my lifetime, I have had the opportunity to issue an altar call to fellow younger nerds as follows: in the nanosecond (10^{-9} second) moment that one passes from this life to the next, one will be all-consumed with the singular thought that one must be united with his or her Creator throughout all of eternity. The most important decision in life is one's need to say "Yes" to Jesus in order to spend eternity with one's maker. As an evangelical Christian, this means the following: did you confess your sins and accept Jesus as your Savior or not in this lifetime? Yes or No? 0 or 1? One's destination in eternity is that simple.

So, too, all of humanity will realize in the nano-second of one's pending death that one desperately must be united with Creator God for all of eternity. Each individual has to say, "Yes" to Jesus. For if one does not profess salvation in Jesus Christ, one's destiny will be to be eternally separated from one's Creator, which is Hell. And, owing to humanity's fallen state in this world, Satan is seeking to keep all of humanity from having the relationship with God that he knows he can never have. Having taught young children through the years, one said to me that Satan simply is jealous of the relationship that we can have and, because Satan can no longer be with God, Satan does not want us to have something that he can never have.

Donald Hustad used to tell the story of a practice in Scotland that required church members to attend confession on a Saturday, whereby they received a token that they presented in order to gain access to partake of communion in corporate worship on Sunday. The point is this: how many of us actively prepare beforehand to encounter God in periodic corporate worship, let alone being ready to participate and partake of communion?

Worship demands the total range of all human beings' psyche at all levels of humanity. The postures of our mental, physical, social, emotional, spiritual, and financial capacities need to be rightly aligned in worship. And, as we already discussed, worship requires a *proskuneo* approach of spiritually bowing to the Godhead.

The use of liturgical dance has often been prohibited in churches in which I have served. But I was able to move around that prohibition by using deaf choirs in worship. Their signing to suitable worship music was so powerfully worshipful as a form of dance.

7. The music of worship includes the use of the sounds of nature from all of creation, both animate and inanimate. In the book of Revelation, the entire gamut of sounds of all creation are present. The revelation of God is found vocally, in the use of non-texted instrumental music, and by the use of the sounds of creation, including the roar of the lion and the sound of rushing water. Our responses to God are always and only logogenic, sung by the congregation, aided by a possible praise team, and accompanied by the use of a single timbre of instrumental music and by the sounds of nature. Instrumental solos or ensembles as response are never found in the music of worship based on practices found in the book of Revelation. But they are revelatory.

Part of humanity's role in the stewardship of creation is in the use of all of creation rightly applied in our worship. But this goes well beyond the music of our periodic worship, regardless of it being personal, familial, or corporate, and extends to all areas of one's life.

8. A sense of unity is perceived via the dynamics of antiphonal and responsorial responses by the performing groups. Corporate worship is always and genuinely congregational in the book of Revelation, and it inclusively unites the variegated levels of creation into a sea of doxological praise to Creator God. Man reminds us that "the principle of Unity is vital in worship" which takes us further than *koinonia* (fellowship).[20]

If we were to be forced to eliminate all musical response from our corporate worship, which would be the last "group to stand?" For the early church, it was congregational singing. Based on evidence in the book of Revelation, in heaven, it will be congregational singing. So, what should it be for corporate worship in today's church? Today, the most important *oda*

---

20. Man, *Let Us Draw Near*, 395–96.

of response in the church's corporate and other worship is congregational singing.

9. Old *proskuneo*, rooted in the Old Testament Hebrew *shetachavah*, motivated by reverential fear of a vertical God-to-slave nature, includes a new *proskuneo*, motivated by the love of a horizontal host-to-guest nature. The master-slave vertical orientation, stressing position, loses primacy and now includes true *koinonia* (fellowship) of a host-guest relationship with our exalted Jesus as Christ, Savior, and Redeemer by the power of the Holy Spirit. While we necessarily are concerned with our theology this side of eternity, once we gain heaven, our theology will meld into a unified doxology as our eternal response to our Creator. So, is it possible, this side of eternity, to seek to focus even more on doxology because we are able to align our various Christian theologies? This is anathema to the various Christian denominational leaders in the church today based on their respective interpretations of Scripture. Yet, it still should be our goal, and perhaps the ultimate work of the Holy Spirit in this age, to draw all of us together as one this side of eternity. Drawing diverse Christian denominations together will require an analysis of the essentials and non-essentials of the plethora of Christian faith traditions as seen through the prism of the Bible. Yet, as the bride of Christ, the Holy Spirit is seeking to bring us together as one no less than on this side of eternity. The Holy Spirit is perhaps "waiting on us" instead of us "waiting on the Lord" (Ps 27:14).

The role of the Worship Pastor or Minister of Music (or of the Arts) in tandem with the Senior Pastor should be one seeking to grow the congregation into deeper, spiritual worship regularly and is paramount. Yet, for fifty years I have suspected with no proof that no less than half of the pastors in the pulpit were likely never called by God to serve. And likely, even a higher percentage of Worship Pastors have not been called by God either. As long as the Worship Pastor "looks pretty, sings pretty, and carries him/herself well on stage," they are hired. Too many simply have remarkably not been trained in how to disciple and grow a congregation spiritually through worship via music and the arts. Worship Pastors along with their Senior Pastors need to possibly ascertain the strengths and weaknesses of their congregations based on the Fruit of the Spirit found in Galatians 5, and then to grow them. While the Fruit of the Spirit is singular, the nine elements of it can be likened to nine facets of a diamond. In seeking to disciple oneself and then one's congregation into deeper spiritual virtues, my preacher son Matthew teaches that the nine Fruit of the Spirit build on one another, that is, to have joy, one must have love. To have peace, one must have love and joy, etc. And in order to have self control, one must have all eight: love, joy, peace, patience, kindness, goodness, faithfulness, and meekness. Self control is mastering one's ego that centers on one's pride that must decrease as the Holy Spirit increases by dying to self moment-by-moment. I have often thought that the least of God reaching down that Christians can experience is the Fruit of the Spirit and the greatest strength of humanity reaching meekly up to God can be found in the teaching wisdom of the Book of Proverbs. I am searching for a Hebrew scholar to assist me in ascribing the New Testament Fruit of the Spirit by their nine facets to the couplets of wisdom found in the Book of Proverbs. By so doing, we might be able to create a Christian Guide to growing in the faith by grace. This could be so important for young Christian men as well as a discipleship guide for all Christians regardless of age.

10. Music in worship dramatically involves all the senses of redeemed humanity and all the collective resources available in all of creation. Christianity is historically tied to its past and is being eschatologically pulled into its future. Music in worship is the eschatological glue or the tractor beam drawing us in our present-day worship to our eternal worship in heaven. Christians are merely passing through the present life, as their citizenship is already recorded in the book of life in heaven.

As the university system was codified at the University of Bologna around 1088, liberal arts subjects included the trivium and quadrivium and were based on the work of Plato and others in antiquity. The trivium was comprised of the subjects of grammar, rhetoric, and logic. The quadrivium was comprised of arithmetic, numbers in the abstract; geometry, numbers in space; music, numbers in time; and astronomy numbers in space and time.[21]

I gave up a piano scholarship to study at Aspen in the summer of 1973 and alternatively studied Eurythmics at the Dalcroze School of Music in New York City. Dr. Hilda Schuster, director of the school for over fifty years before her passing in 1997, taught that Jacques Emile Dalcroze stressed and taught music as consisting of time, space, and energy. Dalcroze understood that this expands upon the liberal arts definition of music. But perhaps, Dalcroze conceived of traditional music as having the ability to transport us to our heavenly home thus through "space" as well. Of course, we do not know if Dalcroze thought of eternity, but vibrations are the energy of our ability to communicate. Perhaps, then, he sensed that music was not just time bound but also had the ability to be conceived in space as well. Humanity has been able to record the "speech" of whales communicating with those

---

21. Man, *Let Us Draw Near*, 395–96.

in the South Atlantic from the North Atlantic ocean and scientists have also recorded the sounds emanating from outer space.

Following my father's military service as a navigator on a B-29 in World War II, he earned an engineering degree at the University of Michigan as a Phi Beta Kappa. In addition to his skills of being astute in math and science, my father also led singing, sang solos, and sang baritone in the church choir. On numerous occasions, I had the privilege of accompanying him on the piano over many years. Upon arriving at age 84, with both Parkinson's disease and Alzheimer's ravaging his body, he had become very confrontational and had no ability to answer questions coherently in a timely manner. His energy level was very short, about fifteen minutes, before he needed to rest again. When, at age 84, Hospice called and said that they expected father to pass from faith to sight within two weeks, I called my siblings and asked them to join him the following week at our father's big church in Texas at 2:30 PM on a Tuesday because nothing ever happens in a big church in Texas at 2:30 PM on a Tuesday. My siblings expected that I was simply going to play our father's favorite hymns, gospel hymns, Gaither songs, and classical anthem solos, such as "The Holy City" and the "Pharisee and the Publican" on the piano that he had sung over his lifetime. What my siblings did not expect was that from the first note that I played, our father sang on pitch and in rhythm and did not miss a word. My siblings were flabbergasted, but I was not. I was profoundly moved, however, when unexpectedly our father sang not just for fifteen minutes, nor thirty minutes, nor forty-five minutes, nor sixty minutes, nor seventy-five minutes, but, robustly, for ninety minutes. It was inspirational! When he was returned to his assisted caring facility, the nurses said that his last two weeks were a joy to be with him as his demeanor changed entirely and he was pleasant and joyful before his faith eventually became sight at his passing. His ability to sing showed me that music in our worship can truly serve to draw us like a tractor beam to our eschatological home with our dear Savior and Lord Jesus Christ, despite our failing condition this side of eternity. While Alzheimer's disease had crippled my father mentally, his music was in his heart and soul and spirit (his *Imago Dei*). Music in our worship is the eschatological glue pulling each and every Christian believer to his or her citizenship in heaven.

God is intentionally social, and it is his reasonable expectation that we *proskuneo* (worship) him in "Spirit and in truth" together in unity and *koinonia* (fellowship), as one in the Holy Spirit. Thus, believers are clearly as spiritual as they are physical. And yet, perhaps, believers are predominately more spiritual, for if they are born once physically, they will die twice, physically and spiritually. But, if believers are born twice, physically and then born-again spiritually, they will die once, physically, for they are alive spiritually for eternity based on Philippians 1:6, which states, "And I am sure that he who began a good work in you will bring it to completion at the day of Jesus Christ."

So, when does one's eternity begin? Most say it is when they die and go to heaven. Wrong! When one genuinely repents of one's sins and accepts Jesus Christ as one's Lord and Savior and seeks in obedience to follow Christ moment by moment and then is baptized (mindful that baptism alone will not save one), one's eternity begins. Therefore, I often say, "then, ACT LIKE IT! Quit moping around!" Yet, we too often in worship are consumed with our seemingly sole attention on our physical state. The spectrum of music for worship rightly Holy Spirit-inspired has the potential to take our mind off our physical condition and to vivify our spiritual souls in periodic worship. The use of music in our personal, familial, and corporate worship should always unify the participants and it should never be divisive.

CONCLUSION

The "doing of music" in our worship should be driven by the sacrificial love which the worshipers purposefully return to the Godhead. The old adage "the Spirit is willing, but the flesh is weak" should no longer be an allowable excuse. Individuals need willfully to be more responsible by being obedient and accountable both to God and each other in the Church; they need to comprehend consciously that they will be held individually responsible for their actions or inactions in worship as in life. I have often thought of the opportunities that God has provided to me to witness to someone and I missed it.

Perhaps not until one encounters dramatic balance in worship as given to us in the book of Revelation, one cannot be transformed by the worship. Part of becoming lost in worship is not just "knowing" the Godhead but in actually "conforming" into the image of the Godhead. This will not change our relational position before the Godhead, but it will free us from the shackles of our finiteness. Doxological worship, rooted in the notion of Christianity's most characteristic rituals as regulative principles found in the Bible, including the book of Revelation, is transformational in character. To be transformed means that we are in a perpetual state of change as we "grow in grace and the knowledge of our Lord and Savior Jesus Christ!" And we cannot help but exhibit Fruit of the Spirit joy! How many of us need to practice doing joy, being the visionary God has called believers to be, and seeking to grow spiritual giants around oneself moment by moment?

Christianity's personhood is as much spiritual as physical. Yet Christianity is often consumed with its seemingly sole attention on its physical state. Contemporary church music, coupled with the old, traditional music, has the potential, as it is empowered by the Holy Spirit, to take Christianity's mind off its physical condition and to vivify its spiritual soul. Although this appears to be possible only on an eschatological level, finite humanity has been provided this Book of Revelation model for doing music in worship not only in the end times, but today, too! "All scripture is inspired by God and profitable for teaching, for reproof, for correction, and for training in righteousness" (II Timothy 3:16). Christianity was perhaps given this glimpse of future worship by the inspiration of the Holy Spirit to the Apostle John so that we may seek to imitate it this side of eternity, although imperfectly. Granted, this imitation may be only for fleeting moments in periodic worship, but how dare we not try! Christians may only transcend their physicality for short-lived moments in time as they hope for their final eschatological consummation as true members of the church—the Bride of Christ. But that is realized eschatology whereby each worshiper is being transformed little by little into his or her individual and collective fullest, as the *Imago Dei* is played out in doxological praise.

Appendices

A. Historical Timetable
B. Dates of Early Playwrights, Philosophers, and Theologians
C. Song Texts
D. References to Music
E. Old Testament Pseudepigrapha
F. Music According to Use as Revelation or Response
G. References to Music—Greek to English
H. Contemporary Definitions for Worship

Appendix A
Historical Timetable

THE FOLLOWING TIMETABLE ILLUSTRATES the various early cultures that coexisted simultaneously:

Mesopotamia	Egypt	Crete/Greece	Rome
Sumerians −2040 BCE	Old Kingdom −2160 BCE	Early Crete −2100 BCE	
Babylonians 2040–1750 BCE	Middle Kingdom 2160–1580 BCE	Middle Crete 2100–1580 BCE	
Kassites 1740–1160 BCE	New Kingdom 1580–1090 BCE	Late Crete 1580–1400 BCE	
Assyrians 1160–625 BCE	Nubians 1090–663 BCE	Dorian Migration 1100–1000 BCE	
Babylonians 625–538 BCE			
Persians 538–331 BCE	Saites 663–382 BCE	Classic Period 600–300 BCE	The Early Republic 509–264 BCE
Greeks 331– BCE	Greeks 332– BCE	Alexander 336–323 BCE	The Republic 509–27 BCE
			Power in Emperor Aided by Senate 27– BCE

Appendix B
Dates of Early Playwrights, Philosophers, and Theologians

Person	Principal Writings
Aeschylus ca. 525–456 BCE	Wrote ninety plays, seven extant, including the following: *Supplicant Maiden, Persians, Seven Against Thebes, Prometheus, Agamemnon, Choephoroe,* and *Eumenides.*
Sophocles ca. 495–406 BCE	Wrote over 125 plays, seven extant, including the following: *Ajax, Antigone, Trachinine, Oedipus the King, Electra, Philoctetes,* and *Oedipus at Colonus.*
Euripides ca. 480–380 BCE	Wrote over eighty plays, nineteen extant, among them: *Cyclops, Rhesus, Alcestis, Bacchantes, Iphegenia at Aulis, Medea, Hippolytus, Trojan Women, Helen,* and *Orestes.*
Aristophanes ca. 445–380 BCE	Wrote forty to sixty plays, of which eleven survive, including the following: *Clouds, Lysistrata, Frogs,* and *Plutus.*
Socrates ca. 469–399 BCE	Wrote nothing of his own. A Greek philosopher and teacher of Xenophon and Plato.
Plato ca. 469–399 BCE	*The Seventh Letter, Lives, Republic* (Books I–X), *Apology,* and *Laws* (Books I–XII)
Aristotle ca. 384–322 BCE	A pupil of Plato; wrote *Logic* and *Politics*
Aristoxenus ca. 350–? BCE	*Harmonic Elements*

Seneca CE ca. 5–65	*Dialogues, De clementia, De beneficiis,* and *Tragedies*
Plutarch CE ca. 46–120	Over sixty writings extant
Tacitus CE ca. 55–117	*The Annals* and *The Histories*
Claudius Ptolemy Origen CE ca. 100–178	*Harmonics*
Pliny the Younger CE ca. 61–113	Ten books of letters
Saint Basil CE ca. 329–379	*Rule*, a Cappadocian theology

Appendix C
Song Texts

VARIOUS AUTHORS MENTION THROUGHOUT this study have identified different *oda* texts in the book of Revelation. They are as follows:

Cullman	5:9, 12, 13; 12:10–12; 19:1–2, 6
Harris	4:8–11; 5:9; 7:10; 11:17–18; 12:10–11; 15:3, 4b
Church, Mulry	1:5–8; 4:11; 5:9–11, 12–13; 11:17–18; 12:10–12; 15:3–4; 18:22–23; 19:1–9; 22:16–17, 20
Wainright	4:8, 11; 5:9, 12, 13; 7:10, 12; 11:15, 17; 12:10–12; 15:3; 19:1–8; 21:3–4

Other hymns texts that I have identified include the following: 7:12, 15–17; 13:10; 14:7, 8, 9–11; 16:5–6, 7.

Obviously, little consensus exists concerning *oda* texts in the book of Revelation. According to my estimation, the following are *oda* texts in Revelation:

Revelation 1:5–8:

And from Jesus Christ the faithful witness, the first-born of the dead, and the ruler of kings on earth. To him who loves us and has freed us from our sins by his blood, and made us a kingdom, priest to his God and Father, to him be glory and dominion for ever and ever. Amen.

Behold, he is coming with the clouds, and every eye will see him, everyone who pierced him; and all tribes of the earth will wail on account of him. Even so. Amen.

> "I am the Alpha and the Omega," says the Lord God, who is and who was and who is to come, the Almighty.

Revelation 4:8:

Holy, holy, holy, is the Lord God Almighty, who was and is and is to come!

Revelation 4:11

Worthy are thou, our Lord and God, to receive glory and honor and power, for thou didst create all things, and by thy will they existed and were created.

Revelation 5:9:

Worthy are thou to take the scroll and to open its seals, for thou wast slain and by the blood didst ransom men for God, from every tribe and tongue and people and nation, and hast made them a kingdom and priests to our God. And they shall reign on earth.

Revelation 5:11:

To him who sits upon the throne and to the Lamb be blessing and honor and glory and might for ever and ever!

Revelation 5:12:

Worthy is the Lamb who was slain, to receive power and wealth and wisdom and might and honor and glory and blessing!

Revelation 7:10:

Salvation belongs to our God who sits upon the throne and to the Lamb!

Revelation 7:12:

Amen! Blessing and glory and wisdom and thanksgiving and honor and power and might, be to our God for ever and ever! Amen.

Revelation 7:15–17

Therefore are they before the throne of God, and serve him day and night within his temple; and he who sits upon the throne will shelter them with *his* presence.

They shall hunger no more, neither thirst any more; the sun shall not strike them, Nor any scorching heat, for the Lamb in the midst of the throne will be their shepherd, and he will guide them to springs of living water; and God will wipe away every tear from their eyes.

Revelation 11:15:

The kingdom of the world has become the kingdom of our Lord and of his Christ, and he shall reign for ever and ever.

Revelation 11:17–18:

We give thanks to thee, Lord God Almighty, who art and who wast, that thou hast taken thy great power and begun to reign.

The nations raged, but thy wrath came, and the time for the dead to be judged, for rewarding thy servants, the prophets and saints, and those who fear thy name, both small and great, and for destroying the destroyers of the earth.

Revelation 12:10-12:

Now the salvation and the power and the kingdom of our God and the authority of his Christ have come, for the accuser of our brethren has been thrown down, who accuses them day and night before our God.

And they have conquered him by the blood of the Lamb, and by the word of their testimony, for they loved not their lives even unto death,

Rejoice then, O heaven and you that dwell therein! But woe to you, O earth and sea for the devil has come down to you in great wrath, because he knows that his time is short!

Revelation 13:10:

If any one is to be taken captive, to captivity he goes; if any one slays with the sword, with a sword must he be slain.

Revelation 14:7:

Fear God and give him glory, for the hour of his judgment has come; and worship him who made heaven and earth, the sea and the fountains of water.

Revelation 14:8:

Fallen, fallen is Babylon the great, she who made all nations drink the wine of her impure passion.

Revelation 14:9-11:

If anyone worships the beast and its image, and receives a mark on his forehead or on his hand, He also shall drink the wine of God's wrath, poured unmixed into the cup of his anger, and he shall be tormented with fire and sulphur in the presence of the holy angels, and in the presence of the Lamb.

And the smoke of their torment goes up for ever and ever; and they have no rest, day or night, these worshipers of the beast and its image, and whoever receives the mark of its name.

Revelation 15:3-4:

Great and wonderful are thy deeds, O Lord God the Almighty! Just and true are thy ways, O King of the ages!

Who shall not fear and glorify thy name, O Lord? For thou alone art holy. All nations shall come and worship thee, for thy judgments have been revealed.

Revelation 16:5–6:

Just art thou in these thy judgments, thou who art and wast, O Holy One. For men have shed the blood of saints and prophets, and thou hast given them blood to drink. It is their due!

Revelation 16:7:

Yea, Lord God the Almighty, true and just are thy judgments!

Revelation 19:2:

Hallelujah! Salvation and glory and power belong to our God, for his judgments are true and just; he has judged the great harlot who corrupted the earth with her fornication, and he has avenged on her the blood of his servants.

Revelation 19:3:

Hallelujah! The smoke from her goes up for ever and ever.

Revelation 19:6–9:

Hallelujah! For the Lord our God the Almighty reigns.

Let us rejoice and exult and give him the glory, for the marriage of the Lamb has come, and his bride has made herself ready;

It was granted her to be clothed with fine linen, bright and pure.

Revelation 21:3–4:

Behold, the dwelling of God is with men. He will dwell with them, and they shall be his people, and God himself will be with them; he will wipe away every tear from their eyes, and death shall be no more, neither shall there be mourning nor crying nor pain any more, for the former things have passed away.

Appendix D
References to Music

Musical Reference	Passage in the text of the book of Revelation
"a loud voice like a trumpet"	1:10
"saying (say, said)"	1:22, 27; 5:9, 12, 13, 14; 6:1, 3, 5, 7; 7:3, 12, 13, 14; 9:13; 10:4, 8; 11:15, 17; 12:10; 13:4; 14:8, 13; 16:4, 17; 17:1, 7, 15; 18:10, 21; 19:4, 9; 21:3, 5, 6, 9; 22:6, 9, 10, 17, 20
"voice like the sound of many waters"	1:15; 14:2; 19:6
"if any one has an ear, let him hear"	3:22; 13:9
"First voice, speaking to me like a trumpet, said"	4:1
"twenty-four elders"	4:4,10; 5:8; 11:16; 19:4
"voices"	4:5; 6:6
"sing(ing)"	4:8, 10
"proclaiming with a loud voice"	5:2
"harp"	5:8
"sang (sing) a new song"	5:9; 14:3
"I heard...voice of many angels numbering myriads and myriads and thousands and thousands...saying with a loud voice"	5:11–12
"cried (crying) out with a loud voice:"	6:10; 7:10; 8:13; 10:3; 18:18, 19
"calling"	6:16
"called with a loud voice:"	7:2
"silence"	8:1

"seven trumpets"	8:2, 6
"seven trumpets and ready to blow them:"	8:6
"blew the trumpet"	8:7, 8, 10, 12; 9:1, 13; 11:15
"trumpets"	8:7, 8, 10, 12; 9:1, 13, 14; 11:15
"blasts of the other trumpets"	3:13
"called out with a loud voice, like a lion roaring"	10:3
"when he called out, the seven thunders sounded"	10:3, 4
"trumpet call to be sounded:"	10:7
"heard a loud voice from (in) heaven"	10:8; 11:12, 15; 12:10; 14:13; 16:1; 18:4
"like the sound of loud thunder:"	14:22
"sound of harpers playing on their harps:"	14:2
"no one could learn the song"	14:3
"said (saying) with a loud voice"	14:7, 9
"calling (called) with a loud voice"	14:15, 18
"sing the Song of Moses"	15:3
"heard a loud voice from the temple"	16:1, 17
"cried (crying)"	16:7; 19:3, 6
"called out with a mighty voice"	18:1
"weeping and mourning aloud"	18:15
"cried (crying) out"	18:18, 19; 19:5
"mighty voice of a great multitude in heaven crying"	19:1, 5, 6
"like the sound of mighty thunderpeals"	19:6
"with a loud voice he called"	19:17
"heard a great voice from the throne"	21:3

Appendix E
Old Testament Pseudepigrapha

IN ORDER TO USE the Old Testament pseudepigraphy to provide a picture of the early church, Charlesworth poses the question: "How can I [we] be certain that the Pseudepigrapha is earlier than the New Testament [era]?" Although the answer is "fraught with imprecision," he categorizes the literature in the following manner:[1]

1. Pseudepigrapha too late for early church research includes the following:

- Three Enoch;
- Apocalypse of Ezra;
- Apocalypse of Sedrach;
- Apocalypse of Daniel;
- Testament of Isaac;
- Testament of Jacob;
- Testament of Solomon;
- Testament of Adam;
- History of Joseph;
- Syriac Menander; and
- Slavic pseudepigrapha (Old Testament Pseudepigrapha preserved only in Slavic).

2. Charlesworth further indicates that one must not use Christian redactions that predate C.E. 150 because they cannot adequately convey the

---

1. Charlesworth, *Old Testament Pseudepigrapha*, 31–43.

intellectual mind and world of early Judaism or the early church. These documents include the following:

- Testament of Twelve Patriarchs;
- History of the Rechabites;
- Martyrdom and Ascension of Isaiah;
- Hellenistic Synagogal Prayers; and
- Four Ezra (also known as 5 and 6 Ezra) to the Sibylline Oracles.

3. Old Testament pseudepigrapha suitable for early church research includes the following:

APOCALYPTIC LITERATURE AND RELATED WORKS

Jewish and Pre-Christian	Probably Jewish and Pre-Christian	Composed from earlier Jewish Tradition and in decades following temple destruction in CE 70.
1 Enoch	Apocrypha of Ezekial	4 Ezra
The Jewish Sibyllines	Apocalypse of Zephaniah	2 Baruch
The Treaty of Shem		3 Baruch

Testaments

Jewish and Pre-Christian
Testament of Twelve Patriarchs
Testament of Job
Testament of Moses

Expansions of the Old Testament

Probably Jewish and Pre-Christian	Jewish and basically contemporaneous with New Testament writings
Letter of Aristears	Joseph and Asenath
Jubilees	Pseudo-Philo

Martyrdom of Isaiah	4 Baruch
Life of Adam and Eve	Jannes and Jambres
Lives of the Prophets	

Wisdom and Philosophical Literature

Pre-Christian	Basically contemporaneous with New Testament writings
Ahigar	Pseudo-Phocylides
3 Maccabees	4 Maccabees

Prayers, Psalms, and Odes

Jewish and pre-Christian	Basically contemporaneous with New Testament writings
Five More Psalms of David	Hellenistic Synagogal Prayers
Prayer of Manasseh	Prayer of Joseph
Psalms of Solomon	Prayer of Jacob
	Odes of Solomon

The Supplement

- Philo the Epic Poet
- Theodotus
- Ezekiel the Tragedian
- Fragments of Pseudo-Greek Poets
- Aristobulus
- Demetrius the Chronographer
- Aristeas the Exegete

Appendix F
Music According to Use as Revelation or Response

PERFORMANCE PRACTICE —TYPE OF SOUND MADE

	Revelation	Response
Vocal		
voice	1:12	
voice of a sound of many waters	1:15; 14:2	19:6
great loud voice of an angel	5:2; 7:2; 10:3; 14:9,15, 19; 17:7; 19:17	
great loud voice of angels, four living creatures, and twenty-four elders		5:11
voice in the midst	6:6	
great loud voice of martyrs	6:10	
great loud voice of all creation		7:10
great loud voice out of heaven	9:13; 10:4, 7, 8; 11:2, 15; 12:10; 14:13; 18:4	
great loud voice as a lion roars	10:3	
great loud voice out of the shrine	16:1	
great loud voice from the throne	16:17; 19:5; 21:3	

MUSIC ACCORDING TO USE AS REVELATION OR RESPONSE

great loud voice of a crowd in heaven		19:1
non-vocal (including instrumental)		
great loud voice as a trumpet	1:10–11	
voice as of a trumpet	4:1	
out of the throne came forth lightnings and voiced and thunders	4:5	
sounds as of harpers		5:8; 15:2
great loud voice of an eagle	8:13	
sound of thunders	14:2	19:6

PERFORMANCE PRACTICE — MANNER SOUND IS PRODUCED

	Revelation	Response
Vocal		
say (λέγω [lego])	1:11, 17; 4:1; 5:5, 9, 11, 13; 6:6; 7:2; 9:14; 10:4, 8; 11:12, 15; 12:10; 14:7, 8, 9, 13, 18; 16:1, 5, 17; 18:4; 19:5, 17; 21:3	4:8, 10; 5:14; 6:1, 3, 5, 7, 10; 7:10, 12; 11:16; 15:3; 19:1, 4, 6
sing (αδω [ado])		5:9; 14:3; 15:3
proclaim (καρυσσο [karusso])	5:2	
cry (εκραζό [ekrazo])	7:2; 10:3; 14:14; 18:2; 19:17	
spoke (ελαλεό [elaleo]) or uttered	10:3, 4	
rejoice (χαιρόυσεο [chairouseo])... and are glad (ευθραινεο [euthaineo])		11:10
responsorial		5:9–14; 11:15–18; 16:4–7; 19:5–8

antiphonal		4:8–11; 5:9–14; 7:9–17; 19:1–4
non-vocal (including instrumental)		
having harps		5:8; 15:2
... in order that they might trumpet (σάλπιζο [salpizo])	8:1, 6	
trumpeted	8:3, 7, 8, 10, 12; 9:1, 13; 11:15	
being about to trumpet	8:13; 10:7	

POSTURES OF PERFORMANCE

	Revelation	Response
sitting		4:4; 11:16
before the throne		4:6; 5:11; 14:3
fall before		4:10; 5:8, 14; 11:16; 19:4
standing		5:6

Appendix G
References to Music—Greek to English

Reference	Passage (Greek to English transliteration with translation)[1]
1:10	Σάλπιγγος salpiggos (of a trumpet)
1:11	λεγούσης legousas (saying)
1:12	ψωνήν phonan (voice)
1:15	ψωνή αὐτοῦ ὡς ψωνή ὑδάτων πολλῶν phona autou os phona udaton pollon (voice of him as a sound waters of many)
1:17	λέγων legon (saying)
3:9	προσχυνήσουσιν ἐνώπιον τῶν ποδῶν σου proskunasousin enopion ton podon sou (they shall worship before the feet of thee)
4:1	ψωνή ἡ πρώτή ἥν ἥκουσα ὡς σάλπιγγος... λέγων phona a prota an akousa os salpiggos... legon (voice first which I heard as of a trumpet... saying)

1. Marshall, *Inter-Linear Greek-English New Testament*; Aland, *Greek New Testament*. When discrepancies occurred between Marshall and Aland, deference was given to Aland.

APPENDIX G

4:4, 10; 5:6, 8, 11, 14; 11:16; 14:3	εἴκοσι τέσσαρες πρεοβυτέρους eikosi tessaras presbuterous (twenty-four elders)
4:5	ψωναί καὶ βρονταί phonai kai brontai (voices or sounds and thunders)
4:6, 8; 5:6, 8, 11, 14; 6:6; 14:3; 15:7	τέσσαρα ζῷα tessera zoa (four living creatures)
4:8	λέγοντες legontes ([four living creatures] saying)
4:10	πεσοῦνται καὶ προοκυνήσουσιν ... λέγοντες pesountai kai proskunasousin ... legontes (will fall [the twenty-four elders] and they will worship ... saying)
5:2; 16:1	κηρύσσοντα ἐν ψωνῇ μεγάλῃ karussonta en phona megala ([an angel] proclaiming in voice a great loud)
5:5	καὶ εἷς ἐκ τῶν πρεσβυτέρων λέγει μοι kai eis ek ton presbuteron legei moi (and one of the elders says to me)
5:8	([four living creatures and twenty-four elders]) ἔπεσαν ἔχοντες ... εκαστος κιθάραν epesan echontes ... ekastos kitharo fell having ... each one a harp)
5:9	καὶ ᾄδουσιν ᾠδὴν καινὴν λέγοντες kai adousin odan kainan legontes (and they sing song a new saying)
5:11	καὶ ἤκουσα ψωνὴν ἀγγέλων ... kai akousa phonan aggelon ... (and I heard a sound angels [and four living creatures and twenty-four elders] καὶ ἦν ὁ ἀριμμὸς αὐτῶν μυριάδες μυριάδων καὶ χιλιάδες kai an o arimos auton muriades murisdan kai chiliades and was the number of them myriads of myriads and thousands)
5:12	χιλιάδων λέγοντες ψωνῇ μεδάλῇ chilisdon legontes phona megala (of thousands saying voice with a great loud)

REFERENCES TO MUSIC—GREEK TO ENGLISH 177

5:13	καί πᾶν κτίσμα ὅ ἐν τῷ οὐρανῷ καί ἐπί τῆς γῆς kai pan ktisma o en to ourano kai epi tas gas (and every creature which heaven and on the earth καί ὑποκάτω τῆς γῆς καί ἐπί τῆς θαλάσσης ... λέγοντας kai upokato tas gas kai epi tas thalassas ... legontas and underneath the earth and on the sea ... saying)
5:14	ἔπεσαν καί προσκυνήσαν epesan kai proskunasan ([four living creatures and twenty-four elders] fell and worshipped)
6:1	λέγοντος ὡς ψωυή βροντῆς legontos os phona brontas ([four living creatures] saying as with a sound of thunder)
6:3	ἤκουσα τοῦ δευτέρου ζῴου λέγοντος akousa tou deuterou zoou legontos (I heard the second living creature saying)
6:5	ἤκουσα τοῦ τρίτου ζῴου λέγοντος akousa tou tritou zoou legontos (I heard the third living creature saying)
6:6	καί ἤκουσα ὡς ψωνήν ἐν μέσω τῶν τεσσάρων ζῴων λέγουσαν kai akousa os phonan en meso ton tessaron zoon legousan (and I heard as a voice in the midst of the four living creatures saying)
6:7	ἤκουσα ... τοῦ τετάρτου ζῴου λέγοντος akousa ... tou tetartou zoou legontos (I heard ... the fourth living creature saying)
6:10	καί εκραζαν ψωνῇ μεγάλῃ λέγοντος kai ekrazen phona megala legontes (and they cried voice with a great loud saying)
6:15	καί οἱ βασιλεῖς τῆς γῆς καί οἱ μεγιστᾶνες καί οἱ χιλίαρχοι kai oi basaleis tas gas kai oi megistanes kai oi chiliarchoi (and the kings of the earth and the great men and the chiliarchs καί οἱ πλούσιοι καί οἱ ἰσχουροί καί πᾶς δοῦλος καί ελεύθερος kai oi plousioi kai oi ischuroi kai pas doulos kai eleutheros and the rich men and the tasstrong men and every slave and free man)
7:2	καί ἔκραζεν ψωνῇ μεγάλῃ τοῖς τέσσαροιν kai ekrazen [allou aggelon] phona megala tois tessarsin (and he cried [another angel] voice with a great loud to the four ἀγγέλοις ... λέγων aggelois ... legon angels ... saying)
7:10	καί κράζουσιν ψωνῇ μεγάλῃ λέγοντες kai krazousin phona megala legontes (and they cry voice with a great loud saying)

7:11, 12	εἰστήκεισαν ... καί ζῷαν ἔπεσαν eistakeisan ... kai zoan epesan ... ([and angels] stood ... and living creatures fell ... καί προσεκύνήσαν ... λέγοντες kai prosekunasan ... legontes and worshipped ... saying)
8:2, 6	ἑπτά ἀγγέλους ... ἐδόθησαν αὐτοῖς ἑπτά σάλπιγγες epta aggelous ... edothasan autois epta salpigges (seven angels ... there were given to them seven trumpets)
8:6	ἡτοίμεσαν αυτους ἵνα atoimasan autous ina ([seven angels with seven trumpets] prepared themselves in order that σάλπισωσιν salpisosin they might trumpet)
8:7	καί ὁ πρῶτος ἐσάλπισεν kai protos esalpisen (and the first trumpeted)
8:8	καί ὁ δεύτερος ἄγγελος ἐσάλπισεν kai o deuteros aggelos esalpisen (and the second angel trumpeted)
8:10	καί ὁ τρίτος ἄγγελος ἐσάλπισεν kai o tritos aggelos esalpisen (and the third angel trumpeted)
8:12	καί ὁ τέταρτος ἄγγελος ἐσάλπισεν kai o tetartos aggelos esalpisen (and the fourth angel trumpeted)
8:13	σάλπιγγος των τριων ἀγγελων των μελλόντων σαλπίζειν salpiggos ton trion aggelon ton mellonton salpizein (trumpet of the three angels being about to trumpet)
9:1	καί ὁ πέμπτος ἄγγελος ἐσάλπισεν kai o pemptos aggelos esalpisen (and the fifth angel trumpeted)
9:13	καί ὁ ἕκτος ἄγγελος ἐσάλπισεν καί ἤκουσα ψωνήν μίαν ἐκ kai o ektos aggelos esalpisen kai akousa phonan mian ek (and the sixth angel trumpeted) (and I heard voice one out of των τεσσάρων κεράτων τοῦ θυσιαστηρίου τοῦ χρυσοῦ τοῦ ἐνώτιον τοῦ Θεοῦ ton tessaron keraton tou thusiastariou tou chrusou tou enotion tou Theou the four horns of the altar golden before God)
9:14	λέγοντα τῷ ἕκτῳ ἀγγέλῳ ὁ ἔχων τόν σάλπιγγα legonta to ekto aggelo o echon ton salpigga (saying to the sixth angel having the trumpet)

REFERENCES TO MUSIC—GREEK TO ENGLISH

10:3	καὶ ἔκραζεν φωνῇ μεγάλῃ　　ὥσπερ λέων μυκᾶται καὶ ὅτε ἔκραζεν kai ekrazen phona megala　　osper leon mukatai kai ote ekrazen (and cried　voice with a great loud as　a lion roars　and when he cried ἐλάλησαν　αἱ ἑπτὰ βρονταὶ τὰς ἑαυτῶν　φωνάς elalasan　ai epta brontai tas eauton　phonas spoke or uttered the seven thunders the of themselves voices)
10:4	καὶ ἤκουσα φωνὴν ἐκ τοῦ οὐρανοῦ λέγουσαν kai akousa phonan ek tou ouranou legousan (and I heard a voice out of heaven saying)
10:7	φωνῆς τοῦ ἑβδόμου ἀγγέλου ὅταν　μέλλῃ　σαλπίζειν phonas tou　ebdomou aggelou, otan　mella　salpizein (voice of the seventh　angel,　whenever he is about to trumpet)
10:8	καὶ ἡ φωνὴ ἣν　ἤκουσα ἐκ τοῦ οὐρανοῦ... λέγουσαν kai a phona an　akousa ek tou ouranou... legousan (and the voice which I heard out of heaven... saying)
11:10	καὶ οἱ κατοικοῦντες ἐπὶ τῆς γῆς　χαίρουσιν ἐπ᾽ αὐτοῖς kai oi katoikountes epi tas gas chairousin ep　autois (and the ones dwelling on the earth rejoice　over them)
11:12	καὶ ἤκουσαν φωνῆς μεγάλης　ἐκ τοῦ οὐρανου λεγούσης αὐτοῖς kai akousan phonas megalas　ek tou ouranou legousas autois (and they heard voice　a great loud out of heaven　saying　to them)
11:15	καὶ ὁ ἕβδομος ἄγγελος ἐσάλπισεν καὶ ἐγένοντο φωναὶ μεγάλαι ἐν τῷ kai o ebdomos aggelos esalpisen kai egenonto phonai megalai en to (and the seventh　angel　trumpeted and there were voices great loud in οὐρανῷ λέγοντες ourano, legontes heaven, saying)
11:16, 17	προσεκύνησαν τῷ Θεῷ　λέγοντες prosekunasan to Theo, legoutes (twenty-four elders worshipped　God, saying)
12:10	καὶ ἤκουσα φωνὴν μεγάλης　ἐν τῷ οὐρανῷ λέγοντες kai akousa phonan megalan　en to ourano legousan (and I heard voice　a great loud in　heaven saying)

14:2	καὶ ἤκουσα ψωνὴν ἐκ τοῦ οὐρανοῦ ὡς ψωνὴν ὑδάτων πολλῶν καὶ ὡς ψωνὴν kai akousa phonan ek tou ouranou o phonan udaton pollon kai os phonan (and I heard a sound out of heaven as a sound waters of many and as a sound βροτῆς μεγάλης καὶ ἡ ψωνὴ ἣν ἤκουσα brontas megalas kai a phona an akousa thunder of great loud and the sounds which I heard was ὡς κιθαρῳδῶν κιθαριζόντων ἐν ταῖς κιθάραις αὐτῶν os kitharozon kitharizonton en tais kitharais auton as of harpers harping with the harps of them)
14:3	καὶ ᾄδουσιν ᾠδὴν καινήν... καὶ οὐδεὶς ἐδύνατο μαθεῖν τῆς ᾠδὴν kai adousin odan kaivan... kai oudeis edunato mathein tan odan (and they sing song a new... and no man could to learn the song μὴ αἱ ἑκατὸν τεσσεπάκοντα τέσσαπες χιλιάδες ma ai ekaton tesserakonta tessares chiliades except the hundred and forty-four thousands)
14:7	λέγων ἐν ψωνῇ μεγάλῃ legon en phona megala ([another angel] saying in voice a great loud)
14:8	ἠκολούθησεν λέυων akolouthasen legon ([and a second angel] followed saying)
14:9	ἠκολούθησεν λέγων ἐν ψωνῇ μεγάλῃ akolouthasen legon en phona megala ([and a third angel] followed saying in voice a great loud)
14:13	καὶ ἤκουσα ψωνῆς ἐκ τοῦ οὐρανοῦ λέγοντες kai akousa phonas ek tou ouravou legousas (and I heard a voice out of heaven saying)
14:15	κράζων ἐν ψωνῇ μεγάλῃ krazon en phona megala ([another angel] crying in a voice a great loud)
14:18	ἐψώνησεν ψωνῇ μεγαλῃ... λέγων ephonasen phona megala... legon ([another angel] he spoke voice in a great loud... saying)
15:3	καὶ ᾄδουσιν τῆς ᾠδὴν Μωϋσέως τοῦ δούλου τοῦ Θεοῦ kai adousin tas odan Mouseos tou doulou tou Theou (And they sing the Song of Moses the slave of God καὶ τὴν ᾠδὴν τοῦ ἀρνίου λέγοντες kai tan odan tou arniou, legontes and the song of the lamb, saying)

16:5	καί ἤκουσα τοῦ ἀγγέλου των ὑδάτων λέγοντες... καί ἤκουσα τοῦ kai akousa tou aggelou ton udaton legontes... kai akousa tou (and I heard the angel of the waters saying... and I heard the θυσιαστηρίου λέγοντες thusiastariou legontes altar saying)
16:17	καί ἐζῆδθεν ψωνή μεγάλή ἐκ τοῦ ναοῦ ἀπό τοῦ τρόνου λέγουσα kai ezalthen phona megala ek tou naou apo tou thronou legousa (And came out a voice a great loud out of the shrine from the throne saying)
18:2	καί ἔκραζεν ἐν ἰσζυρᾶ ψωνῇ λέγων kai ekrazen en ischura phona legon (and he cried in a strong voice saying)
18:4	καί ἤκουσα ἄλλήν ψωνήν ἐκ τοῦ οὐρανοῦ λέγουσαν kai akousa allan phonan ek tou ouranou legousan (and I heard another voice out of heaven saying)
18:22	καί ψωνή κιθαρωδῶν καί μουσικων καί αὐλήτων καί σάλπιστων kai phona kitharodon kai mousikon kai aulaton kai salpiston (and sound of harpers and of musicians and of flutists and of trumpeters)
19:1	ἤκουσα ὡς ψωνήν μεγάλήν ὄκλου πολλοῦ ἐν τῷ οὐρανῷ λεγόντων akousa os phonan melalan ochlou pollou en to ourano legonton (I heard as voice a great loud crowd) (of a much in heaven saying)
19:4	([and twenty-four elders and four living creatures] προσεκύνσαν Θεῷ... λέγοντες prosekunasan to Theo... legontes worshipped God... saying)
19:5	καί ψωνή ἀπό τοῦ θρόνου ἐζῆλθεν λέγουσα kai phona apo tou thronou ezalthen legousa (and a voice from the throne came out saying)
19:6	καί ἤκουσα ὡς ψωνήν ὄκλου πολλοῦ καί ὡς ψωνήν ὑδάτων πολλῶν καί ὡς kai akousa os phonan ochlou pollou kai os phonan udaton pollon kai os (and I heard as a sound crowd of a much and as a sound waters of many and as ψωνήν βροντῶν ἰσχυρῶν λεγόντων phonan bronton ischuron legonton a sound thunders of strong loud saying)
19:17	καί ἔκραζεν ἐν ψωνῇ μεγάλη λέγων kai ekrazen en phona megala legon (and he cried out in voice a great loud saying)
21:3	καί ἤκουσα ψωνῆς μεγάλής ἐκ τοῦ ορόνου λεγούσας kai akousa phonas megalas ek tou oronou legousas (and I heard voice a great loud out of throne saying)

Appendix H

Defining Christian worship in a single sentence is difficult to do, but many authors have attempted to do so through the years. Below are some of the more significant definitions for worship written primarily in the twentieth century. Some authors have not defined worship briefly; in some instances, extended definitions have been summarized, hopefully without losing substance.

> Worship, in all its grades and kinds, is the response of the creature to the Eternal: nor need we limit this definition to the human sphere. There is a sense in which we may think of the whole life of the Universe, seen and unseen, conscious and unconscious, as an act of worship, glorifying its Origin, Sustainer, and End.
>
> Underhill, *Worship*, 3.

> Worship is essentially, as well as etymologically, the recognition of God's worth. It has no direct reference to the edification of the worshipers. It is an offering to God, acceptable to Him and incumbent on man.
>
> Micklem, *Christian Worship*, 19.

> Worship must be in one sense a purposeless act, if it is to be true worship. An action has a purpose if it is done for the sake of something else, but worship is for its own sake, or for the sake of God. That is the same thing, because any activity is doing the will of God when it is truly itself. So there is a sense in which Christian worship. . . has a meaning but no purpose; purpose means acting for a further result. Worship is the gathering up of all activities before God. In that sense it is purposeless. If we try to give it a moral or social purpose, we are destroying its nature. . . In worship we have this mode of valuing a thing for its own sake.

V. A. Demant, "The Social Implications of Worship," 107–8.

To worship is:
To quicken the conscience by the holiness of God;
To feed the mind with the truth of God;
To purge the imagination by the beauty of God;
To open the heart to the love of God;
To devote the will to the purpose of God.
Temple, *The Hope of a New World*, 30.

Worship is man's response to the nature and action of God.
Kay, *The Nature of Christian Worship*, 7.

In Christianity, the Spirit is the future which in virtue of the past actualizes itself in the present. This time-character of the Holy Spirit, connecting him with the history of salvation, manifests itself in the very essence of the Christian service, where it is no myth that is represented, but the historical facts of past time and the facts of the last days still in the future.
Cullman, *Early Christian Worship*, 36.

Worship is dramatic action. The principal actors in the drama of corporate worship are the people of the congregation who are aided and equipped for their role by the leaders of worship—the prompters from the wings. The drama, often scripted, has a structure and sequence based upon the nature of God's dialogical encounter with his people.
Kierkegaard, *Purity of Heart*, 177–84.

It is only possible to enter into fellowship with God on the basis of God's initiative, that is, through revelation. Worship is only possible again since God has made himself known in Jesus Christ. The way to true worship is only brought about through a radical transformation and that God alone makes possible in Jesus Christ.
Delling, *Worship in the New Testament*, 1.

The fellowship of Christian worship is not based upon the passing unities of race or community, but upon God's purpose to "sum up all things in Jesus Christ." It is the fellowship of humanity redeemed in Christ and awaiting the fulfillment of that redemption, and therefore constantly submitted to the judgment and renewal of divine revelation in the present.
Garrett, *Christian Worship*, 10.

Worship is a noble word. The term comes into our modern speech from the Anglo-Saxon "weorthscipe." This later developed into "worthship," and then into "worship." It means, "to attribute worth" to an object. To worship God is to ascribe to Him supreme worth, for He alone is worthy.

Martin, *Worship in the Early Church*, 10.

Worship is the acknowledgment of God's supreme excellence and the expression of man's submission to His absolute dominion resulting therefrom.

French, *Theology of the Liturgy*, 12.

Worship is an end in itself; it is not a means to something else. Karl Barth has appropriately declared that the "church's worship is the *Opus Dei*, the work of God, which is carried out for its own sake." We worship God purely for the sake of worshipping God.

Segler, *Christian Worship*, 4.

I assume from the outset that nothing should be done or sung or said in church which does not aim directly or indirectly either at glorifying God or edifying the people or both. Whenever we edify, we glorify, but when we glorify we do not always edify.

Lewis, *Christian Reflections*, 94.

Worship is the propitious moment of encounter between God and his people. Worship is the peculiar or special occasion of the presence of the Lord in his church.

Pacquier, *Dynamics of Worship*, 18.

Worship is drama. . . Ideally, then, worship needs to harmonize the elements of remoteness and nearness, the ideas of the family and of the symbolic people of God. . . But what is always true is that to lose sight of the dramatic factor in worship is to lose altogether the key to making worship practical as well as beautiful.

Routley, *Worship, Music, and the Church*, 129, 136.

. . . Christian worship is God's revelation of Himself in Jesus Christ and man's response.

Hoon, *The Integrity of Worship*, 77.

. . . The purpose of the church and worship is to relate men to Christ and to relate men in Christ to one another.

Wohlgemuth, *Rethinking Church Music*, 66.

The Christian community assembles for worship on the basis of God's eschatological saving act in Christ which demonstrates its present power in the operation of the Holy Spirit.
      Hahn, *The Worship of the Early Church*, 105.

Worship is a creative encounter of man with God, a living and vital relationship which depends upon the active and unceasing quest of man in response to the call of God.
      Lovelace and Rice, *Music and Worship in the Church*, 18.

Because it is God who always takes the initiative, Christian worship is best discussed in the terms of response. In worship man is responding to God and this is true of the whole of the liturgy, whether it be praise, thanksgiving, supplication, or repentance, whether it be Eucharist or baptism, or liturgical prayer or the celebration of the Church's year. If this is so, worship must be seen in the context of saving history, which is the record of the divine initiative.
      Crichton, "A Theology of Worship," 7.

Christian worship is our affirmative response to the self-revelation of the triune God.
      Hustad, *Jubilate II!*, 64.

Worship is the dramatic celebration of God in his supreme worth in such a manner that his "worthiness" becomes the norm and inspiration of human beings.
      Martin, *The Worship of God*, 4.

Worship is an active response to God whereby we declare His worth. Worship is not passive, but is participative. Worship is not simply a mood; it is a response. Worship is not just a feeling; it is a declaration.
      Allen and Borror, *Worship*, 16.

Worship is the celebrative response to what God has done, is doing, and promises to do.
      Burkhart, *Worship*, 17.

... Worship is a combination of head, hand, heart, and imagination [which] is to say its practice should involve more than hearing, speaking and seeing. God is concerned with the whole person, and it is appropriate to respond with one's whole being.
      Bailey, "From Theory to Practice," 40.

Corporate worship is effective only when each worshiper feels his responsibility for preparation and involvement, and all the worshipers focus on their honor of and submission to the Living God.

        Bailey, "A Biblical Theology of Worship," 15.

Worship in the New Testament was an act of celebration; therefore, the music of the early church was the music of celebration.

        Mapson, *The Ministry of Music in the Black Church*, 3.

Worship is something Christians do communally to praise God.

        Saliers, "The Nature of Worship," 41.

Worship is the believer's response of all that he is—mind, emotion, will, and body—to all that God is and says and does. This response has its mystical side in subjective experience, and its practical side in objective obedience to God's revealed truth. It is a loving response that is balanced by the fear of the Lord, and it is a deepening response as the believer comes to know God better.

        Wiersbe, *Real Worship*, 27.

... A service of worship is a two-way conversation between God and his people with a given pattern and sequence...

        Eskew and McElrath, *Sing With Understanding*, 221.

Worship is the lasting metaphor for the true and perfect, and hence transformed, relationship between creature and Creator.

        Newman, *Worship*, 34.

Christian worship is an individual's, family's, and/or a gathered community's response, via the Holy Spirit, to God's revelation of himself in Jesus Christ.

        Thomas Allen Seel.

Bibliography

Abba, R. *Principles of Christian Worship.* New York: Oxford University, 1957.
Adey, Lionel. *Hymns and the Christian "Myth."* Vancouver: University of British Columbia, 1986.
———. *Class and Idol in the English Hymn.* Vancouver: University of British Columbia, 1986.
Aland, Kurt, et al., eds. *The Greek New Testament.* Stuttgart: United Bible Societies, 1983.
Alfonso, Barry. *The Billboard Guide to Contemporary Christian Music.* New York, Billboard, 2002.
Allen, Ronald, and Gordon Borror. *Worship: Rediscovering the Missing Jewel.* Portland, OR: Multnomah Press, 1982.
Allmen, Jean J. von. *Worship: Its Theology and Practice.* New York: Oxford University Press, 1965.
Altenburg, Johann Ernst. *Essay on an Introduction to the Heroic and Musical Trumpeters' and Kettledrummers' Art.* Translated by Edward H. Tarr. Nashville: The Brass, 1974.
Anderson, Warren D. *Ethos and Education in Greek Music.* Cambridge, MA: Harvard University Press, 1966.
Anderson, Ray, ed. *Theological Foundations for Ministry.* Edinburgh: T. & T. Clark, 1979.
Appleby, David P. *History of Church Music.* Chicago: Moody, 1965.
Arndt, William F., and F. Wilbur Gingrich. *A Greek-English Lexicon of the New Testament and Other Early Christian Literature.* Edited by Walter Bauer. Chicago: University of Chicago Press, 1958.
Arndt, David P., and F. Wilbur Gingrich. "Πρός." In *GELNT* 716.
Arnold, Denis, ed. *The New Oxford Companion to Music.* New York: Oxford University Press, 1984.
Augustine. *Enarrationes in Psalmis (Psalm 72:1).* Quoted in Trench, R.C. *Synonyms of the New Testament* (Grand Rapids: William B. Eerdmans, 1958).
Aylen, Leo. *The Greek Theatre.* London: Associated University Press, 1985.
Bailey, Raymond. "Four Manners of Praying." Unpublished class notes. The Southern Baptist Theological Seminary, Fall Semester, 1987.
Bailey, Raymond. "From Theory to Practice in Worship." *Review and Expositor* 80, no. 1 (1983) 33–52.

Bailey, Robert W. "A Biblical Theology of Worship." In *Music in the Worship Experience*. Nashville: Convention, 1984.

Baines, Anthony. *Brass Instruments: Their History and Development*. London: Faber and Faber, 1976.

Bales, James D. *Instrumental Music and New Testament Worship*. Searcy, AR: James D. Bales, 1973.

Barbour, J. Murray. *Trumpets, Horns and Music*. East Lansing, MI: Michigan State University Press, 1964.

Barker, Andrew. *Greek Musical Writings*. Cambridge, MA: Cambridge University Press, 1987.

Barnhart, C. L., ed. *The American College Dictionary*. New York: Random House, 1964.

Bate, Philip. *The Trumpet and Trombone*. New York: W. W. Norton, 1978.

Bauckham, R. "The Worship of Jesus in Apocalyptic Christianity." *New Testament Studies*, 27 (1981) 322–41.

Baumstark, A. *Liturgie Comparee*. Translated by F. L. Cross. Westminster, MD: Newman, 1958.

Beale, G. K. *We Become What We Worship: A Biblical Theology of Idolatry*. Downers Grove, IL: IVP Academic, 2008.

Beasley-Murray, George R. *The Book of Revelation*. New Century Bible Commentary 35. Grand Rapids: William B. Eerdmans, 1981.

Beckwith, Isbon T. *The Apocalypse of John*. Grand Rapids: Baker, 1979.

Begbie, Jeremy. *Resounding Truth: Christian Wisdom in the World of Music*. Grand Rapids: Baker Academic, 2007.

Benson, Louis F. *The Hymnody of the Christian Church*. New York: George H. Doran, 1927.

Berglund, Robert D. *A Philosophy of Church Music*. Chicago: Moody, 1985.

Berkouwer, G.C. *Man: The Image of God*. Grand Rapids: William B. Eerdmans, 1962.

Bertram, Georg. "ἔθνος." In *TDNT* 2:364–69.

Best, Harold. *Music Through the Eyes of Faith*. New York: HarperOne, 1993.

Betz, Otto. "Ψωνη (*Phone*)." In *TDNT* 9:278–301.

Blevins, James L. "The Genre of Revelation." *Review and Expositor* 77 (1980) 393–408.

———. *Revelation as Drama*. Nashville: Broadman, 1984.

———. *Revelation*. Atlanta: John Knox, 1984.

Borchert, Gerald L. *Worship in the New Testament: Divine Mystery and Human Response*. St. Louis, MO: Chalice, 2008.

Boswell, Matt. *Doxology & Theology: How the Gospel forms the Worship Leader*. Nashville: B&H, 2013.

Bowman, John Wick. *The First Christian Drama*. Philadelphia: Westminster, 1955.

Brockett, Oscar G. *History of the Theatre*. Boston: Allyn and Bacon, 1968.

Brooks, Steven D. *Worship Quest: An Exploration of Worship Leadership*. Eugene, OR: Wipf & Stock, 2015.

Brueggermann, Walter. *The Message of the Psalms: A Theological Commentary*. Minneapolis: Augsburg Old Testament Studies, 1984.

———. *Abiding Astonishment: Psalms, Modernity & the Making of History*. Westminster, VA: John Knox, 1991.

Buecher, Karl. *Arbeit und Rhythmus*. Leipzig: B. G. Teubner, 1909.

Bukofzer, Manfred F. *Studies in Medieval and Renaissance Music*. New York: W. W. Norton, 1950.

Burkhart, John E. *Worship: A Searching Examination of the Liturgical Experience.* Philadelphia: Westminster, 1982.

Buttrick, George A. *The Interpreter's Dictionary of the Bible.* Nashville: Abingdon, 1962.

Carnegie, David R. "Worthy is the Lamb: The Hymns in Revelation." In *Christ the Lord: Studies in Christology Presented to Donald Guthrie,* edited by Howard Hamlyn Rowdon, 243–56. Downers Grove, IL: Intervarsity, 1982.

Charles, R. H. *Studies in the Apocalypse.* Edinburgh: T.& T. Clark, 1915.

———. *A Critical and Exegetical Commentary on the Revelation of St. John.* Edinburgh: T.& T. Clark, 1920.

Charlesworth, James Hamilton, ed. *The Old Testament Pseudepigrapha and the New Testament.* Garden City, NY: Doubleday, 1983.

———. *The Pseudepigrapha and Modern Research.* Missoula, MO: Scholars Press for Society of Biblical Literature, 1976.

———. "A Prolegomena to a New Study of the Jewish Background of the Hymns and Prayers in the New Testament." *Journal of Jewish Studies* 33, no. 1–2 (1982) 265–85.

Chew, Geoffrey. "Song." In *NGD* 17:510–21.

Church, F. Forrester, and Terrance J. Mulry. *Earliest Christian Hymns.* New York: Macmillan, 1988.

Coleman, Robert E. *Songs of Heaven.* Oki Tappan, NJ: Fleming H. Revell, 1975.

Colunga, Juliette. "The Reformation, The Regulative Principle, and the Modern Church: Examining Calvin's Dedication to Purity in Worship (Part I)." Heidelblog. July 30, 2025.

Connolly, Thomas H. "Responsorial Psalmody." In *NGD* 15:759.

———. "Antiphonal Psalmody." In *NGD* 1:481.

Conybeare, Fred C. *The Armenian Version of the Revelation, Apocalypse of John.* Amsterdam: Philo, 1986.

Crichton, J. D. *Christian Celebration: The Prayer of the Church.* G. Chapman, 1973.

———. "A Theology of Worship." In *The Study of Liturgy,* edited by Cheslyn Jones, et al., 3–30. New York: Oxford University Press, 1978.

Cross, F. L., ed. "Theology." In *The Oxford Dictionary of the Christian Church,* 1363. London: Oxford University Press, 1983.

Cullman, Oscar. *Early Christian Worship.* Philadelphia: Westminster, 1953.

Culpepper, R. Alan. *The Anatomy of the Fourth Gospel: A Study in Literary Design.* Philadelphia: Fortress, 1986.

———. *The Johannine School: An Evaluation of the Johannine-School Hypothesis Based on an Investigation of the Nature of Ancient Schools.* Ann Arbor, MI: University Microfilms International, 1985.

Davies, J. G., ed. *The Westminster Dictionary of Liturgy and Worship.* Philadelphia: Westminster, 1979.

Deane, William John. *Pseudepigrapha: An Account of Certain Apocryphal Sacred Writings of the Jews and Early Christians.* Edinburgh: T.& T. Clarke, 1981.

Delling, Gerhard. *Worship in the New Testament.* Translated by Percy Scott. Philadelphia: Westminster, 1962.

Demant, V. A. "The Social Implications of Worship." In *Worship: Its Social Significance,* edited by P. T. R. Kirk. London: The Centenary Press, 1939.

Douglas, Charles Winfred. *Church Music in History and Practice.* Revised, New York: Charles Scribner's Sons, 1962.

Dölger, Franz Joseph. "Zu den Zeremonien der Messliturgie, II: der Alterkuss." Antiqua Christiana (1930) 26–35.
Durant, William James. *The History of Civilization*. New York: Simon and Schuster, 1954.
Earle, Ralph. *Word Meanings in the New Testament*. Grand Rapids: Baker, 1982.
Epperson, Gordon. *The Musical Symbol: A Study of the Philosophic Theory of Music*. Ames, IA: Iowa State University Press, 1967.
Epstein, I., trans. *The Hebrew-English Edition of the Babylonian Talmud*. London: Scovino, 1960.
Eskew, Harry, and Hugh T. McElrath. *Sing With Understanding*. Nashville: Broadman, 1980.
Ferguson, Donald N. *A History of Musical Thought*. New York: Appleton Century Crafts, 1948.
Fiorenza, Elisabeth S. *Invitation to the Book of Revelation*. Garden City, NJ: Image, 1981.
Fleischhauer, Guenter. "Rome." In *NGD* 16:146–62.
Foerster, Werner. "σέβομαι." In *TDNT* 7:168–96.
Ford, John Massyngberde, ed. *The Anchor Bible: Revelation*. Garden City, NY: Doubleday, 1975.
French, Howard, ed. *Theology of the Liturgy*. Bellarmine College Theological Series 4. South Bend, IN: Fides, 1964.
Friedrich, Gerhard. "Σάλπινχ (*Salpinx*—'Trumpet')." In *TDNT* 7:71–87.
———, ed. *Theological Dictionary of the New Testament*. Grand Rapids: William B. Eerdmans, 1971.
Galpin, Francis William. *The Music of the Sumerians and Their Immediate Successors the Babylonians and Assyrians*. Cambridge: Cambridge University Press, 1967.
Gardiner, Cynthia P. *The Sophoclean Chorus: A Study of Character and Function*. Iowa City, IA: University of Iowa Press, 1987.
Garrett, T. S. *Christian Worship*. London: Oxford University Press, 1963.
Gelineau, J. "Music and Singing in the Liturgy." In *The Study of Liturgy*, 440–54. New York, Oxford University Press, 1992.
Gove, Philip, Babcock, ed. "Music." In *Webster's Third New International Dictionary*, 1490. Springfield, MA: G. and C. Merriam, 1976.
Gray, Herbert A. *Religion in Life*. London: Student Christian Movement, 1947.
Greeven, Heinrich. "Προσκυνέο (*Proskuneo*)." In *TDNT* 6:758–65.
Griffiths, Ann, et al. "Harp." In *NGDMI* 2:131–61.
Grout, Donald Jay and Claude V. Palisca, Jr. *A History of Western Music*. 2nd ed. New York: W. W. Norton, 1988.
Grundman, Walter. "εὔσημος." In *TDNT* 2:770.
Guthrie, Donald. *New Testament Introduction*. Downers Grove, IL: Intervarsity, 1970.
———. *The Relevance of John's Apocalyse*. Grand Rapids: William B. Eerdman's, 1987.
Gwaltney, Robert Eugene. "The Concept of the Throne in Revelation." ThM thesis, The Southern Baptist Theological Seminary, 1986.
Ha-Babti, Nathan. *Medieval Jewish Chroniclers*. Oxford: Oxford University Press, 1887.
Hahn, Ferdinand. *The Worship of the Early Church*. Translated by John Reumann. Philadelphia: Fortress, 1973.
Hall, Manly P. *The Therapeutic Value of Music*. Los Angeles, CA: The Philosophical Research Society, 1955.

Harris, Michael Anthony. "The Literary Function of Hymns in the Apocalypse of John." PhD diss., The Southern Baptist Theological Seminary, 1988.
Hartnoll, Phyllis, ed. *The Oxford Companion to the Theatre*. London: Oxford University Press, 1972.
Hatfield, Daniel Earl. "The Function of the Seven Beatitudes in Revelation." PhD diss., The Southern Baptist Theological Seminary, 1987.
Hawkins, John. *A General History of the Science and Practice of Music*. London: Novello, Ewer, and Co., 1875.
Hayburn, Robert. *Papal Legislation on Sacred Music*. Collegeville, MN: Liturgical, 1979.
Henderson, Isobel. "Ancient Greek Music." In *New Oxford History of Music: Ancient and Oriental Music*, edited by Egon Wellesz, I:336–39. London: Oxford University Press, 1957.
Hengel, Martin. *Judaism and Hellenism: Studies in their Encounter in Palestine During the Early Hellenistic Period*. Translated by J. Bowden. Philadelphia: SCM, 1974.
Hill, Andrew E. *Enter His Courts with Praise! Old Testament Worship for the New Testament Church*. Grand Rapids: Baker, 1993.
Holde, Arthur. *Jews in Music*. New York: Philosophical Library, 1959.
Holladay, Carl R. *Fragments from Hellenistic Jewish Authors*. Chico, CA: Scholars, 1983.
Hoon, Paul W. *The Integrity of Worship*. Nashville: Abingdon, 1971.
Hooper, William Lloyd. *Church Music in Transition*. Nashville: Broad, 1963.
Hopko, Thomas. *All the Fulness of God*. Crestwood, NY: St. Vladimir's Seminary, 1982.
Hughes, Edwin Holt. "Music and Theology." In *Worship in Music*, 35–51. New York: Abingdon, 1929.
Hull, William Edward. "The Background of the New Temple Concept in Early Christianity." ThD diss., The Southern Baptist Theological Seminary, 1959.
Hustad, Donald P. *Jubilate II! Church Music in Worship and Renewal*. Carol Stream, IL: Hope, 1993.
Idelsohn, A. Z. *Jewish Liturgy and Its Development*. New York: Holt, Rinehart, and Winston, 1967.
———. *Jewish Liturgy and Its Development*. New York: Holt, Rinehart and Winston, 1967.
———. *Thesaurus of Hebrew Oriental Melodies*. Ktav, Russia: Ktav Publishing House,1973.
Jack, Chris. "The *Proskuneo* Myth: When a Kiss is not a Kiss." In *In Praise of Worship: An Exploration of Text and Practice*, edited by D. J. Cohens and M. Parsons, 8–9. Eugene, OR: Pickwick, 2010.
Jander, Owen. "Singing." In *NGD* 17:338–46.
Jenkins, Ferrel. *The Old Testament in the Book of Revelation*. Marion, IN: Cogdill Foundation, 1972.
Joerns, Klaus-Peter. *Das Hymnische Evangelium: Untersuchungen zu Aufbau, Funktion und Herkunft der hymnischen Stücke in der Johannesoffenbarung*. Goettingen, Germany: G. Mohn, 1971.
Johansson, Calvin M. *Music and Ministry*. Peabody, MA: Hendrickson, 1986.
———. "Some Theological Considerations Foundational to a Philosophy of Church Music." DMA diss., Southwestern Baptist Theological Seminary, 1974.
Jones, Cheslyn, et al., eds. *The Study of Liturgy*. New York: Oxford University Press, 1992.

Josephus, Flavius. *Antiquities of the Jews*. The Works of Flavius Josephus 2. Translated by William Whiston. Nashville: Broadman, 1974.

Jowett, B., trans. *The Dialogues of Plato*. Oxford: Clarendon, 1953.

Julian, John, et al. *A Dictionary of Hymnology*. Revised, London: Murray, 1908.

Karleen, Paul S. *The Handbook to Bible Study*. New York: Oxford University Press, 1987.

Kauflin, Bob. *True Worshipers: Seeking What Matters to God*. Wheaton: Crossway, 2015.

Kauflin, Bob. *Worship Matters: Leading Others to Encounter the Greatness of God*. Wheaton: Crossway, 2008.

Kay, Alan J. *The Nature of Christian Worship*. London: Epworth, 1953.

Keathley, Raymond Haskins. "The Concept of the Temple in Luke-Acts." ThD diss., The Southern Baptist Theological Seminary, 1971.

Kiddle, Martin. *The Revelation of St. John*. Moffett New Testament Commentary Series 15. New York: Harper and Brothers, 1940.

Kierkegaard, Soren. *Purity of Heart Is to Will One Thing*. Translated by Douglas V. Steere. New York: Harper Brothers, 1938.

Kleinig, John W. *The Lord's Song: The Basis, Function and Significance of Choral Music in Chronicles*. Sheffield: JSOT, 1993.

Kümmel, Werner Georg. *The New Testament: The History of the Investigation of Its Problems*. Nashville: Abingdon, 1972.

Lang, Paul Henry. *Music in Western Civilization*. New York: W. W. Norton, 1941.

Leaver, Robin A., and James H. Litton, eds. *Duty and Delight: Routley Remembered*. Carol Stream, IL: Hope, 1985.

Leaver, Robin A. "The Theological Character of Music in Worship." In *DD* 47–66.

LeClercq, Jean. "Theology and Prayer." *Encounter* 24 (1963) 349–64.

Leeuw, Gerhard van der. *Sacred and Profane Beauty*. Translated by David E. Green. Nashville: Abingdon, 1963.

Lewis, C.S. *Christian Reflections*. Grand Rapids: William B. Eerdmans, 1967.

Liddell, Henry George, and Robert Scott. *A Greek-English Lexicon*. Edited by Sir Henry Stuart Jones. Oxford: Clarendon, 1948.

Lietner, Franz. *Der gottesdienstliche Volkgesang im jtidischen und christlichen Alterum*. Translated by Alfred Sendrey. Freiburg i.B.: Herder, 1906.

Lippman, Edward A. *Musical Thought in Ancient Greece*. New York: Columbia University Press, 1964.

Lombroso, Cesare. *Klinische Beiträge zur Psychiatrie*. Leipzig: Verlag von Otto Wigand, 1869.

Lovelace, Austin C., and William C. Rice. *Music and Worship in the Church*. Nashville: Abingdon, 1976.

MacQuarrie, John. *God-Talk*. New York: Harper and Row, 1967.

Man, Ron. *Let Us Draw Near: Biblical Foundation of Worship*. Eugene: Cascade, 2023.

Mapson, J. Wendell, Jr. *The Ministry of Music in the Black Church*. Valley Forge, PA: Judson, 1984.

Marshall, Alfred, ed. *The Revised Standard Version Interlinear Greek-English New Testament*. Grand Rapids: Zondervan Press, 1958.

Marshall, Alfred. *The Inter-Linear Greek-English New Testament*. London: Samuel Bagster and Sons, 1958.

Martin, Ralph P. *The Worship of God*. Grand Rapids: William B. Eerdmans, 1982.

———. *Worship in the Early Church*. Grand Rapids: William B. Eerdmans, 1964.

Mathiesen, Thomas J., trans. *Aristides Quintilianus: On Music in Three Books*. New Haven, CT: Yale University Press, 1983.
May, Herbert G., and Bruce M. Metzger, eds. *The New Oxford Annotated Bible with the Apocrypha*. New York: Oxford University Press, 1977.
McCann, Clinton J. A. *Theological Introduction to the Book of Psalms: The Psalms as Torah*. Nashville: Abingdon, 1993.
McElrath, Hugh T., and Harry Esken. *Sing With Understanding: An Introduction to Christian Hymnody*. Nashville: Broadman, 1980.
McKinnon, James. "On the Question of Psalmody in the Ancient Synagogue." Early Music History, edited by Iain Fenlon, 6 (1986) 159–91.
———. "The Exclusion of Musical Instruments from the Ancient Synagogue." *Proceedings of the Royal Musical Association* 106 (l979–1980) 77–87.
———. *Music in Early Christian Literature*. Cambridge: Cambridge University Press, 1987.
Meagher, Paul Kevin, ed. "Revelation." In *Encyclopedic Dictionary of Religion*, 3:3498. Washington, D. C.: Corpus, 1979.
Meagher, Paul Kevin, ed. "Systematic Theology." In *Encyclopedic Dictionary of Religion*, 3:3442–43. Washington, D. C.: Corpus, 1979.
Mendenhall, George E. "Biblical Faith and Cultic Function." *The Lutheran Quarterly* 5 (1953) 235–58.
Messenger, Ruth Ellis. "Christian Hymns of the First Three Centuries." *Papers of the Hymn Society of America* 9 (1942).
Micklem, Nathaniel, ed. *Christian Worship: Studies in its History and Meaning*. London: Oxford University Press, 1954.
Miller, Hugh Milton. *An Outline of the History of Music*. New York: Barnes and Noble, 1947.
———. *History of Music*. New York: Barnes and Noble, 1960.
Miller, Patrick D., Jr. *Interpreting the Psalms*. Minneapolis: Augsburg, 1986.
Montefiore, Hugh. *Josephus and the New Testament*. London: A. R. Mowbray, 1962.
Moule, C. F. D. *Worship in the New Testament*. Richmond, VA: John Knox, 1961.
Moulton, James Hope, and George Milligan. *The Vocabulary of the Greek New Testament*. Grand Rapids: William B. Eerdmans, 1982.
———. "καρυσσο." In *VGNT* 343.
———. "λέγω." In *VGNT* 372.
———. "προσκυνέο." In *VGNT* 549.
———. "ψωνή." In *VGNT* 680.
———. "χαιρό." In *VGNT* 682.
Mounce, Robert H. *The Book of Revelation*. Grand Rapids: William B. Eerdmans, 1977.
Mowinckel, Sigmund. *The Psalms in Israel's Worship*. Translated by D. R. Ap-Thomas. Nashville: Abingdon, 1979.
Mowry, Lucetta. "Revelation 4–5 and Early Christian Liturgical Usage." *Journal of Biblical Literature* 71 (1952) 75–84.
Newman, David R. *Worship: As Praise and Empowerment*. New York: Pilgrim, 1988.
Nygren, Anders. *Essence of Christianity*. London: Epworth, 1960.
———. *Meaning and Method*. Translated by Philip S. Watson. Philadelphia: Fortress, 1972.
Nyssa, Saint Gregory of. *Commentary on the Song of Songs*. Translated by Casimir McCambley. Brookline: Hellenic College, 1987.

Old, Hughes Oliphant. *Themes and Variations for a Christian Doxology*. Grand Rapids: William B. Eerdmans, 1992.
O'Rourke, John J. "The Hymns of the Apocalypse." *The Catholic Biblical Quarterly* 30 (1968) 49–72.
Pacquier, Richard. *Dynamics of Worship*. Translated by Donald Macleod. Philadelphia: Fortress, 1967.
Pass, David B. *Music and the Church*. Nashville: Broadman, 1989.
Peterson, David. *Engaging with God*. Downers Grove, IL: IVP Academic, 1992.
Phelps, Roger P. *Guide to Research in Music Education*. 3rd ed. Metuchen, NJ: Scarecrow, 1986.
Pike, Alfred. *A Theology of Music*. Toledo, OH: The Gregorian Institute of America, 1953.
Piper, John. "Thoughts on Worship and Culture." https://desiringgod.org/articles/thoughts-pn-worship-and-culture.
Pippin, Tina. "Political Reality and the Liberating Vision: The Context of the Book of Revelation." PhD diss., The Southern Baptist Theological Seminary, 1987.
Poole, Thomas. "Towards a Theology of Music." DMA diss., The Southern Baptist Theological Seminary, 1988.
Price, Carl F. "Hymn Patterns." *Religion in Life* 16, no. 3 (1947) 431–42.
Quasten, Johannes. *Music and Worship in Pagan and Christian Antiquity*. Translated by Boniface Ramsey. Washington, DC: National Association of Pastoral Musicians, 1973.
Rad, Gerhard von. *Old Testament Theology: The Theology of Israel's Prophetic Tradition*. Translated by D. M. G. Stalker. Edinburgh: Oliver & Boyd, 1965.
Riehm, Eduard Carl August. *Handwoerterbuch das biblischen Altertums*. Translated by Alfred Sendrey. Bielefeld and Leipzig: Velhagen & Klasing, 1894.
Risbridger, John. *The Message of Worship*. Nottingham, England: Inter-varsity, 2015.
Robertson, A. T. *A Grammar of the Greek New Testament in the Light of Historical Research*. New York: Hodder and Stoughton, 1914.
Ross, Allen P. *Recalling the Hope of Glory*. Grand Rapids: Kregel Academic, 2006.
Rothmueller, Aron Marko. *The Music of the Jews*. New York: Beechhurst, 1954.
Routley, Erik. *Church Music and Theology*. Philadelphia: Muhlenberg, 1959.
———. *Christian Hymns Observed*. Princeton, NJ: Prestige, 1982.
———. *The Music of Christian Hymnody*. London: Independent, 1957.
———. *The Divine Formula*. Princeton, NJ: Prestige, 1986.
———. *The Music of Christian Hymns*. Chicago: G. I. A., 1981.
———. *Words, Music, and the Church*. Nashville: Abingdon, 1968.
Rowdon, Harold Hamlyn. *Christ the Lord: Studies in Christology Presented to Donald Guthrie*. Downers Grove, IL: Intervarsity, 1982.
Rowley, H. H. *The Relevance Of Apocalyptic: A Study of Jewish and Christian Apocalypses from Daniel to the Revelation*. Greenwood, SC: Attic, 1980.
Sachs, Curt. "The Mystery of the Babylonian Notation." *Musical Quarterly* 27 (1941) 62–9.
———. *A History of Musical Instruments*. New York: W. W. Norton, 1940.
———, ed. *The New Grove Dictionary of Musical Instruments*. London: Macmillan, 1984.
———. *The Wellsprings of Music*. Paris: Hague, 1962.

———. *The Rise of Music in the Ancient World: East and West*. New York: W. W. Norton, 1943.
Sadie, Stanley, ed. *The New Grove Dictionary of Music and Musicians*. London: Macmillan, 1980.
Saliers, Don. "The Nature of Worship: Community lived in Praise of God." In *Duty & Delight: Routley Remembered*, edited by Robin A. Leaver and James H. Litton, 35–46. Carol Stream, IL: Hope, 1985.
Sanders, Jack T. *The New Testament Christological Hymns*. Society for New Testament Studies 15. Cambridge, MA: Cambridge University Press, 1971.
Schlier, Heinrich. "Ἄδω (*Ado*)." In *TDNT* 1:163–64.
Schmidt, K. L. "θρησκεία." In *TDNT* 3:155–59.
Schneider, Marius. "Primitive Music." In *New Oxford History of Music*, 1–61. London: Oxford University Press, 1957.
Scholes, Percy A. "Notation and Nomenclature." In *The Oxford Companion to Music*. 10th ed. London: Oxford University Press, 1970.
Schubart, Christian. *A History of Key Characteristics in the 18th and 19th Centuries*. Translated by Rita Steblin. Ann Arbor, MI: UMI Research, 1983.
Seel, Thomas A. *A Theology of Music for Worship Derived from the Book of Revelation*. Metuchen, NJ: Scarecrow, 1995.
Seel, Thomas A. "Toward a Theology of Music for Worship Derived from the Book of Revelation." DMA diss., The Southern Baptist Theological Seminary, 1990.
Segler, Franklin M. *Christian Worship: Its Theology and Practice*. Nashville: Broadman, 1967.
Seiss, J. A. *The Apocalypse*. New York: Charles C. Cook, 1909.
Sendrey, Alfred. *Music in the Social and Religious Life of Antiquity*. Cranbury, NJ: Associated University Presses, 1974.
———. *Music in Ancient Israel*. New York: Philosophical Library, 1969.
Shepherd, Massey H. *The Paschal Liturgy and the Apocalypse*. Ecumenical Studies in Worship 6. Richmond, VA: John Knox, 1960.
Smart, Ninian. *The Concept of Worship*. London: Macmillan, 1972.
———. *The Philosophy of Religion*. New York: Oxford University Press, 1979.
———. *The Religious Experience of Mankind*. New York: Scribner, 1969.
Smend, Julius. *Vorträge und Aufsätze zur Liturgik hymnologie und kirchenmusik*. Translated by Sigmund Mowinckel. Guetersloh, Germany: C. Bertelsmann, 1925.
Smith, J. A. "First-Century Christian Singing and Its Relationship to Contemporary Jewish Religious Song." *Music and Letters* 75 (1994) 1–15.
Smith, James G. "The Ancient Synagogue, the Early Church and Singing." *Music and Letters* 65 (1985) 1–16.
Smith, James G., and Percy M. Young. "Chorus." In *NGD* 4:341–57.
Smith, William Shepherd. *Musical Aspects of the New Testament*. Amsterdam: Vrije Universiteit te Amsterdam, 1962.
Smithers, Don L. *The Music and History of the Baroque Trumpet*. Carbondale, IL: Southern Illinois University Press, 1988.
Spencer, Herbert. "The Origin and Function of Music." In *Essays*, 18–25. New York, 1904.
Staehlin, Wilhelm. "The Church Hymn and Theology." *Response: In Worship—Music— The Arts* 1 (1959) 22–30.
Strong, James. *The Exhaustive Concordance of the Bible*. New York: Abingdon, 1890.

———. "Worship." In *ECB* 1190.
Strathmann, Hermann. "λατρεία." In *TDNT* 4:62–65.
———. "λειτουργία." In *TDNT* 4:215–22.
Strunk, Oliver, ed. *Source Readings in Music History*. New York: W. W. Norton, 1975.
Stuart, Donald Clive. *The Development of Dramatic Art*. New York: Dover, 1960.
Summers, Ray. *Worthy is the Lamb: An Interpretation of Revelation*. Nashville: Broadman, 1951.
Sweet, Leonard. *A Cup of Coffee at the Soul Café*. Nashville: B&H, 1998.
Swete, Henry Barclay. *The Apocalypse of St. John*. London: Macmillan, 1909.
Tarr, Edward H. "Trumpet." In *NGD* 19:211–25.
Tarr, Edward H. "Trumpet." In *NGDMI* 19:214.
Temple, William. *The Hope of a New World*. New York: Macmillan, 1942.
Thayer, Joseph Henry, trans. "Silence." In *A Greek-English Lexicon of the New Testament*. New York: Harper and Brothers, 1889.
Tilmouth, Michael, et al. "Ode," In *NGD* 13:497–501.
Tracy, David. *The Analogical Imagination*. New York: Crossroad, 1981.
Trench, R.C. *Synonyms of the New Testament*. Grand Rapids: William B. Eerdmans, 1958.
Ulrich, Homer, and Paul A. Pisk. *A History of Music and Musical Style*. New York: Harcourt, Brace, and World, 1963.
Underhill, Evelyn. *Worship*. New York: Harper and Row, 1936.
Unger, Merrill, and W. White, Jr., eds. *Nelson's Expository Dictionary of the Old Testament*. Nashville: Thomas Nelson, 1984.
Vines, W. E. "New." In *VED* 3:109–10.
———. *Vine's Expository Dictionary of Old and New Testament Words*. Edited by F. F. Bruce. Old Tappan, NJ: Fleming H. Revell, 1981.
Wainwright, Geoffrey. *Doxology: The Praise of God in Worship, Doctrine and Life*. New York: Oxford University Press, 1980.
Wainright, Geoffrey, and Karen B. Westerfield Tucker, eds. *The Oxford History of Christian Worship*. London: Oxford University Press, 2006.
Warren, Dwight Allen. *Philosophy of Music History*. New York: American, 1939.
Webber, Robert E. *Worship is a Verb*. Nashville: Star Song, 1992.
———. *Worship: Old and New*. Grand Rapids: Zondervan, 1982.
Wellesz, Egon. "The Doxology in Synagogue and Church." *Hebrew Union College Annual* 19 (1946) 111–32.
———, ed. *New Oxford History of Music: Ancient and Oriental Music*. London: Oxford University Press, 1957.
Werner, Eric. *The Sacred Bridge: The Interdependence of Liturgy and Music in Synagogue and Church During the First Millennium*. London: Dennis Dobson, 1959.
Wesley, John. *A Collection of Hymns for the Use of the People Called Methodists*. London: John Mason, 1779.
Westermann, Claus. *The Living Psalms*. Translated by J.R. Porter. Grand Rapids: William B. Eerdmans, 1989.
———. *The Psalms: Structure, Content and Message*. Translated by Ralph D. Gehrke. Minneapolis: Augsburg Fortress, 1980.
Whaley, Vernon M. *Called to Worship: From the Dawn of Creation to the Final Amen*. Nashville: Thomas Nelson, 2009.

Whirley, Carl F. "The Significance of the Temple Cultus in the Background of the Gospel of John." ThD diss., The Southern Baptist Theological Seminary, 1957.
Whiston, William, trans. *The Complete Works of Flavius Josephus*. Grand Rapids: Kregel, 1981.
White, James F. *Documents of Christian Worship: Descriptive and Interpretive Sources*. Louisville: Westminster/John Knox, 1992.
White, James F. *Introduction to Christian Worship*. Nashville: Abingdon, 1980.
Wiersbe, Warren W. *Real Worship: It Will Transform You*. Nashville: Oliver-Nelson, 1986.
Wilkey, Jay W. "Music as Religious Expression in Contemporary Society." *Review and Expositor* 61 (1979) 507–17.
Williamson, Dave. *God's Singers: A Guidebook for the Worship Leading Choir in the 21st Century*. Nashville: Incite, 2010.
Winnington-Ingram, R. P. "Greece, Ancient." In *NGD* 7:659–72.
Wiseman, Luke, ed. *The Methodist Hymn-Book*. London: Methodist, 1954.
Wohlgemuth, Paul W. *Rethinking Church Music*. Chicago: Moody, 1973.
Wolfman, Ursula Rehn. "Scriabin's Color Symbolism in Music." https://staging.interlude.hk/scriabins-color-symbolism-music/#:~:text=Many%20of%20his%20subsequent%20works,;%20Riccardo%20Muti%2C%20cond.).
Woolf, Bosley, ed. "Catharsis" In *Webster's New Collegiate Dictionary*, 345. Springfield, MA: G. and C. Merriam, 1976.
Wright, LeRoy Evert. "The Place of Music in Worship." PhD diss., Northwestern University, 1949.
Young, Carlton. *Music of the Heart: John & Charles Wesley on Music and Musicians*. Carol Stream, IL: Hope, 1995.
Zerbe, Alvin Sylvester. *The Karl Barth Theology or The New Transcendentalism*. Cleveland, OH: Central, 1930.
Zerwick, Max, and Mary Grosvener. *A Grammatical Analysis of the Greek New Testament*. Rome: Biblical Institute, 1981.

www.ingramcontent.com/pod-product-compliance
Lightning Source LLC
Chambersburg PA
CBHW070323230426
43663CB00011B/2206